The Lie That I Am
A Journey Back to Spirit

by
Mary Beth Smith

DORRANCE
PUBLISHING CO
EST. 1920
PITTSBURGH, PENNSYLVANIA 15238

Dorrance Publishing Co
585 Alpha Drive
Suite 103
Pittsburgh, PA 15238
Visit our website at *www.dorrancebookstore.com*

ISBN: 978-1-6853-7204-0
eISBN: 978-1-6853-7746-5

This book is dedicated to the one who has stood beside me and behind me through every step of my journey. You have helped me make sense of a life that made no sense until you were in it. You have given me permission to be who I truly am, even when I couldn't give that to myself. I AM all that I AM, because you are All that you are. Together we are EVERYTHING! I love you Marsh Smith!

Thank you God for blessing my life so magnificently. I AM Grateful!

Contents

Prologue

Hello, my beautiful readers. Are you ready to examine your life and see it through new eyes? Do you struggle with feelings of being incomplete... not enough? But enough what? Then I believe that you are ready to explore the next set of possibilities on your journey here in this lifetime. Sometimes you'll notice that if I had put a different word in a sentence, it would flow better. What if the purpose is not to have flow in that moment, but to pause and have to think... think a different way. Be a different way. Learn a different way. Then I have succeeded in my wish for you.

While this book is about my life and my experiences, to call it an autobiography would be a lie. As you can tell from the title, I used to believe the lies that I was taught by my family, by society, by my peers—but something inside of me was uncomfortable with the box that I was placed in. It was too small, too constricting. I want more! I need more! I AM MORE! Ever so slowly I noticed how different I was, how differently I saw things from how others saw them. I truly felt every day like I was an alien dropped onto this planet with no instruction book, no one to guide me, and I didn't even speak earthling. Then, as a bonus, I was given learning disabilities so even if I had a guidebook I wouldn't be able to read it.

It is difficult for me to believe that I was chosen for this, and agreed to it. WHAT WAS I THINKING? Then I was dropped into a family filled with so much... dysfunction, which is too limiting of a word, but you get the picture. Yet there was always a strength in my connection with God that couldn't be beaten or logicked out of me. I knew what I knew. I could quiet the connection, I could silence the connection, yet I always knew that it was there and that I could count on it. It didn't always make sense, but it was mine, it was ME! Sometimes as people would talk I could and still do feel the lies in their words. Perhaps a better way to say this is that I could feel that what they were saying was a lie, but they truly believed that lie and would fight to defend it.

I spent my life living in two worlds. The one that helped me to fit in and make sense of why people believed what they believed and did what they did. Where I constantly needed to not be me in order to survive. Where so much of what was said and believed was a lie, but all those lies never made sense to me. The other world was in my head and in my heart. This was where God talked to me, where Spirit played with me, where I was taught God's truth—not human truth, not my truth, but absolute truth. Living in my head was my happy place, things made sense there. It was not about winning or losing, being smart or stupid, being right or wrong. All of that is duality, all of that is of the human density (heaviness). What I learned from Spirit went so far beyond what most humans understand. There is no losing or loser. Love or truth is not part of an interaction where someone is more and someone else is less. We are simply different, and through those differences we can learn from each other so that we can move more and more towards connection and becoming one.

In my head I felt loved. This was not the conditional human love that we are taught, where if you do this I will love you, but if you don't do this, then I won't love you. Really? Do you honestly believe that you can in any way, shape, or form connect love to that? You cannot. There simply is no love in conditions. Love is Love, period. There is nothing you need to do, be, or think for me to love you more than I do in this moment. That is what I learned in my head and in my heart. When I had to return to my life, I would come plummeting down. I had to let go of the God truth in order to survive in this abusive, illogical society where everything seemed to be the opposite of what I knew.

This is the story of how I navigated the obstacles in my life while continually trying to remain connected to my heart, my soul, my God connection. It wasn't perfect, I got lost at times, bought into society's pressures, and had to deal with depression and suicide. Hitting bottom so hard that there really is nowhere to go but up. Learning how to navigate from a place of observation instead of judgment. Learning that I am a very average woman doing extraordinary things because I learned to trust. Trust myself, trust God and to trust my inner knowing. And that in itself takes me from average, to exceptional, to Magnificent! Come join me on this journey of becoming more. Pause along the way and notice what resonates with you and what doesn't. Know that you are not alone on this roller-coaster ride called life, there are billions of us who feel like everything that we think, do, and are is wrong. And know that this is a lie. There... we are calling out your first lie. Everything you think, do, and are is not wrong—it is simply different, you are different! And I am so very grateful that you are. We (the planet and humankind) need your different way of looking at things, we need your different way of doing things. Without you, this planet would be incomplete.

You are not done yet, there is more to learn! There is so much more growing that each of us gets to do—in love, hope, and understanding. I for one would like to do that with all of you. I am so very tired of doing it alone. Are you exhausted from trying to navigate all of this alone? Are you ready to join me and millions, maybe even billions of others who are choosing a different way of being, to start living from a place of truth instead of lies? Are you ready to call out the lies that you allow to define you and in doing so become who you are truly meant to be? Then turn the page and let's begin this journey of truth together!

Chapter 1: The Last

When my parents got married, it was a second marriage for both of them. My sister Connie showed up a year later. She was a novelty. My older siblings saw her as a toy to play with, everything she did was adorable. Each time she learned something new, the whole family was engaged. We even have an old home movie of her sitting on the potty chair with everyone gathered around waiting to clap for her. She was the one that was going to bring the two families together. She thrived with all of the attention, and still does. Mom always talked about how Connie was such a beautiful and delightful baby.

Next came Grant, Mom said Grant was enormous. He was a very sensitive child and felt things deeply, so everyone learned to be kind to Grant so that he wouldn't get his feelings hurt. My siblings always spoke of how you couldn't not love Grant. Grant loved to love. Also, Grant was Mom's only biological son, though we later found out that Mom had given birth to another baby boy who she had given up for adoption years earlier. Did the guilt of giving up that other son make this son even more special? I don't know.

Then came Mary Beth... the last. Not the baby, but the last. When Mom started having contractions with me and called Dad at the firehouse, he was upset because he didn't want to abandon his crew mid-shift. When they got to the hospital, the contractions slowed down, and eventually, they took an x-ray and found that I was breech. As my wonderful, loving mother put it, "You came into the world backwards, and you're still backwards." When the nurse asked my mom what she was going to name her sweet little angel, my mom said, "I don't care as long as it doesn't begin with 'C.' I already have a Connie, a Charlotte and a Christine." So the nurse said, "Why don't you name her after the Virgin Mary?" My mom said, "Ok, but I don't like the name Mary by itself, it needs another name with it." So I was named Mary Beth.

My father was a very quiet, likable guy, but with a quick temper. He met his first wife, Rose, while home on leave from the Army. After he was discharged they were married and had five children. After giving birth to her 5th child, Rose was diagnosed with "female cancer," which she battled for two years. That's what they called it back then, not ovarian cancer or uterine cancer—just female cancer. On the day that she lost her battle, as Dad was walking home to tell his five children the horrible news, he saw a man jump into the river. His instincts as a firefighter took over, and he jumped in to save the man who was trying to commit suicide. That experience haunted Dad for the rest of his life; he could save a stranger who wanted to die, but he couldn't save his wife, who wanted so desperately to live.

Meanwhile, my mother met the love of her life, Gerald, who also served in WW2. They had one daughter named Charlotte. He passed away in a car accident when Charlotte was only one year old. My grandmother moved in with my mother and Charlotte, and they boarded college girls to pay the bills. My mother occasionally helped her sister Marie at her diner. One day at the end of Mom's shift, a customer offered to take her home. My mother never learned to drive, and often took rides from strangers. This man took her somewhere secluded and raped her. My mother had a baby boy from the rape, who she gave up for adoption. This was all kept secret from the kids until all of us were grown with families of our own.

My mother was very religious and prayed to God every day, asking him what she was supposed to do with the rest of her life. Sometime after that, a fireman told my dad about his aunt who was a widow. My father called and asked her for a date. They married three months later. There was no love, no respect, not even much in common, but they needed each other. My mother married to help his five motherless children have some stability. She felt that this was the answer to her prayers. My mom had Connie twelve months later, Grant came fifteen months after that, and I arrived fourteen months after Grant. Mom had a hysterectomy shortly after I was born. I don't know if it was medically necessary, or if Mom's doctor just wanted to have mercy on her.

Being the youngest of nine, when I reached a new milestone as a child, it was something finally DONE for the last time. Thank God, Mary Beth learned to crawl, now I never have to do that again. Thank God, Mary Beth is potty trained, now I never have to wash another diaper. Nothing I did was seen as an accomplishment, but as a duty, checked off a list. Mom couldn't tell me what my first word was, when I cut my first tooth, or what my favorite toy was. Just about the only thing that Mom could tell me was that, "You were wanted as much as I wanted malaria." You see when I was born, I had a life, but it was not a life that was wanted. Day after day and year after year, as I experienced being unwanted, I took it on as my truth. No one had to ask me to or told me to; I did it myself. This is how we begin living our lives as a lie.

As children we are constantly observing and exploring, trying to make sense of the world in which we live. At the same time, we are trying to figure out what exactly our role is in this crazy world. For me, it felt like I was simply struggling to exist, period. The idea of being unwanted was one of the first ways that I defined myself. My world consisted of my teachers who were my parents, my five brothers and three sisters, my grandparents, and occasionally friends and neighbors. This was all I knew from the time that I was an infant until I started kindergarten, when my world expanded. How could I learn what I wasn't taught? I couldn't. So I had to take what I had in front of me each and every day and try to make sense of it as best I could. What I learned was that I was just another kid. I was just another diaper to change and bottle to feed. Did anyone look at me as they changed me? Did anyone speak to me as they fed me? Probably not, because I was nothing special.

My teachers, my family—what did you teach me today? Did you remind me that I am special and extraordinary? Did you even bother acknowledging my existence? Was I placed in a playpen or on a blanket as you walked around me? Don't make eye contact with her; if you do, then you will have to talk to her, or change her, or feed her. Maybe you'll be reminded just by looking at her that you have folded hundreds and thousands of diapers. That's what one of my brothers said about me. He doesn't remember much about me when I was little. I was cute, but mostly he remembered folding my diapers. No one remembers me, ME, Mary Beth. No, I was not something special to be treasured and held. I was something to be tolerated and endured. Every day in our house each child and adult was just doing what they needed to navigate the chaos around them.

When I went to kindergarten for the first time I wasn't told anything ahead of time, not even where we were going. My mother and I walked a couple of blocks from our home, where we entered a magical room. There were paints, colors, paper and more toys than I could have ever imagined. There were also other children my age, and most of them were smiling! I went to play with some dolls, and when I looked up later, my mom was gone. No goodbye, no have a nice day, just gone... and in her place was a beautiful woman who seemed to like me, she even read us stories. Oh, how I loved that day! I wished my mom would never come back, but she did, and I went back to the world of chaos and neglect. To my surprise, I got to go back to the magical room the next day and the day after that. When the weekend came, I remember my disappointment. That was when Connie told me that the magical room was called kindergarten. I loved kindergarten. I remember being so shocked that all the kids there really liked me. What was wrong with them? Didn't they know that I was unlovable? Kindergarten and first grade were wonderful! I got to ask questions, and people explained things to me. Kids in my class liked me, I would even say I was popular. I can remember the boys fighting over me and I was invited to so many birthday parties that mom complained about the expense. You see, Mom never beat me with her hands; she beat me with her words. Mom's words were powerful. Mine were not.

Each day, the people around me were my examples, my teachers. They taught me, and I learned that I was a burden to each and every one of them. If I didn't exist, their lives would be easier... maybe even better. I didn't deserve love, I didn't deserve kindness, I didn't deserve.

4

Were all of these things that they taught to me things that I wanted to learn? No! How do I, now as an adult, unlearn what I was taught? I can't. I can, however, look at all of these lessons that formed the foundation of who I am, and decide if I want to continue to hold on to them as my <u>belief</u> of who I am.

When I was young I noticed that I had a greater understanding of the frequency of things than most people. I've never put those experiences into words like that before, but that is what it boils down to. There were things that I just <u>knew</u> even at a young age. The earliest memory I have was when I was 2 or 3 years old. My sister Connie, my brother Grant and I were on a blanket in the backyard with our mother, and I was playing with a ball. I can see the colors of it blending together as it rolled. I can see the vibrancy and shape of each color, I feel mesmerized by these blended colors, and then stare at them when I hold the ball still. I feel moved by the differences and want to understand why they are the same yet different when still versus moving. I feel myself hesitate because I already know that my mother does not like it when I ask questions. I have too many of them, they never stop. If she answers one, then the questions will keep coming, so she ignores them, hoping for a few moments of peace and quiet, which is unlikely with so many kids underfoot. Connie notices how much I am enjoying the ball, she takes it from me and starts tossing it in the air. I try to get it back, but I'm too little.... I'm always too little. I start to cry, and as always Mom doesn't want to know what happened, she only wants quiet. I was yelled at and Connie was praised. In that moment time stopped for me, and I saw that everything that Connie does is right and everything that I do, and think, and am, is wrong. From that moment until I was 25, I followed Connie around trying to figure out what she did that made her so lovable and right. There are no mistakes, but if there were, that would have been one of mine. To abandon believing in myself and instead take on believing in Connie who made little sense to me, had a huge effect on me. As time went on, I trusted myself less and less. I looked to others for answers to questions I wasn't allowed to ask, so their answers were disjointed and never made sense.

Not only that, but the pool of people I had to learn from was so very limited at that time. For some reason, my mother always wanted to keep me close, so I was not exposed to many people besides my family.

My second earliest memory was when I was three or four, and my mother and I were at the grocery store. Ahead of me, there was a very heavy woman in a house dress, and I could see a big, black owie inside of her body. I knew (and I don't know how, I just knew), that I could reach inside of her and get rid of her owie. So I did, or at least I tried. That's when I found out that it's not ok to touch someone in the abdomen in a grocery store. I was slapped, yelled at and shamed by my mom. She refused to let me go to the grocery store with her for what seemed like years because I was an embarrassment and should not be allowed in public. I tried to explain to my mom what I saw and what I was trying to do to help this poor woman with an owie. Maybe that is the moment that my mother decided to keep me close. As the years went by, I learned that I was different and not necessarily in a good way; this was enhanced by the fact that I had learning disabilities. My mother told me that I should be in an institution, but she was trying to be a good Christian by keeping me at home. I had an older sister who had been institutionalized in high school, so I knew that there was a possibility that I could end up there as well. Every day I struggled to not be me, to not ask questions, try not to want anything, try not to be anything.

I was happiest when I lived in my head, things made more sense there than in the outside world. I started spending more and more time in my closet. I learned that if I stayed in my closet I could find a happy place inside of my head. Out of sight, out of mind. It took my family many years to figure out that I was spending most of my time in my closet. To this day, some of them still don't know this about me. To be honest, what happened in that closet went far beyond out of sight, out of mind. In my closet, I got to spend time with my spirit guide and angels. Growing up, I guess that I thought of them as my imaginary friends. In that space, I was so loved, I was held when I cried, I was listened to and understood, and I actually felt wise. I didn't ask many questions because by that time the pattern had already become part of my survival mode, but I did wonder about things, and sometimes I saw things... almost like a movie in my head. One of the things that I learned from Spirit—that I knew to be absolute truth—was given to me after watching Rodgers and Hammerstein's *Cinderella*[1]. I was lying on my shoes in my closet, and I was told that my Prince Charming was coming for me. I was told that he was going to take me far, far away, and my family would never be able to hurt me again.

That thought, that idea, that promise, kept me going for many years, but eventually when my Prince Charming didn't show up, I lost hope. I started going into a severe depression. The doubts about myself and my abilities, that Mom affirmed daily, started setting in. I observed other people laughing, dreaming about the future, forming friendships and relationships. I lived in a closet. My friendships never lasted long. I saw my mother's prophecies coming true—my mother hated my laugh, so I had to not make a sound when I laughed; I was unlovable; I would never amount to anything; I should never marry; and most importantly—I should never have children. But the thing that I wanted more than anything in the world was to have a little girl, so that I could do things differently. I wanted to be the mom that I wished I had. I wanted my daughter to be curious and ask lots of questions. I wanted to do her hair in pretty styles with lots of bows. My mother didn't even know how to make a ponytail. I wanted to read her stories that would spark her imagination. I wanted to be patient and kind so that she would grow up to be the same. All of these visions and words filled with hope kept me going, but just barely. My depression as a teenager and beyond was so deep and so heavy. The only person that seemed to notice how severe it was, was my oldest sister Christine, who would tell Mom how concerned she was for me. She thought that I needed professional help, but when she would mention it to me, I was terrified of being locked away. I knew that if anyone ever found out what was going on in my mind, they would lock me up and throw away the key. My parents weren't afraid of doing that, and it was a constant fear that I had to live with.

From age 8 to 22, almost every day I asked God to die. No one and nothing made sense to me. No one was honest with each other, and belittling sarcasm was a way of life in my family. People don't realize that there is no God

[1] Rodgers and Hammerstein's *Cinderella*, 1964.

connection in belittling sarcasm, and if there is no God connection, then it really cannot be called Love. When I hear things, feel things, experience things, I feel a vibration or an energy about it (I often refer to this as a frequency), which gives me a greater understanding of it. Does it come from truth or Love? If it's not truth or love then I try to understand and define what it is. People had to repeat things multiple times for me, because the first time things were said, I <u>felt</u> the words, the second time I tried to <u>understand</u> the words. This led to people believing that I was slow. Often when I meet people for the first time I see their soul, and it is so magnificent that I want to be with them all of the time. The second time I see them I meet the human that they are, and I would feel a disappointment.

Chapter 2: I Want to Die

The summer after first grade my life fell apart, and that's when I started asking God to let me die. A male relative of mine began sexually abusing me. He was so much older and bigger than me. At first I didn't tell anyone, I just left my body and went somewhere less scary. What I didn't realize until much later was that a part of me had to stay behind and experience that awful pain and abuse each time. Thank God, I can't remember much of it, but I do remember bits and pieces.

How can any man think that he has a right to put his penis in someone just because he has "needs" that we mere women couldn't possibly understand? What man has the right to take away a child's innocence because he has a hard-on? None, I tell you! My choices were taken from me again and again until all that was left was a bitter shell of a little girl. No one wanted to be around me. I didn't even want to be around me, or inside of me.

Last year I was diagnosed with endometrial cancer—I wonder why. My baby was delivered by emergency C-section so that she wouldn't have to touch my violated vagina. It's amazing what I created through all the pain and anger and resentment that I held within me. I was married for ten years before my husband could touch me in the middle of the night without me instantly going to a place of fear and panic. All because of a very selfish Asshole that only thought of his own NEEDS and desires. What makes him or any man think that they have that right, I just do not understand. What gave my relative the right to take my hopes, my dreams, and my innocence? He had no right at all. And yet he did.

When I started second grade, I didn't even recognize myself. I felt that my life was sad, and this is the moment that I really started believing I had nothing to live for. My belief that I was here to be used and abused took on a whole new meaning. I had no one in my life that showed me love, nor did I feel that I deserved love. I felt that I was all alone in a world that made no sense. That year I had Sister Constance as my teacher, and she reaffirmed my new beliefs about myself. Everything I did was wrong, everything I felt was wrong, everything that I was, was wrong. I sucked my thumb until I was fourteen; Sister Constance taught me to do it in private. When I twirled my hair, Sister Constance made me stand in front of the class and mess my hair up. She only confirmed what I thought was the truth... I am worthless. At seven years old, I had already labeled myself as stupid, unlovable, a victim to be abused and alone.

Once when my father was spanking my siblings, he said I was next. I said, "But I didn't do anything wrong." He responded, "Are you sassing me?" At that moment I was able to see into my father's heart, and I could feel the pain and disappointment he felt about his life. I turned to him and said, "You can spank me if it will make you feel better," and I meant it. I was okay with him beating me with a belt if that would alleviate some of his pain, because by this time I firmly believed that I deserved to be beaten.

Gifts from God don't always feel like gifts at the time, but sometime later—it could be years or minutes—you understand the divinity in the experience. That happened for me in 2015-2016 when I was called for jury duty. At the time I was suffering from severe anxiety and I was trying to not rely on medications to control it. I didn't know what to do, what if this gave me a panic attack? What if it got so bad that I couldn't figure out how to take care of myself? That had happened before, and stress amplifies the anxiety. While I was having these thoughts, I felt the hand of God on my shoulder, and I knew that there was something that either I or someone else needed to get from this experience. So

I showed up at the courthouse at the appointed time with my medication in my purse, just in case I needed it. When we had all been called in and the formalities were done, we were told that the defendant was charged with sexually abusing two minors. My head instantly started spinning. Holy crap, how was I going to be able to do this? That's when I thought of the sweet innocent little girls not having a voice and no one believing them because they were children. I suddenly felt stronger and more empowered, I would be their voice. I felt like I was speaking for the little girl inside of me that no one ever believed when she tried to tell people what was happening to her. Eventually, they asked if any of us had personal experience with this kind of thing, or if we knew someone who had gone through it. I raised my hand high—no more hiding, no more pretending it didn't happen. When they called on me, they asked if it was myself or someone I knew. I told them that it happened to me. Then they asked if I felt I could be impartial. I said I hoped that I could be. They talked to other potential jurors and asked them more questions, and then the defense attorney asked me if I could be unbiased in a case involving child sexual assault. Could I listen to the testimony and not allow my own experience to affect how I rendered a verdict? I responded with a very loud and clear NO. The defense attorney asked to have me dismissed. The prosecuting attorney stepped in and asked if I could keep an open mind and look only at the facts and then render a verdict. I responded yes. Then the defense attorney used the word unbiased again, and I said NO, I couldn't be unbiased. The judge stepped in and reworded the question so that it didn't include "unbiased" and I had to respond that yes I could. So the judge said I could stay. We continued until it was time to pick a jury.

Not surprisingly, I was one of the first five people to be let go. As I sat in my car shaking and crying from shame and guilt because I wouldn't be there to help defend those poor little girls, I was told by Spirit that others were going to do that for them. That I had done what they had hoped that I would do, I stood up for that little girl inside of me. I stood before a judge, attorneys and potential jurors and said that if I had to choose between adults and small children, I will always fight for the child. In that moment, that little girl inside of me that had to endure all of the horrific abuse was given a voice and even some small amount of justice, and I felt so free. It took at least 30 minutes before I was calm enough to be safe to drive home. I needed that 30 minutes to cry and scream and let out as much pain and anger as I possibly could. I needed that 30 minutes to celebrate that I finally was strong enough, and powerful enough to speak the truth about what happened to me and let go of the shame. What did I have to be ashamed of? If someone should feel shame, it should be him, not me. Thank you, God, for giving me the strength to see it through and for giving me the opportunity to heal another layer of pain.

My father was a very, very hard worker who worked two full-time jobs in addition to doing odd jobs for people just to keep a roof over our heads and food on the table. His favorite job was being a fireman. Firemen are like a family of their own. They tease each other, confide in one another, they celebrate and even cry with each other. My dad worked 24 hours on and 24 hours off for five days, and then had four days off. On his days off, he would do maintenance for what would now be called a property management company. We usually got to see him for an hour every other day unless his day off was Sunday, then he would often do odd jobs for people. Occasionally we might do something as a family such as visiting relatives. My father never graduated from high school because he had a difficult time reading, which impacted how he viewed himself throughout his life.

When I was nine or ten, Mom went to the hospital to have her gallbladder removed. While she was gone Dad went into a rage. That was a very bad day in our house. He put his foot through the kitchen floor and his fist through a 1.5-inch-thick dresser. He beat all of us kids that day, he even broke a plastic brush on my back. When his anger was finally spent, he loaded us up into our VW van and took us to an amusement park. It started to rain before we arrived, and they had closed the park. At that moment I saw what no one else could. I saw how sorry Dad was that he took out his anger and feelings of helplessness on us. I now understood his pain and frustration on a whole new level, and it allowed me to feel such compassion for him from that moment on. I may have had a one-sided relationship with my father, but at least I had a connection to someone.

When I was 16, a fireman that worked with Dad stopped by the house to drop off some tools that he had borrowed. He said to me, "Boy, are you lucky to have this man as your dad." His words intrigued me. I asked him, "What do you mean?" He said, "Are you kidding me? They don't make 'em better than your dad! There's nothing he won't do for someone. He has the biggest heart of anyone I know." All I could think about that night was what that fireman had said. My dad was kind and generous? With a big heart? I wanted to experience this side of my dad that the firemen knew. So the next day when I heard the garage door open, I ran to the door before Dad could come in, and I locked it. But it wasn't me who locked that door, it was like I was on the outside watching some other part of me lock the door.

When Dad realized that the door was locked and he couldn't get in, he said, "What the hell?" He then knocked and I answered, "Yes... how can I help you (giggle, giggle)?" He responded, "Let me in, Mary Beth." I said, "I would love to let you in, Daddy, but first you have to say the magic words: 'I love you, Mary Beth, please let me in.'" He replied, "Like hell." He then reopened the garage door and went around to the front door, where guess who was waiting for him. I locked that door too, and again I watched myself do it, as though it was someone else. He tried the door and swore again. I said, "Come on, Daddy, you can do it... 'I love you, Mary Beth, please let me in.'" He said, "Over my dead body." He next went around the house to the back door. I thought, *Oh, crap,* as I watched myself lock it. I knew I was going to die if and when Dad ever got into this house. The other me wrapped the curtains around my face and under my chin, and when he approached, she said, "Guess who?" He said, "I'm going to break down this Goddamn door and then we'll see if you're still smiling." She said, "Go ahead, but guess who is going to have to fix it and pay for it! Come on, Daddy; you can do it! 'I love you, Mary Beth, please open up the door.'" He yelled, "I love you, Goddamn it, now open the door." She said, "Close enough," and unlocked the door, hugged him and said, "I love you too, Daddy! That wasn't so hard, was it?" He grunted and went into the kitchen.

I went into my room and relived everything that had just happened. The thought that there was a part of me that was so brave and knew just what needed to be said and done was incredible. That night at dinner, Dad said, "Please pass the beans." I said, "Oh, no, Daddy, it's 'I love you, Mary Beth, please pass the beans.'" He laughed, and in a sarcastic voice, he said, "I love you, Mary Beth, would you please pass the beans?" My reply was, "I love you too, Daddy, I would love to pass you the beans." This continued for the entire meal. My mother hated it and made all kinds of negative comments, but it didn't stop Dad and I from having our fun. All night we said I love you before he'd ask me to turn the channel, or get him a cup of coffee. It was the best night I had ever had.

When I went to bed that night, I understood that I had given my father a gift that day that went beyond any gift he had ever received. I gave him the gift of LOVE! A love so pure in its innocence and so unconditional—there is nothing that he had to be, do, or think for me to love him more than I did right then and there. From that day on, my father was a changed man. On that sacred day, I was allowed to love as I had never been allowed to love before. I was finally allowed to show a small piece of who I truly was, and it felt GOOD! That is when my dad became Daddy, a name I had never called him before. I also got to hear my DADDY say that he loved me for the first time that I could remember!

Chapter 3: Noticing and Learning

If grade school was difficult for me, high school was even worse. In grade school, I got away with a lot as far as reading and learning, because mine was the only grade ever in the school's history that had so many kids in it that we were separated into three classes until we got in the upper grades where they just shoved more desks in the two rooms until we all fit. Because of this there were not enough books to go around. If a teacher was ambitious and mimeographed pages from the book for us, we got to see things, read things, and learn things. But usually, the teachers read stuff from the book, and we did work on the board. So my learning disabilities were not as evident.

I had my first science class in 10th grade. I got a D. My brother Grant said I couldn't take earth science because it was for the potheads who had limited brain cells. So I spent many a lunch hour with my science teacher because I was holding up the class. I was constantly putting my hand up asking questions, like: What is an atom? What are genes? What does chemistry mean? I knew next to nothing, but my teacher loved my enthusiasm because I wanted to hear about everything. Science felt like, finally, someone was explaining WHY to me. Why is the grass green? Why am I so different from my siblings? Why is it difficult to breathe around fire? Holy cow, a new world opened up for me and then it closed just as quickly. Because of my poor grade I couldn't continue to take science. And then, I learned that if I took Drama, I didn't have to take an English class, which meant I graduated high school without ever reading a book. Drama was by far my favorite class. I was encouraged to express my feelings in drama. I could go to the depths of the pain I felt. I could make people laugh. But most importantly, I got to be someone else for a little while. My life disappeared for an hour a day and I became someone else. Usually, I played wacky old ladies. Once, my history teacher asked my drama teacher how to get me to talk. My drama teacher's response was, how do you get her to shut up?

Before I could start high school, I needed a physical. When I showed up for my appointment, my doctor was surprised. He said he hadn't seen me since my 6-month checkup. He showed me my chart, which had only a couple of pages in it. He said I had never gotten my shots as a child and had to get them before I started high school. Ok, I said, not looking forward to the experience. Again, why was I never taken to the doctor?

Next, he asked me questions about my health. One of the questions was, do you have headaches? I said I don't know what that is. He said that it's pain you experience in your head. I said, "Well, everyone has that." He asked me how long I had had pain in my head. I could tell he thought I was a little simple in the brain. I said definitely 8th and 7th grades, and yep, 6th for sure. I'm not sure about 5th grade. He was shocked. You've had pain in your head for all those years? I said, "Yes, I thought everyone did." In my thoughts I was wondering if I even knew what pain was. Maybe what I had was something else? No, I knew what pain was, I had experienced it enough. He said we need to get an x-ray to see what is going on in there.

Next time I saw my doctor, he said I had something called polyps in both my sinus cavities and they needed to come out. I ended up having surgery. They said there must have been so many sinus infections to have created such large

16

polyps over the years, and they had never been taken care of. I could feel his empathy for what I had suffered. He told me to come back any time I was feeling pain anywhere in my body. I remember being so surprised at his words. Maybe there was someone that would take care of me if I was sick? Was that possible?

The day before I started high school, my brother, who was a year ahead of me, told me that I was not allowed to talk to him or acknowledge him in school. No one—not even the teachers—were allowed to know that we were related. So again I need to be invisible.

In high school, I started putting on weight. Food was my friend (another lie I told myself to make it ok). What it really meant was I was stuffing my emotions. Obese people hardly ever feel full. At least that is something I learned later on. In high school, I was about a size 16 at my largest point. So, just before my senior year, I started a weight loss program I paid for myself. I took a bus to Brookfield once a week to show my menus to the nurse. I lived on 500 calories a day. And there was something about if you ate this meat, you could only have these fruits and these vegetables. I bought most of my own food for this diet, because Mom said it cost too much for her. I got down to a size 9. I know that men aren't going to understand these sizes, but you women will. So my senior year, I looked pretty amazing. I wore big baggy clothes for several months, and then my sister Charlotte did a wonderful, surprising thing—she took me shopping and bought me a pair of size 9 designer jeans. When I walked down the hallway, no one recognized me, not even my best friend Lindie. Thank you for that, Charlotte—what a beautiful gift you gave me.

Because I hadn't mentally accepted my weight loss, when I went to pick up my senior pictures, I saw this beautiful portrait in the window of the photography studio. I thought, boy I wish I were that beautiful. I never even recognized the girl in the picture as me. But there I was, on a 2'x3', bigger-than-life picture. I love my senior picture. My dad must have loved it too, because when he died, inside his wallet was a picture of my mom before she had children, and my senior picture, and boy, did that touch my heart. So here I am with this beautiful new body and what I later considered a pretty face when again, my world fell apart. I fell asleep walking down the steps at school. I was ok. Thank you, God! Then my hair started falling out. I had a pretty big bald spot in the back under my top layers of hair. Our doctor couldn't figure out what was wrong. I had electrodes attached to my head. I had brain scans looking for tumors. Nothing. No clue as to what was wrong, but I was sleeping 16+ hours a day. I stayed home two or three days a week, partly because of my severe depression with suicidal thoughts and partly because I was so physically exhausted.

Finally, I was diagnosed with hypothyroidism. By the time I was diagnosed, I was up to a size 22. Can you imagine how low my self-esteem was after going from a size 9 to a size 22 and losing half my hair in six months? At 18 years of age, it felt devastating!

Something that impacted the way I saw my role in our family happened when I was about ten. I found out that most of my siblings were my half-brothers and sisters. It wasn't that anyone was hiding it from me; it was just that no one explained it to me. Once a year, we went to Rose's grave. I thought Rose was a beloved aunt. Mom mentioned Gerald a lot, but I thought he was her favorite brother. Then, during my grandparents' 50th wedding anniversary, they had a photographer there to take pictures of different groups, including all the grandchildren. I went up and got in the group, and Grandma told me to get out. This picture is only for their grandchildren. I didn't understand. I asked Mom, and she said Grandma and Grandpa probably only want their biological grandkids in the picture. What does that mean? She explained that only some of my siblings were born to Grandma's daughter; Charlotte and the three littlest of us were born from her, while the other five were born from Rose. I ran into the bathroom crying. Someone had to come find me when it was time to leave.

I asked Connie if she knew that we were not related to our big brothers and sisters. She said, "Yes, we are, but we are only half-brothers and sisters." "How could I not know this?" I asked. She said, "I don't know—it's not like people don't talk about Rose and Gerald." "Who are they?" I asked. "Rose was Dad's first wife and Gerald was Mom's first husband." "Are you kidding me...? Mom and Dad were each married before?" I went into my closet and stayed for a very long time. Suddenly things were making more sense. I was an imposter in their family; this must be why my older siblings didn't like me. There are fifteen years between

Christine and myself, and my siblings started leaving home when I was three. They never really talked to me or acknowledged me. It wasn't until I was in my 50s and we were all together at a family function that I finally had the guts to ask my siblings why they didn't like me. What did I ever do or say that made them not want me to be a part of their lives except at family functions? My beautiful brother Ken spoke up and said, "You didn't do anything except to be born last. You are the little sister. We are supposed to ignore you and tease you." I cried that night in my husband's arms. Are you kidding me—50 years of neglect and I had convinced myself again and again that I was unlovable and that wasn't the truth at all. I was just the little sister. How do I go back and correct decades of beliefs that I'm not good enough, that I'm not worthy, that I don't matter?

So much of what we believe about ourselves comes from corrupt data—corrupt information. WE turn it into our beliefs. WE allow it all to fester inside our hearts, inside our minds, until WE become someone unrecognizable to who we truly are in our soul. We have to call out the lies and old beliefs that we have carried around for decades, maybe even lifetimes. I'll give you an example: I am unlovable. This is a lie! I am very, very lovable. I have a huge heart. I love helping the homeless and giving to food banks. I love telling stories that inspire people to think differently and then they can even choose to be different. I love connecting to the difference I make on this planet. I love paying it forward. I love being a baby whisperer. I love me! So how can I be unlovable? That is a lie and I no longer allow that lie to be part of my thoughts, part of my beliefs. I turned that lie into my belief of who I am. And every time that thought or feeling comes up I choose to look at it honestly and call it out as the lie that it is!

Why do we still believe all these lies from our childhood? How are they serving us? If they don't serve us, then why are we still living from that place? I truly hated my mom. Until one day, my very, very wise and wonderful sister-in-law Janet asked me why I hated my mom. I told her that she is so mean and hateful. She tries to put others down to bring herself up. It's my opinion that she loves pushing everybody's buttons. Janet said, "What if her sole purpose was to push people's buttons?" Holy crap—mind-blowing moment! My response was, "Then she has fulfilled her purpose magnificently!" After that, my mother's words

19

didn't have as much power over me as they used to. Her words still hurt, but they weren't as powerful. Thank you, Janet! My heart has been magnificently touched by your presence in my life and in my family. I AM Grateful!

Chapter 4: Is My Birth Something to Celebrate?

Ok, now I want to set things straight regarding my siblings. NONE OF MY SIBLINGS EVER PURPOSELY NEGLECTED ME! They were simply moving forward on their own paths, living their own lives. That is what they are supposed to do. The way that Spirit has explained it to me is that I needed to feel so neglected that I would go inside (both inside my closet where I felt safe, and inside myself where God resides) and connect with God. Only then could I truly come to a place of learning truth and redefining my new relationship with God. So, thank you, my precious sisters and brothers, for moving on and living your lives, so that I could live mine with God. It is all a matter of perception. I perceived them not sitting down and having big heart to heart conversations with me as neglect. I perceived them not wanting to know about my life, as my life doesn't matter. I perceived them not asking me to join them when they did things as them not wanting to be with me. I was WRONG! I was loved by them. Maybe not in the way that I wanted to be loved, but I was loved in the way that they were able to love me. So again, I want to apologize to my sisters and brothers for believing that you did wrong by me. I understand the truth now, and it feels so much better. I also apologize for grouping all of my brothers together. Each and every one of them is so very different, and to group them together is an insult to the unique individuals that they are.

How we perceive people, words, and even situations is important. How much of what we experience with a person is true and how much is our own clouded perception? At first, looking at these things can be very daunting, but one word at a time, one experience at a time and we can change the way we see things and the way we say things. Every time I do this, I feel a little more success because it is so huge. At first, I felt like everything I was saying was wrong—but that's not the truth. There might be a better way of saying it or just a different way of saying it. Another thing that was not easy for me was really looking at what someone said to me and using that information to learn and grow to become a better version of me, instead of going into victim mode.

When I was young, I realized that I couldn't read the way my classmates could. I couldn't understand what people were saying if they used a lot of words that I didn't know. This is why I bought into that belief that I was stupid (which is a lie). But in 1997, my spirit guide "Charles" told me that part of the reason why I was given these learning disabilities was so I wouldn't read other people's stuff, other people's beliefs. I wouldn't do what all the self-help books told me to do. They wanted me to be my own person—find my own way that worked for me, so I could later teach what I had learned to others. And because it came from my own thoughts and experiences, I would resonate with it more completely. So now I am able to accept my learning disabilities as a gift from God. Wow, what a change! In doing that, and experiencing that, I learned that I had a unique way of looking at things. I could take my thoughts and experiences to a totally different place. As an adult, this has served me well in all aspects of my life. I believe it has also assisted me in trusting myself and my choices more.

Birthdays are another place that my perception is off. My 10th and 16th birthdays were so difficult for me; my family forgot both of them. When my girlfriend Nan's mom found out that my family forgot my 10th birthday, she went out and bought me a store-bought cake and she had a little party with just her, Nan and me. I felt so special. But my 16th birthday was a nightmare. For a girl's

Sweet 16 birthday in my hometown back then, we got a corsage with 16 small sugar cubes on it. It sounds hokey now, but back in the 1970s, it was special. All my friends had had their birthdays in September and October, so by the time my birthday rolled around in January, I knew the routine. The first thing that would happen is when I got to school, my locker would be decorated and inside would be balloons and signs. But on my 16th birthday there were no decorations, signs or balloons. I figured my friends must be changing it up because of everyone having the same thing for their birthdays. At lunch, it would be a birthday cake and singing, presents and corsage. I get to lunch and Dinah was missing, so I thought, oh, she must be getting the cake. When she arrived, she said, "Sorry I'm late, but it's my mom's birthday and I needed to get her a card." I said, "I know. Your mom and I have always had the same birthday." All my friends looked at each other like oh, crap, I forgot—did you remember? They all apologized, and I tried to pretend that it was ok, but I've always felt my birth wasn't a good thing and this certainly wasn't helping me to heal that.

After school, my brother Grant was supposed to pick me up and take me to get my hair cut. It was below freezing, and I was wearing a dress. This was before cell phones, and I just had to trust Grant would remember, but he didn't. It was four miles or more that I had to walk. My tears froze on my face, and by the time I got to the salon, they were closing for the day. My stylist took one look at me and felt so sorry for me, but he needed to get home, so instead, he asked me to be a model at a show of the latest hairstyles. I would get my hair cut for free and it would be a lot of fun. I agreed and walked home.

When I walked into the house, Mom asked me what took me so long. Just as I started to tell her about the worst birthday of my life, Mom stopped me and said, "Just a minute, I'll be right back." When she left the room, I knew exactly what she was doing. I picked up the extension phone and listened to my mom ask someone at my dad's property management job if they could please get a message to my dad. She asked him to stop and pick up something for Mary Beth's birthday. My parents had forgotten my birthday, too. None of my brothers or sisters came over for cake and ice cream, because there was no cake and ice cream. When Dad got home, Connie was with him. She opened my closet door to find me on the floor crying. Connie asked me what happened. As I started to tell her what happened, she got that same look that I had seen so much that day and excused herself for a few minutes. When she came back, she had a plan. I was to get dressed because she was going to take me out to celebrate my birthday.

Connie took me to Burger Chef. It was a hamburger joint that both she and Grant worked at. The whole crew sang happy birthday, and Connie put a candle in my hamburger. After dinner, she took me to a grocery store, and I was to wait in the car. When Connie finally came out of the store, she had a Sweet 16 corsage and a bag of licorice. She had called while I was in my closet and asked them to please, please make a blue Sweet 16 corsage for a young girl who just had the worst birthday on record. They said they couldn't in that amount of time. Connie must have been very persuasive because there it was in my hand. I couldn't believe that Connie had done that for me and I was so very touched.

Connie then took me to an R-rated movie, so I couldn't wear my corsage or everyone would know that I wasn't old enough to go in. Just knowing that she had done that for me was enough. Mom and Dad ended up giving me two turtlenecks. I had asked Mom when I was seven or eight why I don't remember my birthdays from when I was younger. She said, "We didn't do anything for your birthday until you noticed, then we had to start."

All of this and so much more led me to believe that my being born was not a good thing if the people in my own family didn't feel it was worth celebrating. I did have a sweet birthday moment in 4th grade. The night before my birthday, we had company. Some firemen had come over. I interrupted them and asked Mom and Dad what treat was I going to take to school tomorrow for my birthday. I don't remember what their excuse was, I only knew I wouldn't be handing out a treat... again. But the next day I was called to the door of our classroom. There stood that same fireman from the night before with a whole box of full-size Hershey candy bars for me to give my class. I was so excited that I don't even know if I ever thanked that dear, sweet man. When was the last time you did something like that for another person? My therapist Robert taught me that he always tries to do the next right thing. It's now a lifestyle I try to live by, and it has had a huge effect on my life.

Chapter 5: My First Introduction to the Man I Would Marry

At the age of 22, I had decided that I had had enough. Enough pain, enough hopelessness, enough sadness. I had been asking God for so long to die, it was time to take action, and I picked a day and time when no one would be home. I was living with my oldest sister Christine at the time, and the most difficult part was traumatizing someone I loved with finding my body, but the thought of living one more day was more than I could take. As soon as Christine and her family left, I got out my pen and paper to write my suicide note. "To whom it may concern…." What a way to start a suicide note. I wasn't even crying. I had been detached from life for so long. I had talked to my brother Grant about ending my life, and he said, "Mar, I don't know what to say. Is it really that bad?" When I talked to my sister Connie about it, she said, "If you could just lose five pounds, I'm sure that would make you feel better." My sister Christine said she was really, really concerned about me and wished I would seek professional help.

I paused in my writing when I heard a voice say, "Are you sure you want to die?" Wow, that question surprised me, not hearing a voice asking me the question, but the question itself. I had to think about that for a moment. My response finally came. "If this is going to be my life, then yes, I do want to die." He asked, "What would it take for you to stay?" Again, I had to think. I knew I had to be more honest in this moment than I had ever been in my life. I said, "I've heard of this thing called happy, and I would really like to experience that before I die." I had experienced happy moments, but they were few and far between. I was talking about living from a place of happiness. He seemed to understand this. I felt so much peace in his presence. I felt loved and seen (all the way to my soul) and really heard. Like my pain was his pain. I felt like someone finally understood, but I didn't know what he understood. He said, "What would you say if I told you that there is a man coming to you. This man is going to love you no matter what." I responded without hesitation, "I don't know what those words mean. So far, the people that say they love me only cause me pain. I have had enough of that." He said, "Yes, you have." Then he showed me a vision of a man—MY MAN. He had dark blond hair, and blue eyes that sparkled when he smiled. For some reason, I knew that he was 6 feet tall, and I saw that he wore a navy blue uniform. I didn't look at much except those eyes and that smile. I nodded my head, and the connection was broken. I was back into the heaviness of being fully me again, but suddenly I felt something strange as I ripped up my suicide note. Later, I realized what it was—it is called Happy! My problems were still there, my pain was still there, but they were different. They were less heavy, less all-consuming, just... less. And I felt my whole life change in those moments. Thank you, God! Thank you, God! Thank you, God!

I looked for my blond-haired, blue-eyed, 6-foot-tall answer to a prayer. I asked my dad to introduce me to some firemen or policemen. He had been retired for many years, but he had to know someone, right? After about six months, I convinced myself to trust God's time, not my time. I had moments of doubt, but when I connected to the energy of that promise and the vision, all doubt faded away.

In the meantime, I was laid off from my job and couldn't find another. I was back living with my parents in the basement. When I went to job interviews, they seemed to really like me, but when they saw what I made at my last job, they would say, "You wouldn't be happy here." I would say, "Try me." My sister Connie transferred down to Tennessee. She asked me if I'd come down and be her receptionist for a while because hers had just quit. I said no thank you. My parents encouraged me to go. Mom even told me that it was my responsibility to take care of Connie. I reminded her that Connie was 2 ½ years <u>older</u> than me. My dad just wanted no more kids living with them to deal with. So off to Tennessee I went.

The cultural change moving down south was a surprise. The people were really nice, even if they called me a damn Yankee every day. Connie and I worked really well as a team, and I was enjoying going to work. I hadn't been there long when Dad let us know that he needed quadruple bypass surgery on his heart after having a heart attack. I wanted to leave immediately for Wisconsin, but Connie said we couldn't leave because there was too much going on with the business. Besides, this surgery is a piece of cake now, and the doctors know what they are doing. I said fire me if you want to, but I need to be there for Daddy. I hopped on a Greyhound bus. My ticket was paid for with quarters I took from the soda machine at work.

A few days later, my father had double bypass surgery. It was supposed to be quadruple bypass surgery but the procedure took so long that the surgeon ran out of time and couldn't complete it, as the heart can only be stopped for so long. I was the only one of his children that was sitting in that waiting room with Mom. Later in life, the other kids had their chance to step in and help Dad. This was mine, and it was so very special and sacred to me. While he was in ICU, I got to spend 15 minutes out of every hour with him. Mom couldn't handle it; she ran out of the ICU screaming that he looked dead. As I visited and spoke to him during those 15-minute visits, I noticed some things. The first was I knew that he was going to live (I know, what I know, that I know). The second was that each time I came in, the improvement in him was really remarkable. The third was every time I told Dad that I had to leave, he would shake his head almost violently and tears would come down (Dad couldn't speak because he was on a ventilator). Later, I asked him why he did that. He said that he was so scared that he would never see me again, or hear my voice, and he was so afraid. Up to that point, I had never felt more connected to a human being than I did in that 24 hours with Dad. He was able to leave the ICU about six hours before they normally do, because he was doing so well that they had no reason to keep him there.

Unfortunately, 48 hours later my father didn't even remember that I had ever been there, and the sadness of that engulfed me. I had to keep telling myself that it didn't matter. What mattered was that he was going to live. To say that it was that easy to let go of, would be a lie.

A month later Mr. Smith came into our dance studio in Tennessee for lessons. I said, "Oh, he is cute but way too young for me." I thought he was four years younger than me. It ends up that he is four years older than me. The second time Mr. Smith came in, his teacher was in the office closing a sale, so I did the warm-up dance with him. I looked into those beautiful blue eyes, and I KNEW! As we danced, I said, "It's you!" He said, "What's wrong with me?" I said, "Nothing, Mr. Smith, you are perfect!" I know it sounds ridiculous, but I couldn't wait for the dance to end so I could call my sister Christine to tell her. When she answered, I said, "I met him, Christine, I just met him." "Met who?" I said, "HIM." "HIM, him?" I said, "YEP!" "Blond hair, blue eyes, 6 feet tall and wears a navy blue uniform?" I said, "Yep, except for the uniform."

I waited for six weeks, but he never asked me out. I couldn't understand it. I thought this was a done deal. When the studio had a bonfire and hayride outing, I went and stood next to Mr. Smith and was trying to figure out what to say, when I heard, "Mr. Smith, would you go out with me?" I wanted to scream, "NO, HE'S MINE!" Then I heard him say, "I thought you couldn't date students, or you would lose your job?" Oh, my gosh—he's talking to me (I must have been the person that asked him out, but I didn't say a word!). I explained that I had already given my one-month notice and that I would be done by Christmas (this was Dec. 7th). "In that case," he said, "I would really like to go out with you. Would next Saturday work for you?" I couldn't believe I had to wait for a whole week.

It was time for the hayride. My new sweetheart's name was Marsh. We managed to (wink, wink) accidentally sit next to each other with our feet dangling off the edge of the hay wagon. My hands were cold, so Marsh did such a romantic thing. He gave me his left glove while he wore the right glove, and then he took my right hand and held it and wrapped our clasped hands with his scarf. I wanted to cry. Who does such a sweet, romantic thing? My gift from God, that's who!

Chapter 6:
The Last First Date I'll Ever Have

Marsh called me and we spoke a couple of times during the week. He said he would pick me up at some specific time in the early afternoon. I was so excited, and I managed to get Connie out of the house so I wouldn't have to worry about her catching us. When the appointed time came and went and no Mr. Smith... I got pretty worried. About 20 minutes late, he finally shows up. Should I answer the door? You see, I had a dating rule. If a guy can't show up on time, then I am obviously not his priority, so I would have my mother tell them that when they didn't show up on time, I made other plans. I was not going to waste my time on someone that didn't care enough to show up on time.

It ends up that Marsh had accidentally left my address at home and didn't know which apartment was mine. He asked at the apartment complex office about Mary Beth Roberts, but Roberts was a made-up name for work and of course, he didn't know that. He said that as he drove around the apartment complex, he suddenly just knew which one I lived in and rang the doorbell... and was right. Talk about guidance!

I answered the door, and Mr. Blue Eyes was holding a white carnation. Aaawww! Ok, all is forgiven. He informs me that he thought we could go to the zoo. Are you kidding me? I love the zoo! How did he know? The zoo in December was something I had never done. I was so ready for this, except I was wearing heels. Oh well, at least they were comfortable heels. He took pictures of me, which gave me permission to take pictures of him. I love pictures of people. And now, even if I never saw him again, I would have his picture to remember this day. We had peacocks walking around us. Marsh pointed out things to me and explained things to me, and he really listened when I talked. My face hurt from smiling so much. It was a perfect first date. He even took a picture of us using the timer button thingy on his camera.

I need to let you guys in on something very special. The night before this first date, we had our regular Friday night party at the dance studio, and Marsh showed up in... his "Navy" navy blue uniform. Yes, folks, my guy is a Sailor! Mr. Red, White, and Blue (Navy blue) through and through!

Now back to our date. I could tell when Marsh suggested dinner after our time at the zoo, that it was one of those things where he's going to wait and see how the zoo went before he mentions dinner. That way if it's a disastrous date, he could leave. While eating dinner, I decided to test Spirit's theory of "he's going to love you no matter what." I told him about my vision of him as I was writing my suicide note. I could see he wasn't very comfortable with it, but he didn't run for the door so that was good. I then ordered a salad, which I never eat on dates as they are too messy. Again I was testing and didn't even realize it. Boy, am I silly. Marsh must have been enjoying himself as much as I was because he suggested we go to a movie next. I was in heaven. I asked him how he knew that I would lose my job if I dated a student, and he said that he had asked his teacher about me. That perked me up. I was wondering why he never asked me out. I felt so much better now that I knew he was interested in me too. Fun fact about Marsh—he has never asked a girl out for the first date. We have all asked him out. We women know a good thing when we meet it!

At the movie theatre, Marsh asked me if I won. I said, "Won what?" He said that "if the numbers on your ticket stub total 21, you win a prize. It can be a free popcorn or movie ticket, whatever they want to give." I told him that "I had never heard of that," and he said, "Oh, yeah, it's nationwide." So, I totaled them up and nope—we hadn't won. After about our 10th movie, we finally got 21. We were in West Virginia, and Marsh told me to go claim my prize. As I was walking up to the concession stand, I turned to look at Marsh one more time because I couldn't get enough of him, and I saw his shoulders shaking from laughing so much. I knew then that he had been teasing me all along and I smacked him on the arm. He was so proud of himself that he could keep it up for that many months. My guy has a brilliant sense of humor. Just good, clean fun, never done with malice and that means so much to me after my upbringing. During the movie, Marsh took my hand. It was amazing how at 24 years of age, I was wishing and hoping that he would hold my hand again like he did on the hayride. But it was so much more. I don't know if you know this, but the hand is very sensitive. He was stroking and making circles on my hand and I was melting. I mean, if there hadn't been a chair in front of me, I swear I would have been on the floor. Oh, Thank You, God! When he kissed me, it was pure heaven on earth! Yes, Yes, Yes, it was an absolutely perfect first date. Marsh asked me out again for a week later. Guess what I said?

Because Marsh didn't ask me out earlier, I was running out of time. Our second date was on Dec. 21, and I was leaving in a couple of days to move back home. How was this going to work? We were at a dance showcase on the 22nd and I knew Marsh was going to go home to West Virginia for Christmas, so I asked him what he thought about us going to West Virginia for Christmas where I could meet his family. Then we could travel on to Wisconsin for New Year's where he could meet mine. He said I don't think so. I was disappointed, but I was so grateful for the two dates we'd had, so I said ok. I went off to help some other students from the studio. About an hour later, Marsh came up to me and said, "My mom is really looking forward to meeting you." Marsh had called his mom collect from a pay phone at the event. I had so many butterflies in my stomach I think I could have taken flight.

So I packed up my stuff, and we were off. It was a long drive, and I was going to see mountains for the first time. I feel like I asked Marsh a million questions. I was waiting for him to get frustrated. I was waiting for him to ask me to shut up. He never did. I kept telling God, "You really did an excellent job of picking this one for me. Thank You!" He knew so much about history and different states, the capitals, presidents, horticulture. If he didn't know something, he'd say, "We'll have to look that up," and sure enough, he went to the library in his mom's hometown to find answers. When we went through the Smoky Mountains, I was disappointed because it was dark. He told me to roll down my window. When I did, I said, "It smells like there's a fire." He smiled and said, "You may not have seen the Smoky Mountains, but at least you got to smell them." And then he explained why they smell like that. If this was a dream, I never wanted to wake up.

When we finally got to his parents' house, I was very nervous. His mom was so young and so welcoming. Marsh is four years older than me, but his mom was 15 years younger than mine. His stepfather had a good sense of humor, but I could tell all my talking was driving him crazy. I tried to stop, but Marsh encouraged my questions. What's a girl to do? On Christmas, his youngest sister, Mandy, came over with her husband, and his stepsister was there. Everyone was waiting for the big announcement that we were getting married because Marsh had never brought a girl home before, except his girlfriend in high school. Boy, were they surprised to hear that we had only had two dates. Mandy was very protective of her big brother. To see the way they talked to each other was so beautiful for me to observe. That is what I had always wanted from my brothers. There was so much kindness and respect. It was a wonderful Christmas and a wonderful visit.

Next stop, Wisconsin. My mother fell in love with Marsh immediately. Dad didn't say anything good or bad. My brothers tried to tease him a little, but they saw Marsh as pretty serious with people he doesn't know. Connie's reaction was embarrassing. How could I date a student? She was so disappointed in me. On and on she went. Connie ended up not talking to me for over a year because I had the gall to go against her and be so selfish. My happiness was unimportant. What mattered most to her was a bunch of strangers in another state. My disappointment in her overwhelmed me. It was all me, me, me from Connie like always. My relationship with Connie was never the same after that. This ended up being a good thing, because I needed to stop needing Connie's approval and start approving of myself.

Chapter 7:
Where Do We Go from Here?

Eventually, Marsh had to get back to his military school in Tennessee. Marsh was an electronics tech. His job was to fix the equipment that analyzed data. I was so sad to see him go, but I would never forget him. I didn't want to force myself on him anymore. He needed to make the next move. I needed him to show me how important this relationship was or wasn't to him. Finally, he asked me if I would be interested in going back to Tennessee for ten weeks while he finished school. There was only one problem. Marsh had already given notice on his apartment and was due to move into the barracks when he got back. Well, he'd figure something out. My staying with Connie was definitely out of the question. I went back down south with him and he rented a furnished trailer, and we played house for ten glorious weeks.

One evening while living in this trailer, Marsh and I went for a walk after he got home from school. I remember this like it was yesterday. We ended up walking through a plowed cotton field. The sun was getting lower in the sky when Marsh asked if I'd like to watch the sunset with him. Are you kidding me, of course I would. I plopped down on the ground, but Marsh said, "What are you doing?" I was a little embarrassed (this was my first time watching a sunset). I jumped up and said I'm sorry, I thought you meant here. He said yes, but you're facing the wrong way. I looked at him and looked at the sun and I had no idea as to what I was supposed to do. He turned his back to the sun and sat down, and patted the ground next to him. He then told me to pick something in front of me to watch the sunset on it. There wasn't much to choose from in a large, open field, so I chose a big old tree. He said now watch the sun slowly set on every part of that tree. And we did. When it was about to set on a knothole, Marsh said, "What do you think lives in there?" I said "I have no idea." He spoke softly in my ear. "I wonder if it's an owl, or maybe a family of squirrels." I felt like I could climb into that knothole and see. Then he whispered, "Do you see those last couple of leaves hanging on to the branch that the sun is setting on?" I nodded. "How much longer do you think they'll last?" I just shook my head. I was almost in a trance feeling the oneness with this tree—our tree. Finally, the sun set on the last bit of the tree, and I cried. I had never been into nature really, but in that moment I felt so connected to that tree. I can't even put it into words. It was one of the most spiritual moments of my life so far. How can it be possible that a man that knew so much, could be interested in little ol' me? I loved the way Marsh saw and experienced things differently just like me... but with his own twist to it.

Finally, it was graduation day for Marsh. As his Commanding Officer addressed the audience, he informed us that the men and women who were able to graduate from this school were in the top 2% of the most intelligent men and women in the armed forces—officers or enlisted, that is how difficult this course was. Marsh graduated 5th in his class. His Commander said that roughly 70% of the people that started this course had dropped out or failed. God, are you sure that I'm the right one for this highly intelligent man? I asked Marsh later, "How can you be with someone who's not smart, when you are so smart?" His reply was, "I'm book smart and you are people smart. I would love to have your ability of being able to talk to people. Do you have any idea what a gift that is?" My answer—NO. It's just what I do and who I am. Is this special? Am I special?

Marsh asked me if I'd be interested in spending the next four weeks on vacation with him. Our first stop was a stay with his navy friends Don and Marie in Norfolk, Virginia. During our first couple of days, we just hung out in their home.

Finally, I spoke up and said, "Aren't there some historical places around here?" He just laughed and shook his head—time to research what was nearby. We started with the Norwegian Lady, a monument to an 1891 shipwreck. My father is 100% Danish, so I was very emotional when I read about it. We walked on the boardwalk and I got to see the ocean for the first time, and I was in awe of her power, and yet I could feel her playfulness. Yes, the ocean and I were going to have a love affair, that I was certain of. We saw various forts and went to historical Williamsburg for two days because there was so much to see and learn. Of course, I had so many questions, and if Marsh didn't have the answer, there were plenty of people around that enjoyed sharing their knowledge. To stand in the room where our constitution was written was... no words. Every politician should have to visit Williamsburg before they take office. I had never been more proud to be an American. Our last tour before heading out was to the navy carrier *USS America*. As we drove down to the dock, we saw ship after ship. Destroyers, frigates, submarines. They were so huge, and suddenly war seemed so very real. Not a movie or a game on a computer. There were thousands of sailors on the ships and walking around, and I realized that each one of them was willing to sacrifice their life for what I had just read and learned about in Williamsburg. My father (who repaired planes in WW2), Grandfather (who took care of the horses in WW1), and my brother Grayson (who fought in Vietnam and came back a different man) were all ready to make the greatest sacrifice for a country that they believed in, for a democracy that they believed in. Wow—I wished they were there at that moment so I could hug them and look them in their eyes and say thank you. Thank you for your willingness. Thank you for your bravery. Thank you for being related to me.

As I saw ship after ship, my legs started to shake. Finally, we were at the carrier *America*. I was too scared to do this. Then I looked at the man who held my heart. He was so proud to be able to share this with me, and I found new strength. Five thousand men (back then, only men were allowed on carriers) lived on this ship. They were gone for six months at a time. If Marsh went to sea, this is the ship that he would be on. Be strong, Mary Beth, you can do this. Did you know that a carrier has three elevators that can bring several planes at a time up to the deck? Their wings are folded so they fit into the hanger deck and onto the elevators. I still managed to ask a few hundred questions and really was fascinated, but in the back of my head, I kept hearing war, War, WAR! When we got back to Don and Marie's house, Marie took one look at me and told the boys that we girls needed to talk. As soon as the door closed, I started sobbing. I just met the man of my dreams—actually better than a dream. I couldn't lose him to war. How can I marry a man that could go off to war? War was so very, very real now. Bombs are real, and they kill real people. This is not a game. How can people enjoy playing war? Please help me, God, to understand. How do I move forward with this relationship? How do I move forward with my life now that I have this new understanding?

Marie was magnificent. I can't remember all that she said, but she let me know that it is an honor and a privilege to be married to a military person. Not everybody can handle it. There is a lot of divorce, something like 40% in the Navy because they are gone so long, and when they come home, they find the family has just continued to live their lives without them. It's difficult to fit back in for a few months and then you're gone again. You just have to find a way to make it work for you and your family. By the time we finished talking, I was exhausted, but I felt better. I still had concerns, but for now, I would take it one day at a time. I wanted to live every day that I had with Marsh to the fullest. Before we left Virginia, I got to meet Marsh's beloved Aunt Mary Jo, Uncle Luke and their boys. I felt very scrutinized by Aunt Mary Jo. Marsh had a special place in her heart, and I knew I was going to have to prove myself; I just hoped I would be in his life long enough to do that. We were about to go back to his mom's home when I said, "How far is Washington, D.C., from here? Could we stop there on our way to West Virginia?" Even as far back as this, it seems that Marsh had a difficult time saying no to me.

I hope that every American at some point has an opportunity to go to Washington, D.C. I could have spent months there because there was so much to see, learn, and experience. The Capitol was so impressive. I felt like a groupie looking for stars I knew. I loved the Lincoln Memorial—I didn't want to leave. I could feel Lincoln's burdens and his sadness. At the Jefferson Memorial, I was mesmerized by his words. That man had a gift, and I'm grateful that he used it to start this country of ours. The Washington Memorial was ok, but I didn't feel that it expressed much about the man that was our first president. The White House looked to be about one quarter the size I thought it would be. My absolute favorite part of our trip was the Vietnam Memorial Wall. So much pain and conflict was felt there at this wall. So much unresolved pain. So many mementos. I felt my brother and all he must have gone through over there. Marsh explained a lot about the war. Marsh had joined up just before the end of the Vietnam War. The war ended right after Marsh got out of boot camp. Thank you, God! Back then when Marsh was in the military, they always had to wear their uniforms when they traveled. He spoke of how shocked he was that people would spit at him because he wore a uniform. Things certainly have changed over the years. Thank you, God!

On to West Virginia. By now, I felt that Marsh and I were more than in love. He was a part of me and I was a part of him. I wanted to know and experience everything with him and through him. Abby, Marsh's mom and I had some incredible talks. Because I asked so many questions, I heard stories that even Marsh didn't know. The most surprising and eye-opening was the story of when Marsh became sick at age 11. His Aunt Mary Jo had mentioned the difference in Marsh before and after his surgery. What I learned from Abby helped me to understand better this man that I had grown to love so much. When he was 11, he suffered from severe constipation. It got so bad that they sought medical help. The only tool they really had to help Marsh way back in the hills of West Virginia was an x-ray machine. The x-ray showed a mass in his colon. The interpretation from the doctor was that Marsh had a tumor and needed an operation. After cutting open this sweet child and taking out a section of his colon, and stitching him back up, they said it wasn't a tumor after all, simply poop. The next day the doctors said that he could start back up on solid food. A few days later Marsh was in extreme pain though getting little sympathy from the on-duty nurse, but eventually it was back to the x-ray machine. As they were raising the table to get an image with him standing up, Marsh's incision broke open. There stood this 11-year-old little boy holding his intestines in his hands. Both young techs ran out, though one had enough sense to come back and lower the table before Marsh went unconscious. They took him to his room and covered his stomach area with a towel while they tried to reach the surgeon. 8 hours later they located the surgeon, and Marsh was wired back up. Yes, I said wired. Marsh said they put wire the thickness of a coat hanger in one side and out the other and twisted it so that it would never open up again. So my cutie pie now has what looks like 13 belly buttons. Infection set in. Marsh was unconscious for a very long time according to his mother. Finally, the doctor told Abby that she needed to prepare for the worst. He wasn't coming out of his coma and nothing was improving. The next day, Marsh opened his eyes, sat bolt upright in bed and told his mom that "It's ok. Everyone really likes me here." She said that Marsh described heaven to her before falling unconscious again.

About a year ago, Spirit showed me something so very special. Marsh was sleeping next to me, and he was holding my hand (something he often does), and the vision started. I was shown that this was when he was in the hospital bed unconscious. He went from lying on a hospital bed to getting up and floating to a very gently sloping hill covered in grass and wildflowers. The sun was shining, and even I could feel the gentle, caressing breeze. There was a little girl chasing butterflies. Marsh went to join her. When she turned around, I saw that it was Morgan, our daughter. She was about four, and Marsh looked to be about six. They ran and jumped and played. The smiles on their faces were radiant! It seemed like hours and hours of just loving being a child, and loving being together, rolling down the hills, picking flowers and making them into chains (even in heaven, Morgan is making things—I had to giggle). The peace and love between the two of them was so evident. Then Morgan took Marsh's hand and led him to a spot and sat down. Marsh sat down next to her. She looked him in the eyes and said, "You have to go back." Marsh said, "I don't want to go back. I want to stay here with you." She told him that if he didn't go back, she couldn't be born. She needed him to be strong and brave for her. Without hesitation, he said he would. They hugged each other and the vision ended.

Abby said that about 24 hours after Marsh had spoken to her about heaven, he came out of his coma. He lived, but he was changed. The hospital staff had no respect for the shy, reserved young boy that he was. They thought nothing of exposing his body as a freakish amusement for anyone and everyone to look at. He withdrew into himself until he was hardly recognizable. All his relatives spoke about Marsh as before and after the surgery, and now I had a better understanding of why.

I feel with all my heart that one of the gifts I was to be in Marsh's life was for him to be able to move forward without feeling this emotional pain left from his surgery. I kissed his 13 belly buttons to make them all better. I had Dad show Marsh his beauty mark (his scar from his bypass surgery), and Marsh said, "That's nothing, look at mine." He lifted his shirt, and for the first time, he displayed his scar with pride instead of horror and shame. At that moment, something in Marsh shifted. I am grateful, I am grateful, I am eternally grateful. Thank you, God!

Spending time with his family assisted me in knowing another side of Marsh. Marsh is a very private man. You have to catch phrases when you can, to ask about later; he doesn't like sharing. At our wedding, his mother and stepfather gave us $1000. I was in shock. His mother said, "After all Marsh did for me and his brothers and sisters, it's the least I can do." I asked her, "What did he do?" Marsh said, "Mom, that's enough." She said, "No, son, Mary Beth is your wife now and you need to start including her." So she told me how part of the reason Marsh joined the Navy was that the Navy would provide food, clothing and a place to live, so Marsh could send a good portion of his pay to his family so that they no longer needed to move back in with relatives when they ran out of money. I can't imagine anyone in my family ever doing such a selfless thing, and it changed who I wanted to be.

Our time in West Virginia wasn't all talking. One day Marsh was outside for a long time in the snow. I looked out the upstairs window and saw that he had stamped out with his boots a huge heart, and inside it was "I 'heart' M B"! How incredibly sweet was that! Oh, how I love this man! Another time, he and I were building a snow fort using a trashcan to shape large blocks. I had never seen it done that way, but it was very efficient. Suddenly, his mom, who had those pink sponge curlers in her hair and a fishing hat on top of that, was pelting us with snowballs. She had a whole pile of them next to her, and she was laughing so hard as she kept letting them fly. It only took Marsh a couple of seconds to join in the fun. It took me a bit longer. You see, I was hoping that someday this woman would be my mother-in-law. You don't hit a mother-in-law with snowballs... do you? Well, eventually, I joined in. I didn't hit much, but I sure had a good time. I wondered if my mom even knew how to make a snowball?

A few days later, Marsh's cousin Jake came to visit. I believe Jake is several years younger than Marsh. He was a big guy, with a true West Virginia hillbilly beard, and looked like a biker dude with his leather coat and tough-guy look. I watched as the funniest thing happened. Marsh goes up to Jake, and says in this adorable little boy voice, "Do you want to make bubbles with me?" Jake had no idea how to respond or what Marsh was asking. Marsh explained it to him, and then these two grown men went out in the cold March snow with a bucket of Joy dish soap mixed with glycerin and water. Using bent coat hangers as wands, they made huge bubbles that shattered like glass when they popped because the air was so cold. Jake had the best clean fun he'd had in who knows how long. I think Marsh had another fan after that day. You see, one of Marsh's gifts is he touches lives just by being a nice guy who just has a kind heart. He does kind things all the time, and never even understands the difference he just made in a person's day. I've watched it happen thousands of times.

Finally, Marsh's leave was almost over. The plan was to take me back to Wisconsin and he would fly out to his next duty station from there. Have I mentioned that his next duty station was Pearl Harbor, Hawaii? It was so difficult to let him go, but I really didn't have a choice. I was going to go to a place in Michigan called Creative Health Institute and help my brother Ken and his wife Janet. Marsh and I promised to write to each other, and I hoped he meant it. Because of my past, I really didn't feel I deserved more than I had already received. Every day had been a love story dream come true. I needed to trust God and trust our love for each other. Can I do that?

Chapter 8: The Longest Three Months of My Life

After six weeks at Creative Health Institute in Michigan, my dad came to pick me up because I needed to get ready to go to Hawaii! Yep, it seems that Marsh missed me as much as I missed him. He did such sweet things while we were apart, like sending me a huge calendar so I could count the days until we were together again. He set up a time while I was in Wisconsin that we would be able to go out and look at the full moon at the same time. It was something like midnight for me and 8 P.M. for him. Marsh let me know repeatedly that I was only coming for a vacation. The max that I was allowed to stay was six weeks. He was paying for my ticket.

Plane trips to Hawaii tend to be at night, so you can hopefully sleep on the flight and arrive in the morning with a whole day of tropical fun ahead of you. All I cared about was seeing Marsh and feeling his arms around me. When I was little, we three little kids would sit on Dad's lap while he slept in the rocking chair. As I laid my head on Dad's chest, I felt there was no place safer on the planet. I feel that same way when I lay my head on Marsh's chest. I know in my heart that this man that I love more than I thought possible will do anything and everything to keep me safe.

There Marsh stood at the gate with a white carnation and pink rose lei for me. What a sight for sore eyes. He had the rest of the day off to spend with me. He was trying to pretend that this short vacation for the two of us was not that big of a deal, but the truth was that it was a huge deal for both of us. He had to get permission to move out of the barracks. Find an apartment that he could afford. Move all his stuff in and unpack. Not to mention buy a car, which happened to be automatic even though he preferred stick shift. I don't drive a stick, so I wonder why he got an automatic car? The next six weeks were heaven with some tension thrown in. It was difficult to get settled in when Marsh was constantly reminding me that I only had six weeks. I think it was to remind himself as much as it was to remind me. Most of the time we just tried to fit in as much fun and love as possible. He worked Monday through Friday, and when I arrived, there was a serial killer on the loose! I kid you not! Marsh asked me to stay in the apartment and not to interact with strangers until this person is caught. Ha-ha, like that's going to happen. I have six weeks to see everything I possibly could and I was going to make the most of it.

I had never been a big museum girl because it was not something my family did. Here in Hawaii on the island of Oahu, I went to every museum I could find, and I loved sharing what I had learned with Marsh when he got home. Visiting Iolani Palace was a favorite of mine. This is the only real Palace in the United States. They described how they would wake the king and queen by chanting. Slowly, the chant would get louder and louder, and one window shutter at a time would be slowly opened until the king or queen were awake. I learned about King Kamehameha, who had united the islands into one kingdom. It was a very violent history. Unfortunately that is a pattern on this planet. The state capital is behind the palace, and everything about its architecture is symbolic of the islands, representing the ocean, the volcanoes and the royal palm trees. I love to hear and experience the meaning behind things. Banyan trees separate the capital and palace. Banyan trees make me very happy because they feel very old and wise. For some reason, when I am in their presence, I feel like they are sharing their wisdom with me. There were even band concerts once a month at a gazebo by the palace. For a girl who had to take buses everywhere, having so many things close together was wonderful. Marsh's favorite thing about the area was the library. That man loves books, which translates to loving libraries. I didn't understand this love in his life. I'd rather be out experiencing life, than reading about others out there experiencing life. Boy, have I changed! I now enjoy both.

My first luau was so exhilarating. The food, the stories, the dancing, the singing, and on top of all that there were fire dancers. Everywhere I looked was a new thing to take in. I was so mesmerized. Marsh loves watching me in awe. I felt like I had experienced so little before I met him, and now every moment felt like an adventure, and Marsh Smith was my guide.

A mere day or two before I was supposed to leave, Marsh asked me to stay longer. This wasn't permanent, and he could ask me to leave at any time. I decided that if I was staying, I'd better get a job. I decided I would like to try being a dental assistant. I am very good at putting people at ease. Where are they most uncomfortable? The dentist's office! I found a position working for five dentists that were willing to train me. I loved talking to the patients. Finding out about where they came from, what they miss most about home, etc. I think the dentists would get frustrated with all my talking, but the patients loved it. Soon, the dentists noticed that the days I was assisting them were always completely booked.

Marsh and I continued to discover the island. Marsh said we should focus on one part of the island at a time and do everything we can in that area. That way, it would take years to do it all, so there are always new things to experience. Marsh enjoyed snorkeling at Hanauma Bay while I enjoyed feeding frozen peas to the fish. It's a nature preserve now, so many of the things we were able to do back then are no longer allowed. I loved Sea Life Park. It may be small, but the dolphins and penguins were always so entertaining. The dolphins had such fluidity and grace, and the penguins were just plain funny. In all the times I had been there, only one penguin had ever managed to leap through the hoop. We both loved Pali Lookout, but sometimes I could feel the warriors and the fierce battles that had happened there centuries ago, so my legs would feel weak and shaky. The Polynesian Cultural Center was a dream come true for a girl with a lot of questions. You get to visit different "villages" that represent the Polynesian Islands of Fiji, Tonga, Samoa, New Zealand, and of course Hawaii. In each village, they showed how a village from that particular island used to look, the games they played, the food they cooked, crafts they made, the traditions they had. In the evening was the most incredible grand finale with everyone doing their native dances in their native clothing. I was so happy that I squealed like a small child. Again, I could have spent days there.

After a year, I decided I needed to go home to get my stuff. I quit my job and decided to make it a long trip so I could go down to Tennessee to see Connie and try to heal our wounded relationship. Then over to West Virginia to see Marsh's family and back to Wisconsin. While I was in Tennessee, Marsh called and we had a pretty long talk. He decided that he didn't want me to come back to Hawaii. He really needed some time to just be a "sailor" in Hawaii. Spending 24/7 together was just too much for him. He loved me, and if I had my own place and we were dating, that would be a whole different situation. But having me in his space constantly was more than he wanted. I told him I understood, and if he ever changes his mind to give me a call. If I'm still available, I would love to see him again. I also told him that he needed to contact his family to let them know that I wouldn't be showing up in a couple of days. And that was it. I cried and cried, and then tried to figure out where I was going to live and what I was going to do with the rest of my life. How do I go from living in paradise with the love of my life—my gift from God, to living in my parents' basement? After two days, Marsh called and said he couldn't do it. He wanted me back even if it meant 24/7 in his space. He tried to do it without me, but nothing was as much fun as it was with me. My response was that I wasn't going to hurry back. I wanted him to really think about what he wants because it is difficult constantly feeling like my life is in his hands and he decides if I stay or go. I needed to feel more secure. He said he would try.

There was a strain on our relationship when I finally returned to Hawaii. I had been gone about six weeks. I needed to feel like I belonged. Marsh got a set of mattresses instead of a futon. I got a dresser with mirrors on it. Slowly it was becoming "our home." Yet no matter how hard Marsh tried, always in the back of his mind was his desire to be free. We still went out exploring and playing. Everyone always asked when we were going to get married. Every time I asked

God if he was sure that I was supposed to be with Marsh, within a few minutes I either got a shooting star or a double rainbow. I would say ok, but you might want to have a conversation with Marsh because he doesn't seem to agree. About 1 ½ years later, we split again. I moved into a women's hostel, I guess it was called. Marsh paid my rent and we saw each other a couple of times a week, but I was miserable. I shared a tiny room with another girl. Then one of the women I had worked with at the dental office offered me a room, but before long I think my depression was putting a damper on her marriage, so back to Marsh I went. I felt there was no place on the planet that I was wanted. When I had returned to Hawaii from Wisconsin, my father gave me a set of luggage. He said, "Notice the size, Mary Beth. Big enough to come for a visit, but not big enough to stay." My sister Connie told me again and again that I absolutely cannot move home with Mom and Dad. They don't need my shit, and they were so happy with all of the kids out of the house. Five years later, Connie moved into Mom and Dad's basement with a newborn baby and a husband. But she only stayed on and off for nine years, so I guess that made it ok. I was so angry that it was ok for her, but not for me. These double standards were getting old.

2 ½ years had gone by since our first date and the old belief of not being enough or even being wanted returned. Marsh had never yelled at me or belittled me, he just always wanted his own space. I told God that if he didn't ask me to marry him for Christmas, my birthday, or Valentine's Day I needed to move on. It was time to stop living from a place of unwantedness. I know that God wanted us to be married, and I wanted it too, but I also wanted a family. I wanted children! So Valentine's Day came and went. Marsh's coworkers said it was leap year, and the girl can ask the guy. I did. His response was... if I tried to create the most perfect woman for me, she couldn't compare to you. But I just can't do it. So that payday I started putting some money aside for my plane ticket back to Wisconsin.

On February 24th, Marsh and I went to Maui to see the baby whales. Every year all these humpback whales come from Alaska to Maui to have their babies. When the babies are older and strong enough, they do the long trip back to Alaska. We were watching the whales on a glass-bottom boat. That means that there was a huge window in the bottom of the boat that we could look through.

We had to pick a place and drop anchor, as the boats are not allowed to follow the whales around. So when we got all settled, I would focus on a baby whale and watch how protective its parents were. I laughed and cried at this beautiful miracle of life. I was in love... with whales. I went below deck to use the bathroom, and when I came out a whale was passing below the window in the bottom of the boat. I felt a moment of panic, and then I was fine. This whale was so close it felt like it was only a couple of feet from the bottom of our boat. All he had to do was breach and we would be goners. As he swam under us, this huge eye slowly moved right across the window like he was checking us out (like he was checking me out). I can still see and feel that eye looking at me right through to my soul. It felt like a soul connection. I was sad when the adventure came to a close. We spent the night in Maui, and that night our daughter was conceived. I knew the moment that it happened, and I told Marsh. He laughed it off, so I let it go and even forgot about it.

Surprise, surprise, I began feeling sick. I went to my doctor, and he asked if there was a chance I could be pregnant. Well, of course I'm pregnant. I need to stop telling God what to do. I knew that God wanted me to be with Marsh, and I got impatient and now look at what happened. I need to stop thinking that I know better than God. I must admit that I was so excited about finally being a mom! Knowing that this baby is going to be part Marsh and part me, means it is going to be perfect. I hope it has Marsh's intelligence and sense of humor, and I hope it has my way of being with people. If this child could be blessed with those gifts, it will never have to struggle like Marsh and I have. And if I could have a healthy baby girl, then all my prayers would have been answered regarding my baby.

Now how do I continue to save money for my flight and manage to leave Hawaii before Marsh figures out I'm pregnant? I'm about six weeks along, which means I only have about 2 ½ months before I need to be gone, and where am I going to go? I wonder if Marsh's mom would be willing to let us stay there and not tell Marsh. Don't be ridiculous, Mary Beth, that is never going to happen. Christine's family only has three bedrooms and five people, so that's not an option. The only option is Mom and Dad. Crap. I was told that prince charming was going to take me far, far away from that, and now I'm considering subjecting my baby to that nightmare? When I talked to Christine, she said that I needed to include Marsh in the conversation. This is his baby, too. I explained that I never wanted to get married because I had to. She said that sometimes we don't have much of a choice. But if Marsh doesn't want ME, why would he want the baby and me? And what if he decides that he doesn't want me, but he <u>does </u>want the baby? I am not willing to risk having to give up this baby! I need to stop sending this baby all of this stress. They need to feel loved and wanted every moment of every day!

About a week later, Marsh said, "What are we going to have for dinner?" Silly me, I didn't even hesitate. I said, "I don't know about you, but I'm having a tuna fish and pickle relish sandwich." Marsh's response was, "I knew you were pregnant." You see, Marsh has a rule—no kisses for me if I eat tuna or licorice, so I never eat them when he's around. Sometimes a pregnant girl has to do what a pregnant girl has to do.

His next question was, "So, when are we going to get married?" Are you kidding me? Just like that—when are we going to get married? I told him that I don't believe in getting married because I am pregnant. I think he was in shock. Marsh has this adorable way of looking down and not saying anything when he knows he is in the wrong. Ok, it would be adorable if I weren't so angry or frustrated when he does it. Finally, he says, "So what are we going to do?" I told him, "I don't know." I explained how I had been trying to save for a plane ticket home. I explained now that we have lived together for a couple of years, I know that I would be a good wife to some man. I want to be with someone who actually wants to be with me and appreciate me. Again, he looks down. "I do love you, Mary Beth, and I think you are going to be a really great mom. This baby is very lucky to have you."

How do I respond to that? Believe it or not all this just somehow evolved into setting a wedding date even though he never actually proposed. I still don't really understand how this happened. From there, it was going to every jewelry store on Oahu to find the perfect diamond. As Marsh put it… "You have to wear this ring the rest of your life. It has to be perfect!" The setting was very simple, it looks like two M's and when the engagement ring and wedding ring are together they form another M. For Mary Beth and Marsh.

We called his parents and mine with the good news. We also told them about the baby at the same time. I don't like lying or even hiding the truth. We put a wedding together in four weeks, and it was so much better than I had hoped for. Of course, my parents didn't come. Mom doesn't fly and Dad doesn't... I want to say that he didn't have the money, but I felt he could have gotten it but it wasn't his priority. I didn't want anyone at our wedding that wasn't there with happiness and respect for our marriage. So, on my side, we paid for my sister Christine to come and officiate, and she did an incredible job performing the ceremony. Christine spoke from her heart and with the conviction of her love for Marsh and I, and her love of God. She was the absolute perfect person to join us in marriage. My best friend Ann was my Maid of Honor. She was one of those unique people who know how to truly listen to everything I have to say and still loves me when I'm done. On Marsh's side was his mother and stepfather, and Marsh's brother who was a Marine stationed in Hawaii at the time. Marsh's brother was his Best Man. Marsh's sister-in-law and nephew, and Marsh's entire Command showed up with their spouses. Marsh's Captain was there in his dress whites and he was beaming.

The morning of our wedding, which was such a sacred and holy day for me, I would be fulfilling my promise to God, and God would be fulfilling his promise to me. The promise we made as I was given the vision of this man that was coming into my life and would love me no matter what. This tiny baby forming in my body was bringing us together in more ways than I thought possible. I know that Marsh loves me, but he always holds a little back, like if he ever allowed himself to love me fully, he would lose a battle he has going on inside of him. I really cared most about just three of us at the wedding—God, Marsh and I. Everything else was an extra blessing.

The place we chose for the wedding was Haiku Garden on the other side of the island. It backed up to the mountains, and we both love the feeling of security that comes from the mountains. It had a beautiful pond with a gazebo on it, and several different settings to have the ceremony. We chose to have the ceremony under a little tiki hut. I wore a ¾-length wedding dress since we would be outside in the heat. Marsh wanted to wear his military dress white uniform. I thought that would be way too much white, so I asked him to wear a baby blue tuxedo shirt and white pants. I wanted the man (Marsh Smith) to marry me, not the sailor (Marsh Smith) to marry me. Now that I look back, it doesn't make as much sense as it did in my head at the time. He should have been allowed to wear what was important to him—this was his wedding, too.

After the ceremony, Marsh's brother and sister-in-law sprayed "Just Married" on the hood of our car in shaving cream. As we drove, it was flying up onto our windshield and wouldn't wash off with the wipers. We were going through the Likelike Highway tunnel and could barely see out the windshield. Somehow Marsh managed to keep us alive. In the car, he told me, "I can't believe you let me drive myself to the wedding. I almost didn't show up." I held back the tears as we drove to our apartment, where we had a small reception on the huge patio there. One of Marsh's coworkers said something about how she noticed that Marsh looked like he was going to run for it at one point during the ceremony. Marsh laughed and said that he almost did several times. Then he told everyone how he couldn't believe I let him drive alone to the ceremony because he almost didn't show up. After everyone left except our house guests, I said I was tired and needed a rest. I closed the door to our room and then I cried and cried. Again Marsh didn't want to be married to me. What should I do? I really wanted to run away. If we had been on the mainland, I probably would have, but here in Hawaii, I couldn't afford it on my own. I yelled at God that he got what he wanted, but now I'm stuck in a marriage with a man that doesn't want me. Will this feeling of not being wanted ever end? Now go out there, Mary Beth, and pretend that your heart isn't breaking.

The next day Marsh's mother and stepdad, Christine and Ann along with Marsh and I headed for our honeymoon on Kauai. We stayed in a three-bedroom condo, and my heart was able to let go of some of the pain. Kauai is my heart center. I don't know how else to put it into words, but Kauai is where my heart can breathe and I guess even heal. In no time, I was feeling happier and laughing, but always in the back of my mind I knew Marsh didn't want to be married to me.

Abby and my sister Christine got along so well. When Abby found out that there were only ten years difference in their ages, she acted like a kid again.

We spent several days going to waterfalls, beaches, the Grand Canyon of the Pacific, and Kauai's own rainforest. It was a very magical honeymoon. I bet that you are wondering why we took so many people with us on our honeymoon. Well, they spent a lot of money and took the time to fly in for our special day. We didn't want to just abandon them on Oahu and go off on our own, so we took them along with us. I'm grateful we did because we were surrounded by people who loved us. After doing all the planning of the wedding alone, it was nice to experience things with our loved ones. Marsh and I had the rest of our lives to honeymoon.

Chapter 9:
And Baby Makes Three

With the wedding behind us, we can focus on our baby coming. I LOVED being pregnant. I loved knowing that I was sharing everything with my baby, my thoughts, my food, my moods, my voice, my wisdom, everything. The first thing we bought was a rocking chair. It had to be the perfect height for breastfeeding. Next was a very thick children's songbook. Every day when I came home from work, I would sing to the baby. I guess the baby loved it because as it grew inside me, it would be impatient if it took me too long before I'd start the next song. I would be singing away and then I had to flip several pages because I didn't know the next couple of songs, and it would kick and kick until I started singing again. But when I saw that it was almost time to start dinner, I would let the baby know this is the last song, and then I need to make Daddy some dinner. The strange thing was once I would say that, it never kicked when the song was done. Even in the womb, we had a very smart child.

I loved to sing. It was a sign that I was happy. My favorite songs were ones I made up—they were also Marsh's favorites. Full disclosure—I think I enjoy making up songs because it was ok to sing off-key and that was the only key I sang in... off. Even before our baby was born, I would talk to it constantly. I would put two items up to my belly and ask which one, and the one it kicked is the one I'd choose. The Spaghetti Factory was a huge favorite of mine during my pregnancy. I wondered how someone can eat the same thing three times a week and never tire of it, but I did. We both wanted a girl so much. Me, because I wanted to right the wrongs from my own childhood. Marsh, because he said he was not a big sports fan and didn't know how to teach a boy any of that. I had to remind him that girls play sports too.

When I was five months along, I woke up with a little spotting of blood. I called my OB/GYN's office and told them. They asked—how soon can you get here? I sped to their office. The doctor came in and listened to the heartbeat and looked at my vitals and said everything looks good. I said, "What about the spotting?" He said, "What spotting?" He looked at my chart and said, "Oh, yeah, I guess I should take a look." I had red flags flying all around me about this guy. I kept hearing "run away, run away" in my head. So after my appointment, I went to the obstetrics ward at the hospital and asked to speak with the head nurse. When she came out, I told her that I am far from home and don't know anyone. My OB doctor doesn't seem to have his act together, and I need to find a new one. I have spotting going on, and I need a really great doctor. She told me she couldn't help me—she was sorry. I said what if it were your daughter in a strange place. Wouldn't you want someone to help her? She hesitated and then gave me the name Dr. Tani. I called him from a payphone and set up an appointment. That ended up being one of the many good decisions I have made in my life.

Everything was progressing as it should. Dr. Tani was always asking questions about my diet, and he ran a lot of tests. My weight gain didn't fit what I was eating. I was so grateful that he was keeping a steady watch over me. Then during a three-day holiday weekend, I started having problems. It actually started Friday morning. I woke up with excruciating pains. Nothing I did alleviated the pain, and the pain wasn't coming and going like contractions. Then the pain just stopped. I went into the doctor, and he said some things were slightly elevated, but nothing that should cause the symptom that I described. He told me to keep him posted. I was fine all day, and then at 2 A.M., I had pain for a couple of hours. This continued all weekend, but each morning the pain lasted longer. Tuesday morning at 5 A.M. I couldn't take it anymore, and we called the doctor. He met us at the hospital. He ran more tests and said he was concerned. They were going to give me some medication to hopefully help me to stabilize. I asked about the baby. He said the baby seemed fine, but he ordered an ultrasound just to make sure. That little stinker of ours crossed its legs so we couldn't see if it was a boy or a girl. She did that at her ultrasound at ten weeks also. All I cared about was that it was ok.

Marsh and I had no boys' names picked out in case it was a boy. I wanted to name it John Doe Smith. Marsh said he wasn't leaving the hospital until the baby was officially named because he didn't want the kid to hate us. I thought he would have a really great sense of humor. What an icebreaker, "Hi, I'm John Doe Smith." Marsh said if it was bald, we could name it Arnchubald Smith. Oh, this kid was going to have a sense of humor with two parents like us. But if it was a girl, she would be Morgan Smith. About a year into our relationship, a friend of Marsh's was talking about his kids coming to visit. I asked what their names were. The girl was Morgan. Marsh and I snapped to attention and looked at each other and mouthed, "Morgan." On the way home, I said, "Oh, my gosh, if I ever have a girl, I'm going to name her Morgan." Marsh said, "I know, I can't believe how much I like that name, too." I asked if he knew any Morgans, and he said no. I haven't met any Morgans either, which means that it holds great potential. Morgan sounds smart and connected to nature and pretty—not ditzy beautiful. Marsh agreed. Of course, with my learning disabilities, I spelled it Morgain.

Each time Dr. Tani arrived at the hospital and ran tests, he was more and more concerned about the results. As he left Tuesday night, he said, "We are trying to stabilize you so the baby can grow a little longer. Right now, the baby is about six weeks too early. Its lungs aren't fully developed and we don't want the baby on a ventilator if we don't have to." Marsh went home to bed and said he'd check on me on his way into work in the morning. I spent the night talking to our baby, trying to convince it to stay inside and "cook" a little longer. As Marsh was leaving the hospital to head to work on Wednesday morning, he met Dr. Tani. He told the doctor that I was so happy to have finally gotten a decent night's sleep.

Marsh asked how I was doing, and the doctor said he didn't know yet, as he had just arrived and hadn't seen the latest test results. So Marsh went on to work and I waited for the doctor. When he came in, he had two men standing behind him.

My doctor was trying to explain things to me, but everything was swirling. He said I had something called HELLP syndrome. It's a very severe form of pre-eclampsia. He explained that these men were here to ambulance me to Kapiolani Women's and Children's Hospital because they were better equipped to handle a case like mine. I said I need to call my husband—I NEED MARSH. I was not going anywhere until I was able to tell Marsh what was going on. Of course, Marsh wasn't at work yet, so I had to leave a message for him to meet me at a different hospital and that it wasn't good news. Please hurry! When I got into the ambulance, I told them that I wanted lights and sirens, the whole works. They said that they were told not to do that. They needed to keep me as calm as possible. I said, "Then I better get the works because if I don't, it might stress me."

When I arrived at my new hospital, everyone was whispering. The nurses were all excited about working with Dr. Tani. He didn't work at this hospital except for extreme cases. I also learned that his skill level was off-the-charts amazing, and everyone loved learning from him. I think someone informed me that this was a teaching hospital, and would it be ok if students observed my case. Of course, if someone can learn from this experience, then by all means, please do. Everyone was running around in a panic. They were shaving my lower abdomen? What the heck was going on? AND WHERE IS MY HUSBAND!! The nurse said the doctor would be in soon to explain things to me.

When the doctor showed up, it wasn't MY DOCTOR! Where was Dr. Tani? It turned out that this doctor was my anesthesiologist. Dr. Tani was prepping for my surgery. "What surgery! What is happening? I need my husband; he can explain this to me." I was told he hadn't arrived yet. My anesthesiologist needed to ask some questions, and I needed to make some decisions. It seems my liver was shutting down, and my platelet count was dropping. I believe my platelet count was 40. Normal is 150-450 (150,000-450,000/mm3, this is Class 1 HELLP syndrome, and has the highest risk for death). If my platelet count dropped any more, I would bleed to death. That got my attention! Ok, what do we need to do?

He said, "We have a couple of options, we can put you under and you will probably vomit in your sleep, it will go into your lungs and you will die." I said, "No, thank you. Next choice." He said, "We can make a small incision on your arm, and if it clots within a certain timeframe we could do an epidural and maybe you could live long enough to see your baby." I said, "Next option." He said, "Those are your only two options." I said, "Death or death are not very good options." He was so uncomfortable. I didn't know what to think or decide. Then I remembered how much I wanted this baby, and if I could meet our baby, even for a moment, then that's what I wanted to do. I asked him if the baby was going to be ok. He said, "We hope so, but we need to get that baby out as soon as possible. Ok, let's do the epidural and let's do it now." He had me sign some paperwork, and he left. I remember saying to someone, "No one dies in childbirth anymore. Modern technology, I thought, prevented that."

I was crying when Marsh finally walked in the door. He had been in the wrong waiting room, and no one knew what he was talking about. He thought I hadn't arrived yet. I tried to tell him everything I had been told. He was in shock. He didn't know what to say. Finally, Marsh said, "I need something to eat." I said, "Are you kidding me... I haven't eaten in 36 hours and I'm dying and you need a candy bar?" And then I got from Spirit (but I didn't know that back then) that he needed a moment alone to just... assimilate all he had been told.

When they showed up with my gurney and we were going down the hallway, Marsh was holding my hand, and I said, "Wait, I can't have a C-section, I skipped that chapter in all the books I read." The nurse chuckled and said, "You're getting the crash course. You just need to lay there, and we'll do all the work." I said, "What about Marsh's cheer he's been practicing?" I looked at Marsh, and he shrugged and sang his cheer that we came up with when we got in trouble at Lamaze class. It seems that laughter is frowned on in Lamaze because laughter tightens the muscles. The reason for Lamaze is to relax the muscles. We got yelled at in every class. Marsh and I love to laugh all the time. So, as we were going down the hall, Marsh was singing, "Push it out, shove it out, waaay out!" The nurse laughed and said, "Try this, Marsh... Pull it out, pull it out, real slow."

As we approached the surgical unit, Marsh had to go to a different area to wash up and then put on surgical scrubs. It helped me to know that he would be by my side in five minutes. The room was really buzzing. I don't remember seeing Dr. Tani when I rolled in, but I was pretty distracted. They got me on the table and were strapping me down under my chest and both my arms and legs. That was when I noticed that I was seizing. I was flailing all over the place. I suddenly noticed a light over to my right. As I focused on it more, I saw my brother Ken. What was he doing in my C-section? Suddenly, Ken turned into a beautiful, blond Angel. She smiled so sweetly at me. That's when it really sunk in that I was going to die. I felt so very at peace. There are no words to describe how calm and at peace I felt. She was moving closer. She just looked into my eyes, my soul, and smiled. Suddenly, I said, "Wait a minute. All my life, all I ever wanted was to be a mom. I'm a few minutes away from achieving that, and you are going to take me away? No way! I want to meet my baby before I go." Then the angel moved into the corner. I couldn't believe no one was mentioning the beautiful shimmering Angel in the room. As I studied her in the corner, I realized, hey—if that worked, maybe I could get some more time. So, I said, "Do I really have to go? I really think that I could be an amazing mother. I'd really like to be given the opportunity to try. If at any time you decide that I'm not doing a good job, you can take me." I noticed the water coming from my eyes, but I couldn't wipe it away because my arms were strapped down. I said, "Please let me try? I want to live!" And she smiled one last time and then disappeared.

The anesthesiologist made a small incision on my left forearm, and we all watched to see how long it took to clot. It was so quiet in the room. It sure seemed like a very long time to me. Finally, he said it had clotted, we can do the epidural. They untethered me and had me lie on my side to do the epidural in my spine. I asked him how good he was at target practice. I heard some laughter. He said he was better when the room was quiet. I said, "Then maybe we need a better anesthesiologist." He laughed and said, "You've got the best." I said, "A little talking shouldn't be a problem, then." I forgot that the shaking from my seizures could make it more difficult. Next thing I knew, I was rolled over and strapped in again. Pretty soon, he pinched me above my chest and asked if I could feel that. I said no. And then I said, "Hey, how much am I paying you to pinch my boobs?" The whole room was laughing loudly. I heard a nurse or someone say, "I thought she was dying?" Another person responded, "She is." I turned to them and said, "Yes, but if the only thing my child hears from me before I die is my laughter, I've just given them my greatest gift."

I looked around and said, "Hey—where's my husband? He should be here by now." They said that he's being prepped, it's ok, he'll be here soon. I felt like there were moments when I was very alert, and other times I was drifting. I saw Dr. Tani, and I said, "Ok, Doc, be careful with that incision. I need my bikini line preserved." I weighed about 250 pounds, so that got another chuckle. He said, "Oh, are you planning on wearing a bikini?" I said, "It could happen. Maybe not today, but it could happen!"

I asked for Marsh again, and finally, he came in. I was so relieved. Marsh said that when he came in, he saw Dr. Tani praying in the corner. They asked Marsh how he wanted the mirror adjusted so he could see better. He said he didn't want to see. He just wanted to look at me. I saw how surprised he was by my trembling seizing body. I said, "They said this is normal, but I don't know." Finally, when he really looked me in the eyes, we were able to communicate with each other, and we both felt better.

Shortly after that, I heard a very, very faint baby cry. I said, "Oh, honey, someone just had a baby, isn't that wonderful?" He had no idea what I was talking about. Eventually, I said, "Shouldn't we have a baby soon?" And someone calmly mentioned that we had a baby girl. I couldn't believe it—we got our girl! Our little girl named Morgan. Thank you, God! How do I thank You enough? Not only did my baby make it, but it was a girl! Thank you, thank you, thank you, God! I am so grateful. They stopped and showed me this tiny face in a blanket. They asked Marsh to follow the baby. He didn't want to leave my side, but they kinda scooted him out. Later, we were told that the reason why Marsh was kept out in the corridor for so long and not brought into my delivery room was that they have found that the dad is more likely to reject the baby if he witnesses the mother dying. So, they kept him out of the room as long as possible, but when they saw how much more stressed I was because he wasn't there, they decided it was worth the risk in this case.

With Marsh out of the room, they closed me up and wheeled me to the recovery room. I had huge pads on both sides of my gurney because of my seizing. That way, I wouldn't hit the rails and injure myself. When Marsh arrived, I wanted him to describe every detail about our little girl. He smiled at me and said, "She's uglier than sin." I couldn't believe he said that to me. And then I remembered a conversation we had about babies while I was pregnant, and he said that he thinks all newborns are uglier than sin. That was his way of bringing some normalcy into a moment that was anything but normal.

I wanted to call everyone and share the news with them. I have a picture of me on the gurney with thick pads, talking on the phone telling my parents. I was only allowed that one call; they didn't want me to overdo it. Marsh called his parents. We asked our parents to call everyone else for us because we were a little busy healing. When asked what the baby's name was, I was grateful that the nurse told me what the two most common spellings were, and asked which I wanted, or if I wanted something more unusual. So, I guess Morgan was named by a nurse too, in a way. Another pattern.

I was not allowed to meet Morgan properly for three days. They were concerned that seeing her would stress me, and I would start seizing again. Every night for five nights, they didn't think I would make it. For some reason, when they would take my blood pressure at around 9 P.M., it would be so high that they expected me to code at any moment. Looking back, I wonder if it was the thought of Marsh leaving me and going home that sent it up so high. Marsh's presence has a very calming effect on me. We have witnessed this many times in the last 34 years and is another reason why I guess God really knew what he was doing when he brought Marsh into my life.

Marsh and I developed a routine when my blood pressure would go up so high. He would ask for two ice packs and tell the nurse to just leave us. He would put one ice pack behind my neck and the other at the base of my spine. Then he tried to sing soothing songs to me. We found the thing that worked best was him telling me stories of all the things that we were going to do and experience with our baby girl, Morgan. Then, at about 6 A.M. they would come in, and my blood pressure was so much better. Marsh would then sleep for an hour on the floor in my room, go home for a shower and change of clothes, and come back and we would do it all over again. Because I wasn't allowed to see our baby girl, I was sending Marsh over all the time to visit her. I didn't want her to feel abandoned. After her first 24 hours of life, they did a spinal tap on her. They thought she might have meningitis, but the test came back negative, thank you God! I was in a pretty big fog as you can imagine. I only took one pain pill through all of this because I didn't want to give Morgan any more drugs than was absolutely necessary through my breastmilk.

The moment finally arrived—I was going to hold my baby girl for the first time. She was three days old. We had to scrub up to our elbows for several minutes, and then put on an isolation gown. Morgan was in Intermediate ICU. She had an IV and was living in an incubator. She looked so small in that huge, sterile box. Morgan was born weighing 4 pounds 2 ounces. Because she was allergic to the formula they gave her, she went down to 3 pounds 9 ounces. We couldn't take her home until she reached 4 pounds 8 ounces. Once I was released from the hospital I began pumping milk for her. I never really had my milk come in fully, so we always had to supplement.

When I was talking to her as I watched the nurse get her ready for me to hold her, I cried. I was ALIVE! And I was about to hold my precious baby girl for the first time. Thank you, God! I felt so guilty that because of me, our daughter had to come so early. How can I live with that guilt? Oh, what was I thinking; Morgan and I were alive—that's what matters, end of statement. Still, every once in a while, I felt that old guilt of "I did this to Morgan." I'm so sorry, my baby girl. Please forgive me?

Her doctor said the stress that I was experiencing all those nights before she was born was probably what helped her lungs develop enough that she didn't need to be on a ventilator. Personally I believe it was God assisting us.

So the big moment finally came. She was so, so small; how do I hold her? I don't want to crush her. I found that when the front of her body was against the front of my body, she seemed to feel more safe and relaxed. We had to get her fed and burped in 15 minutes, so she wouldn't lose too much of her body heat and have to burn valuable calories to try to get her body temp back up. Morgan has always had a low body temp—is this why? It was so difficult for me to surrender my baby to the nurse. I stayed and watched her as long as they would allow me. I was told that if I stayed too long, then they might not let me come back very often. On day three and four, I only got to see her once a day, and then on day five, it was twice a day.

My sister-in-law Janet suggested I put an amethyst in her incubator. My first day home, I got one and sterilized it, because otherwise, they wouldn't allow it in the incubator. After about two weeks, Morgan's energy had sucked all the purple color out of the crystal and it cracked inside, though not on the outside. I was a patient for five days after her birth, she stayed in the hospital for 20 days after her birth, and she had to be fed every three hours. We were there for every feeding except the 4 A.M. feeding, and when they threatened to do tube feedings, we came for that one, also. Marsh did not want Morgan to have his gag reflex from having tubes shoved down her throat. I drove the nurses so crazy that they let Morgan come home at 4 pounds 6 ounces just to get rid of me. Why can't they turn down the fluorescent lights in the ICU at night? Why does rock music have to be played so loud? This is my baby, and I will fight for her highest good. So, on November 1st, our baby girl got to come home.

One more very important thing I want to mention about Morgan's birth before I close this chapter… Spirit told me about 20 years after Morgan's birth that I needed to ask to live that day. That for most of my life, I had asked to die. For me to shift the energy of that, to undo the damage I had done by choosing death over life, it had to be reversed. And at that moment when I asked the Angel to live, I succeeded, God victoriously, in shifting that energy—that belief. My life is sacred, and I choose to live it in the most honoring way I know how, by living a life filled with gratitude. Thank you, God, for my life. Thank you, God, for my daughter's life. Thank you, God, for my husband Marsh. It is good!

Ten years after Morgan's birth, we returned to Hawaii. It felt like coming home to me. Everything felt so bright and full of life. We took Morgan to our favorite hangouts to share our love of this special place with her, of course, that included the Byodo-in temple. We taught her how to feed the sparrows and we fed the koi. While there I felt a greater connection to the multitude of religions "God" energy. It is all creator energy, just with different titles and traditions. As the years have progressed, I have a greater understanding of the connection we all have to "our" creator energy and the love and knowing we receive from it. It is all oneness. We are the ones that need the labels, not our creator. We are the ones that need to separate through our religions and beliefs. It is all Love, period. Our creator is Love, period.

Morgan went off exploring on her own at the Byodo-in temple, just wanting to be in the energy and take it all in. They had a small grove of bamboo that Marsh and I had never seen before. Morgan found it, almost like she was being drawn to it... pulled in by an invisible force. She stood in the middle of the grove and started to sway with the bamboo. It was mesmerizing to watch them and also listen as the bamboo creaked. In that moment, I witnessed Morgan become one with nature. I understood why later in life, Morgan wanted to get married there. Unfortunately, it just didn't happen.

Morgan had a fun teacher in school that year, that the "gifted" kids met with once or twice a week as she helped them to expand their way of thinking. This teacher had a 20-inch-tall Cat in the Hat[2] stuffed animal that she gave kids to take on their traveling adventures along with his journal. We turned it into a very special part of our trip. Morgan took really fun pictures of him and wrote in the journal like it was him speaking, not her. Her teacher was ecstatic with the results and had Morgan present it to the other kids in her class. She took pictures of him stuffed in a suitcase with part of him hanging out like he was trying to escape. She made little signs to put in the picture to express how <u>he</u> felt. When we went to Pali lookout, off to the right there is an area where the wind comes up the side of the mountain so strongly that you can totally lean into it and it will hold you up. Well, Cat, of course, had to have his picture taken there. We did a luau, and Morgan posed him as if he had eaten too much.

[2] Dr. Seuss (Theodor Geisel), *Cat in the Hat*, 1957.

We went to the Polynesian Cultural Center, and just like her mom, Morgan was so interested in learning everything. She even got a real Tahitian hula skirt made from very thin bark strips. It is so beautiful and vibrant.

We stopped off at my old dental office to see everyone that I had worked with 12 years earlier. I didn't know if any of them would remember me. What I learned was that I'm pretty unforgettable. They welcomed us with open arms. They were disappointed that I didn't give them a heads up that we were coming, and asked us if we could come for lunch the next day. When we arrived, they had a birthday cake for Morgan and had ordered a beautiful lunch spread for us and all the staff. My heart was so touched by their kindness. When we make a difference in life, it comes back to us tenfold, and I opened my heart to receive.

Another stop I wanted to make on Morgan's birthday was at Dr. Tani's office to thank him for saving both mine and Morgan's life that day ten years ago. As we entered Dr. Tani's office, it was easy to see that he was very busy. Good, I am grateful that his practice has flourished, he deserves the very best. As I approached the receptionist, I realized I didn't know what to say. I was suddenly so emotional I couldn't speak... only tears. Even as I write this, there are tears in my eyes. This man had fought to save my life. A life that I had thought for so long was worthless. Dr. Tani hadn't thought so, and he did everything in his power to save us. How do I express to this stranger at the desk that wasn't there back then and didn't know me? Suddenly, I felt this was ridiculous. We can't go back. How many hundreds of babies had Dr. Tani delivered since then? If he didn't remember me, this would be really embarrassing, and it would put another chink in my heart. Marsh stepped in.

Marsh held strong and wouldn't let us leave until we at least tried to see him. It was almost like this was the main reason Marsh had come on this trip. Did he know in his heart how important this was for me? Or was this important to him? I don't know. The receptionist did go back to tell Dr. Tani that Mary Beth Smith and her family were here to say hi to him. He came rushing through that door in a few minutes with the biggest smile I had ever seen on him. He is a quiet, humble, amazing man. He was taking a pair of exam gloves off his hands. He rushed forward, eyes twinkling, and he hugged me. I cried. He turned to my hubby and said, "Marsh, it is so good to see you again." Then he looked at Morgan and smiled. He said, "This must be Morgan all grown up." How had he remembered all our names? Then he looked me in the eyes, and he said, "It is so good to see that you are doing ok. I have wondered how you were from time to time. Your case is the scariest case I have ever had, and I am still surprised at how well everything turned out." We talked for another 5 minutes or so and then he had to get back to work. He thanked us for stopping by.

How, how did he remember all our names? How did he remember so much after ten years? Thank you, thank you, God! I am truly grateful. And thank you, Dr. Tani. You will always hold a special place in my heart. I see your magnificence!

Chapter 10: Baby, Come Back!

Once we got baby Morgan home from the hospital, I felt like I didn't want to ever leave the house again. I just wanted to hold my baby girl until this whole new lifestyle felt real. I kept waiting for someone to knock on the door and tell us that we had gotten the wrong baby. She was so perfect. She made small mew sounds when she wanted or needed something. I was beginning to think that she didn't know how to cry. When we went to the doctor's office, she proved to me that she could. Morgan's doctor told me that because she was a preemie, she would probably have something called growth retardation (she would always be small for her age), and she would be much slower at learning than other children. I said, "Thank you for your opinion, but we have connections with people in high places (God), and I don't think that will be true for Morgan." By three months of age, Morgan was at 100% for weight and 90% for height. So much for that doctor's theory. I'm grateful I didn't buy into his beliefs. I bet Morgan is too.

Three days after Morgan came home, we were on to our next crisis. Morgan was eating and started choking, the milk came out of her mouth and nose, and she was having trouble breathing. For some reason, I called her doctor instead of heading to the hospital. That decision may have saved her life. I love my guided life! The doctor's office told me to take the blue suction bulb that we had gotten from the hospital and suction Morgan's nose. I did that, and she was breathing better, but something was still wrong. I put her in her car seat and headed to the hospital. As I was driving I looked over and Morgan wasn't moving and it looked like she wasn't breathing. I was rubbing her chest as I drove faster and faster while yelling, "Morgan, wake up. Come on, sweetie, we've come through too much for you to leave now. Morgan, Morgan, come on, Morgan, come back to Mommy. I love you so much, Morgan. Please don't leave me." As I pulled into the emergency room entrance, Morgan opened her eyes and smiled at me. Oh, my gosh, I couldn't believe it, she seemed perfectly ok. I was shaking and crying as I carried her into the emergency room. I told them everything that had happened. They ran some tests and said everything seems to be normal. I laughed at their choice of words and said nothing about her life so far has been normal, but thanks for the encouragement.

When Morgan was about 12, I was telling someone this story when Morgan interrupted me. She said, "I remember that. You were so scared until I opened up my eyes and breathed again." How could she remember that, she wasn't even a month old, and I hadn't gotten that far into the story, but things like visions and guidance were pretty normal in our lives by that time. Morgan is very connected, but as far as I know, she has not opened herself up to her true potential, but she'll get there if she wants to.

The next time we went to the doctor, Morgan got her 3-month shots. My dad was visiting at the time. Morgan had a temp and screamed for over 24 hours; that was when I learned she could cry. I learned it was an allergic reaction to pertussis. I read what could happen if she ever got the pertussis vaccination again, and I wasn't willing to risk it with her. When she was supposed to have her second vaccination, I told the nurse that she gets the DT shot, not the DPT. The nurse asked what her reaction had been and I told her. She said, "I'm sure she'll be fine." I said, "That's not your decision, it's mine and my husband's, and we insist on her getting only the DT shot." She rolled her eyes at me and left to get the shot. My guidance was kicking in again. When she returned and put the serum into the syringe, I stopped her and asked to see the bottle. She hesitated but finally handed it to me. And there it was, DPT! I picked up Morgan and said we will be finding a new pediatrician and left the office. The doctor called me later to apologize, but it felt right to leave and not look back. I had to take a stand for my child until she was old enough to do it for herself.

My dad visiting us during that time was a dream come true for me. With me being the youngest, and Dad not having the best health, I had been concerned that my children might never get to know their grandpa. That made me feel sad, but here we were with Dad rocking my daughter like I had seen him rock all of my nieces and nephews. I kept thanking God that I was able to experience this with them. He even fell asleep as they were rocking. It felt just like when I was safe in his arms as a child.

I was able to take Dad to my favorite island of Kauai, but mostly we saw everything there was to see on my island of Oahu. I was so happy and proud to share my new life with my daddy. It was perfect timing because Marsh had to travel to another country while Dad was visiting, and it was wonderful having reinforcements. On Dad's last day there, he said, "Boy, it sure would have been nice to have gone deep-sea fishing." Are you kidding me? I kept asking if there was anything special that he wanted to do and he said, "I'm just here to spend time with you and your family." I called some boats, but they were already out for the day. Another missed opportunity. When Dad got home, I called to make sure that he made it ok. Mom said, "Oh, yes, he's fine. He just hopes he never has to look at another waterfall as long as he lives." Why do I even try? That's what I kept saying, why do I even try. It cost us a lot of money to fly Dad out here and take him all over, and he didn't even really appreciate it.

I focused on Morgan, and that was such a pleasure. I spoke to her constantly, not because I wanted her to have a large vocabulary (which she did), but because I wanted her to be curious about everything around her. I wanted her to understand that you can learn something from anything and everything— and it worked. One of my favorite stories from when she was little was about whenever we would go into our backyard. There was a big dog in a neighbor's yard behind a tall fence that barked and barked. When we heard it, I would always point and say, "Dog, arf." One time when we were on a walk, Morgan pointed at a bush and said, "Gog, arf." I said, "You're so silly, Morgan, that's a bush, and it doesn't say arf." She pointed to the bush and said, "Gog, arf." The next time we went into the backyard and the neighbor's dog barked, I pointed and said, "Dog, arf arf." Then I noticed that I was pointing at a bush. Morgan had never seen the dog; she had only heard it. How silly am I!

For the first 1 ½ years, when Morgan cried she would vomit, and it would come out of her nose and mouth, so we couldn't trust her with just anyone to suction her and watch that she didn't stop breathing. Because of this, Marsh let me stay home to raise Morgan even though money was very tight. I loved being Morgan's mom. At night, Marsh would come out to check on me and I would be rocking Morgan and she would be asleep in my arms. He would say, "Honey, Morgan needs to get some sleep. You need to put her in bed." I would whine, "But, when I put her to bed, she keeps waking up different each morning." She grew so fast and was so smart. At 6 months old Marsh came home from work just as I was feeding Morgan green beans. He said Morgan when Mommy feeds you green food like that you need to do this... and he did that spitting raspberry maneuver. Well, surprise, surprise, Morgan actually understood him. Every time I fed her green beans, peas or broccoli she would give me the raspberry maneuver and spit it out. Marsh was so proud to have taught her that. How could she know what green was at 6 months old? At her one-year checkup, the doctor asked if she was talking yet, and I laughed and said yes. She asked how many words were in her vocabulary. I said, "I don't know. She repeats almost everything I say. I guess at least 100?" The doctor laughed at me, and Morgan reached for me and said, "Mum-mum, go bye-bye now." I said, "Honey, in a little bit, we aren't done here at the doctor's office." Her reply was, "Yes, all done. See Daddy, yes?" The doctor was shocked. I started pointing to things in the room, and Morgan named them. Water – table – light – shoe – head – fingers – nose – paper. The doctor said she has never heard such an articulate child before. I said, "I know, she is extraordinary."

When Morgan was thirteen months old, my brother Ken and his wife Janet, stopped for a couple of days on their way home from New Zealand. We went for a walk, which included walking through a tunnel under the street to get to the other side. It had a great echo. Morgan and I loved to make animal sounds when we walked in that tunnel. Ken started doing a chant, and Morgan started chanting, too. Ken went crazy over that. He asked me when I had started chanting. I told him, "I have never chanted a day in my life." "Then how did Morgan know this chant?" I had no idea. When we got back home, Ken asked if he could take Morgan into the backyard to do some chanting. I said he'd have to ask her. She said, "I'm gonna go outside now, 'kay?" When they finally came back in, Ken said that she was a little Dalai Lama. I said that's nice. He said, "I'm serious, Mary. She sat on my lap and didn't move for two hours, and all we did was chant. She knew how to do it, and she sat perfectly still. I swear she was a Dalai Lama in a past life." I said, "Well, that would explain a lot about her."

Morgan just felt like such an old, wise soul. She knew things and understood things that were beyond me. I used to ask Mother Mary to help me to raise Morgan in the best way possible. Then our next obstacle arrived. Morgan was 15 months old, and as we went for a walk, I was carrying her and my back went out. I got us home because we were only two houses away. I laid on the couch, and for the rest of the afternoon, Morgan brought things to me until Daddy came home from work. He took me to the doctor. It ended up that I had two slipped discs. Marsh stayed home a couple of days, but it wasn't getting better. I was on muscle relaxants and that helped somewhat as long as I didn't move. When Marsh went back to work, I kept Morgan on the bed with me all day. My 15-month-old daughter was taking care of me. Marsh put food for us on the bottom shelf of the fridge. He tried to have everything within reach, like diapers, wipes, phone, and remote. We had toys and books on the floor by the bed, and Morgan would bring me the activity that she wanted to do up onto the bed throughout the day. After several weeks, I said this isn't fair to Morgan, so Marsh found a home daycare near our home. It just happened to be a woman from our Lamaze class.

Morgan seemed to be adjusting really well, but I was a mess. We couldn't afford daycare, and I wasn't getting any better and the guilt of it all was setting in. Marsh had taken orders to Japan, and we were leaving in seven months. How were we going to make all of this happen? I started having very real conversations with God. Not the begging kind, but more like the curious kind. Why do I keep creating health issues? What is that all about? My sister Christine's words were always in my head, "Everything happens for a reason." What could the reason be behind this? I needed to take care of our little girl. She needed me, and I needed her. How was this going to work? And most importantly, how could we work on fixing this? I found that I really, really like talking to God. During that timeframe, I started to read a book titled *Conversations with God*[3] by Neale Donald Walsch. Many days, Marsh would come home and find the book thrown across the room. I had such difficulties reading. I could not go on to the next word until I knew what this first word meant. My reading was agonizingly slow and frustrating. He used a lot of words that I didn't know, and now on top of everything else, I felt stupid again. Morgan would probably pass me up by kindergarten (another lie). If it was a good day, I may have gotten a page read. That's how I started talking to God more consistently. If it worked for Neale Donald Walsch, maybe it would work for me.

One day as Marsh got himself and Morgan ready in the morning, I kissed them goodbye and tried to go back to sleep. With my bad back that can be quite difficult. Shortly after they left, I heard Marsh moving around in the house. Did he leave Morgan in the car? He wouldn't do that! What was going on? Why was he being so quiet? Usually, he would say something like, "Crap, I'm going to be late. Where did I put that?" This was eerie quiet. I said, "Marsh, is that you?" No response. "Marsh?" (louder). "MARSH, ANSWER ME!" Nothing. I tried to turn over to look, but it takes a long time with an injured back. But as I did turn, I saw a man with black hair slowly walking out of our bedroom. Oh, shit! What do I do? I grabbed the phone and dialed 911. They said, "Fire, police and ambulance, how can I help you?" I said, "There is a man in my house, please send help." They asked for my address. I told them, and said to please hurry, he's right outside my bedroom door. She asked if I had anything there to protect myself with, and I said, "Yes, it's called 9-1-1!" I had to whisper as softly as I could. She asked if the bedroom door was open or closed. I said open. She asked if I could close it. I told her I had a hurt back and couldn't get out of bed. I explained that is why our door was left unlocked so that different neighbors and friends could come in and help me get to the bathroom and get me food. "Please hurry!" She said they should be there soon. I asked her to please not make me talk too much. I don't want him

[3] Neale Donald Walsch, *Conversations With God*, 1995.

to know I'm on the phone with you. She said, "I'm going to stay on the line with you until the police arrive." She kept asking me questions to keep me focused and give me something else to think about. Suddenly I heard more voices. I said, "Oh, shit, there's more of them. Please, please hurry." I heard some guy say, "What are you doing there?" The guy by my door said, "I'm waiting for my friend." New guy: "Who's your friend?" The guy by my door said some name I didn't know. Finally, the new guy came into my room with POLICE on his jacket, and I just started bawling. I couldn't stop. He asked me if a—whatever the name was the guy had said—lived here. I said, or rather I wailed, "NNNOOOO." They asked if I had invited him in. I said, "NO." Finally, they arrested him. There were several policemen in the house. They asked me so many questions. I thanked the dispatcher again and again. She wouldn't hang up until a policeman identified himself to her.

The policeman said that me talking on the phone is probably what saved me. The guy was waiting for me to get off the phone. When they came in, his "zipper was open, and he was ready for action." When all their questions were answered, I called Marsh's work. I was shaking and I could hardly speak. Everything was finally hitting me. When someone at his command answered, I asked to speak to MMMMMAAAARRSHHH. They said, "Mary Beth, is that you?"

"YYYYYYYEEESSSSSSS."

Marsh's Captain got on the phone. His voice was calm but direct. "Mary Beth, I need you to talk to me."

"MMMAAARRSHH!"

He said, "Marsh isn't here yet, talk to me. What happened?" I tried to tell him what happened as I experienced uncontrollable sobs and then hiccups. He said that the moment Marsh arrived, he would send him home, and he was not hanging up this phone until Marsh spoke to him. When Marsh finally arrived, he got on the phone and after several "Yes, sirs," he hung up. He then held me and let me cry.

The next day I wanted Marsh to take me to the police department. I wanted to see this guy's mugshot. The police told me that they couldn't do that because of his rights. I couldn't believe that this guy's rights were more important than mine. What kind of insane world is this? I don't understand. I was so traumatized by this experience that there were times I was filled with rage and other times I felt like a complete victim. In the meantime, we had to prepare to move to Misawa, Japan. I was still bedridden, and Morgan was still in daycare.

Then one day, while I was lying in bed trying to figure out what I need to do or think or be to shift this back injury and be whole again, I realized that if I shifted my attitude maybe that would help. I have been carrying all this victim junk around for so long that I can barely remember that there is another way of being. So, I thought I would start with forgiveness. That is something that I have never been good at. So let's work on this forgiveness thing. I needed to think of someone that I felt had wronged me, correct? Ok—the obvious one is Mom. No, too big, too much, not going to happen with my first time working on this. I need to start smaller, much smaller. For some strange reason, my Aunt Mae came to mind. Gee, where did that come from? Yes, Aunt Mae would be a perfect beginning. I love my guided life.

Aunt Mae was one of mom's many sisters, she was known for just blurting out such mean and insulting things that I found her very difficult to be around. How do I do this forgiveness thing? Ok, Aunt Mae, I forgive you for being a really mean person. Nothing. Well, that didn't feel or sound very sincere. Poo, how do I do this? So I closed my eyes, and I really thought about Aunt Mae. I pictured her. I saw her home. I saw her daughter Susie, who had severe Down syndrome. I saw her husband, Uncle George, who for as long as I could remember, was in bed unable to move or speak. He had had a stroke, and Aunt Mae cared for him all day every day. For how long, I wondered? Ten years, twenty years? I had never bothered to ask. Why hadn't I? Was I so self-absorbed that I never asked questions or used common courtesy? Oh, yeah, I wasn't allowed to ask questions. But with regards to Aunt Mae, that would be a *yes*. Was I like that with everyone? No. Was I like that with most people? *Yes*. Wow. I don't like where this is going, or how it feels. Maybe that means I'm on the right track. So, how do I change this? How do I become more like my sister Christine? She is the best example that I can think of. Christine is kind to everyone. Christine always asks people how they are doing and really listens and responds to their answers. I want to start becoming more like Christine. Wait a minute. I've gotten into trouble before trying to imitate a sister (Connie) and not being myself. Am I going to go down that same rabbit hole? *No*. This is different. I do not want to become Christine; I just want to follow her example of being a kind and caring human being. *Yes, that should be ok.*

Ok, so connect to Aunt Mae again, but this time try to be more like Christine. Think about what Aunt Mae is like. Think about how difficult her life might be. Holy cow, this feels like I'm on the right track. I can see how every moment of every day she is serving her family. Her husband's needs and her daughter's needs have to always come before her own. That is so selfless, Aunt Mae. How do you do that day after day, year after year? Could I do that? Wow, what an incredible woman you are, Aunt Mae. When was the last time you did something totally selfish? When was the last time your needs came first? Can you even remember a time when you weren't taking care of others? Mom used to tell me that you and Aunt Ruth would send home a dollar every week so that she could be the first and only child in her family to graduate from high school. Even back then, you went without, so my mom could have a better life. The tears were flowing so hard. What else have you done where you put others first? I know you give a lot to your church. Your relationship with God is what keeps you going, isn't it? What does that relationship feel like for you? When did it start? Have you always had a relationship with God?

The questions and sometimes the answers continued until there were no more questions, only LOVE. I felt only love and respect for this woman that I have the honor of calling Aunt. I saw what an example she was for me now that my perception of her had shifted, and I was so very grateful. How could I have never seen this before? I want to do this with everyone that I know. Is what I just experienced forgiveness, or is it something else? Something more? I don't know, but I can certainly feel God's hand on my shoulder and his presence in my heart. I certainly feel love in my heart, and I am so very, very grateful! Thank you, God. Thank you, Aunt Mae. What an incredible human being you are!

Well, the story doesn't end there. I cried myself to sleep basking in the immense love that I had just experienced. I was startled awake by the telephone ringing. When I answered it, it was my mother. She said, "You are not going to believe what just happened. I just got off the phone with your Aunt Mae. She wants to send you $1000 to help you and Marsh out while you are stuck in bed." Talk about a confirmation from God that I was on the right track. Guess what, it doesn't end there, either.

When I got off the telephone with Mom, I got out a pen and paper and I wrote to Aunt Mae. I told her about the experience I had just gone through. I told her how honored I was that she was my aunt. I thanked her for seeing me, seeing something special in me. I asked her to forgive me for having ever judged her. I thanked her for her prayers and well wishes and also for the money. I told her the money would be used to pay for Morgan's daycare until I was healed enough to take care of her again myself. All this and so much more was included in my letter. I sent it off with so much love in my heart. My mom called me a couple of weeks later. She said that Aunt Mae loved my letter. "In fact, it meant so much to her that she has called everyone she knows and read it to them. You really have a way with words when you want to, Mary Beth! Anyways, she is going to send you another $1000! She knows that you really need it and she is having a Mass said for you to help you with your back."

I continued to write Aunt Mae from time to time over the years, and when she passed away, my Aunt Marie said that one of her most prized possessions were my letters. She kept them in her nightstand, and they had water spots on them from where she cried as she read them. During the meal after Aunt Mae's funeral, people all around me were trying to one-up each other on how mean and bitter Aunt Mae was. After a while, I couldn't take it anymore. I stood up and said, "I can't believe you people. This is Aunt Mae's funeral. How dare you talk about her like that? Who here, if you needed $5, she gave you $10, and how many of you did she have a Mass said for you? I am so ashamed to call you my relatives." I just walked out—I had had enough. My Aunt Marie came out and offered me a ride back to my parents' house. I was very quiet in the car until Aunt Marie spoke up and said, "You're coming to my funeral, right?" We both laughed. We had such an enlightening conversation, where Aunt Marie said that both her and another aunt would talk to my mom all the time about how it was not ok the way she favored Connie over me. I WAS SHOCKED. Someone had noticed that and said something? Someone spoke up for me? It wasn't all in my head like Mom always told me!

Finally, I found someone that fixed my back. He was an acupuncturist, and it took me almost an hour to get from the car into his office. The first thing he said to me is, "Why don't you feel supported?" The tears came, and I realized that I was frustrated because Marsh had taken orders to a foreign country and never even talked to me about it beforehand. He just made the decision for all of us. Again I felt like what I wanted, or needed, didn't matter (another lie). This poor wonderful acupuncturist just listened and assisted me in letting go of all this junk that I had been holding onto. Then he did his acupuncture needle magic. This was one wise man.

I have since then learned the importance of healing the emotional aspect in order to heal the physical. It is so very, very important that we look at what triggered a physical ailment or disease so that we can release all of it. Of course, I didn't learn that more fully until about five years ago. I had been collecting clues about it over the years, but I didn't understand how all the pieces fit. Then about five years ago, my sister-in-law Janet helped me and helped me and helped me until I was able to let go of my ailment and move forward again. I'll be explaining it more thoroughly later in the book. For now, know that I walked like a normal person out of the acupuncturist's office with absolutely no pain... until I got out of the car at home and walked back into my old limited beliefs. All the pain and discomfort came back, but this clue told me that this back issue was going to be temporary. I just needed to follow the breadcrumbs until I was fully healed. It wasn't a matter of if I would be healed, but when. Again I knew what I knew, that I knew, and it was good!

Remember the conversations we've had about perceptions? Well, let this be a lesson for you. I perceived that Marsh was being utterly and completely selfish taking orders to Japan without talking to me first. How dare he say he loved me and then not involve me in the conversation? That's not love—blah, blah, blah. Guess what, he actually did it because he loved me. About 25 years later, I was talking to my therapist Robert about how difficult it was for me that Marsh didn't talk to me about taking these orders before he accepted them. I told him about how my back was misaligned (think about those words...I was misaligned. And I was MISALIGNED IN MY HEAD AND HEART WHICH CAUSED MISALIGNMENT IN MY BACK), for ten months and how it was then on and off for at least another year or more. And then I heard the word "lie" come to me from Spirit, and I saw the vision of the truth. I saw how when we were first together and Marsh would talk about Japan (he had been stationed there before), he would light up and he'd go into these stories... I told him I wish I could experience something like that. I felt so alive with the idea of living in a foreign country and learning why they do what they do. I told Marsh that it would be a dream come true. And because Marsh loved me so much, of course, when the detailer (the person who assigns military members with a new duty assignment) mentioned Japan, Marsh jumped on it. I couldn't believe what I saw and heard and felt 25 years after the fact. Marsh wanted to make me so happy. He chose Japan because he loved me! Marsh felt this would be wonderful for Morgan to experience also.

When I came home from my appointment with my therapist, I asked Marsh if he took orders to Japan because I had told him when we were first together that I wished I could live there and experience some of the things he had gotten to experience. Marsh said, "Yes." I said, "Why didn't you tell me that? Why did you let me believe all these years that you were selfish, and you didn't care about what I wanted?" He said, "Because what you said was true. I didn't ask you what you wanted. I had an idea in my head and I just went for it."

My honey is a man of few words, but sometimes those words can really change what I think, feel, and believe on so many levels. So in that moment I was able to let go of 25 years of holding on to a "lie"! I work on letting go of old lies, beliefs, and patterns all the time. The more I work on it, the more of them I notice. So again, it was my "perception" that Marsh didn't love me enough. It was my "perception" that someone outside myself had wronged me. And it ended up being the exact opposite. Thank you, God, for giving me an opportunity to correct this "wrong." I love you, Marsh! Thank you for your patience with me.

Chapter 11: A Foreigner in a Foreign Land Called Military Life

Marsh sent Morgan and me off to Wisconsin a couple of months before we left for Misawa, Japan. It was so wonderful seeing everyone again. He had the Navy pack us out early, while he moved into the barracks. That way our household goods would arrive a couple of months sooner. It can take up to six months for someone's belongings to arrive at an overseas duty station. Part of the reason why we packed out early was because I was still really upset about this guy who had entered our home when Marsh went to work. I was living from a space of fear and it was consuming me. I wish I knew then, what I know now. It is always beneficial to face my fears and deal with them so they don't fester in my body and my mind.

I wasn't looking forward to a 14-hour flight with a 20-month-old child and a hurt back going into a country where I didn't speak their language. What the heck was I doing? On to a new adventure, I guess. Morgan did phenomenal on the plane. I think that her having to spend so much time on the bed with me as I healed, assisted her in the long flights. We stayed in a hotel right outside the base for a couple of weeks. We then moved into a tiny apartment in the center of town until we could get military housing. While we were living out in town, one day I was slowly making my way to the bathroom when I collapsed to the floor. I could feel nothing from the chest down. Morgan was trying to help me up, but that was not working. I army crawled to the toilet using my arms, and I somehow eventually got myself onto the toilet by pushing and pulling with my arms. I was determined that I was not going to urinate on the floor. The position on the toilet must have helped (or maybe it was God) because the feeling in my lower body came back. The doctors said that eventually the paralysis would become permanent. I knew that this would not be permanent, but I also did not know what it was going to take to shift from a place of being a victim and dealing with health issues to living from a place of total and complete perfect health.

I decided to work more consistently on my spirituality and connecting to my body to try to understand what it needed to be whole again. I focused on finding the good in as much of my life as I possibly could while still being honest. It was a slow process, but eventually, I noticed getting up and going to the bathroom, or getting food, was not as painful. From there, I was able to experience hours where I was pain-free, which eventually led to an entire day where I only felt discomfort. What an incredible shift, thank you, God. Eventually, I was ok for several days and then would have to spend part of a day in bed. Each month, my time in bed became less and less until I was, God victoriously, healed, and to this day, I only spend a couple of hours a year dealing with back issues. What seemed to help me transform the most, was when I just noticed my back and didn't judge it, no anger and no hate allowed. I would send it so much love and let my back know how important it was to me. Not in a judgmental way, but a loving, kind way. I realized how connected we are to our bodies on levels that no one seems to talk about. When my back hurts, it hurts me, too... not just physically, but mentally and emotionally. This was huge! It's all connected.

We experienced our first real earthquake tremor while living in our apartment out in town. When you are lying in bed, you can feel the earthquakes more. There is a feeling of helplessness that happens with an earthquake. There is no warning siren like we usually get for tornadoes, no seven-day plus warning like you get with hurricanes. It just BAM hits, and you can be anywhere doing anything. Experiencing earthquakes helped me to realize how much I like to be in control. I am a Capricorn through and through.

Because of my back, we needed a bigger vehicle that was higher off the ground, and it needed to be automatic. Poor Marsh spent weeks looking and had to walk so many miles every day until he found the right car. Finally, he found one and it was perfect. Next came moving into our military housing. We were on the far north side of the base in a fairly new 4-plex. On this Air Force base they actually measure the height of the grass. If it's too long you get written up. I was told that three writeups and you got kicked out of military housing and had to pay the expense of living out in town out of your own pocket. We were on the ground floor, which was a blessing for my back. The other three families all had little girls around Morgan's age. Shannon was about two years older than Morgan, but you would never know it. Morgan was so smart and strong within herself and it showed. We learned from experience that we had to have Shannon empty her pockets before she left our house because she liked to take things. One day when Morgan was three, Shannon asked if she could have one of her toys to keep. Morgan said, "No." Shannon said, "I won't be your friend if you don't give it to me." Morgan thought about it for a moment and said, "That's ok, I have other friends." I was so proud of her. Carol lived above us, and she was six months younger than Morgan and was very quiet and shy; she and Morgan got along so well. Katie lived across the hall from us. She was about four months younger than Morgan. She was a wild, loving, carefree heart and that gave Morgan permission to be a carefree child too. The four girls would play in our common area in the entryway, and it was wonderful for everyone. Katie's parents bought a Little Tykes slide and climbing thing for them all to play on. It was a wonderful, supportive environment, and I was so grateful for all of those families.

In military life, there is something called a DW. I was a DW. I was not Mary Beth Smith, I was now DW Smith. Dependent Wife to Petty Officer Smith (Marsh was not an officer, he was enlisted, this was simply what they called his rank in the Navy). I practically did not exist. This was a very difficult adjustment for me. Marsh had to write permission slips for everything. He had to give me permission to take books out of the library. He had to give me permission slips to pay the bills when he was away on military assignments. This was insanity! This was not helping my self-esteem and healing my back.

Morgan went to daycare two days a week. On her first day there, she came home with a note. She had bitten a little boy. He wouldn't listen to her words maybe because he didn't have her vocabulary. He kept trying to take something away from her, and she got frustrated and bit him. Marsh was so proud, and to be honest, I was too. Morgan was not going to be a doormat, and that made us so happy. When she moved into the two-year-old room, they had little toilets in the bathroom. Morgan loved those things; they fascinated her. She came home from daycare and announced, "I not wear diapers no more." That day she potty trained herself. She still wore pull ups at night, but she was determined. She had very few accidents and loved big girl undies. Like I've said before, Morgan was an exceptional child and an exceptional gift in our lives. Morgan was very popular at school. She had a way of being a mediator with the children, and she loved rules. She has so much respect for people who follow the rules.

Soon after Morgan turned two, we had our first big snowfall. This was the first time Morgan had gotten to experience snow because we came from Hawaii. Our first year in northern Japan, we had 210 inches of snow that winter! To give you an idea of how much snow that is, Denver, Colorado, averages about 60 inches of snow per year. Morgan was so happy. She and Daddy played in the snow for hours. The next morning when she woke up, most of the snow was gone, and Morgan was not happy about that. She wanted to know where it went. I told her it melted. She didn't understand. I let an ice cube melt in a bowl. Not good enough. Marsh explained the evaporation process to her. She still needed more, so Marsh taught her one of his favorite things: looking something up at the library. There he was able to show her multiple books and pictures to help her understand the whole evaporation process. When she returned to her 2-year-old's classroom on Monday, she tried to explain it all to these poor, lost 2-year-olds. The teachers just laughed. How am I ever going to be able to teach a child like this? She was just so intelligent!

On Tuesdays, we had story time at the library. Afterward, Morgan was allowed to get as many books as Mommy could carry. Morgan loved reading, and I wanted to encourage that. After about six months, Morgan asked me where my books were. I told her that I like reading Morgan's books. Not good enough, of course. She insisted I had to have an adult book before we left the library because Morgan likes things to be fair, so I grabbed one at random. All week she asked me about reading my book while she made-pretend reading hers. This wasn't working. So the next week I chose a novel called *A Tree Grows in Brooklyn*[4] by Betty Smith. It took me 15 weeks, but I finally finished my first novel at 30 years old. Morgan was so proud of me, and I was proud of myself. My 2-year-old daughter was teaching me how to read, and reading over 100 books a week to her was certainly helping. When Morgan was two, she wanted me to teach her how to read. She was already so serious, and I didn't want to push her to grow up too fast, so I promised her I would teach her when she turned three. I have learned that there is a very big difference between pushing and allowing. I should have <u>allowed</u> Morgan to read at age two; now I understand that it was me that wasn't ready. The day Morgan turned three, she informed me that she was not little anymore and wanted to learn to read. She already knew the sounds the letters make. As I taught her the ABCs while she was helping me through my back issues, I always included what an "A" looked like, what it sounded like, and the sign language for it. By 22 months of age, Morgan knew her ABCs, she could point each letter out to me, she could tell me the sound that each letter made, and she knew most of the signs for them. Looking back at that, she really was ready to read at age two. So, here we are at three years old, and I would point to things. "Morgan, there is a tree. What letter does 't-t-tr-reeee' begin with?" Then we started sounding out whole words. One day we were driving in town, and Morgan was sounding out a word and she yelled, "Toyota!" Yes, that was the first word Morgan read, "Toyota," on the back of a truck in front of us. Marsh and I laughed and hooted. "Yes, Morgan, that says 'Toyota.'" By the time Morgan started kindergarten, she was frustrated with how slow I read, but she was patient with me as only Morgan could be.

That first Christmas in Japan, I wanted to do something special for the locals that helped us when we had lived out in town. I found out that most of the local Japanese loved chocolate cake with chocolate frosting. Using foil 9x9 pans, it was so easy, as one cake mix made two cakes. For Christmas, we made 20 cakes

[4] Betty Smith, *A Tree Grows in Brooklyn*, 1943.

and delivered them. I wanted Morgan (and even Marsh) to understand the importance of saying thank you to people that help you out. I was teaching a gratitude attitude. Everyone was so pleased and surprised. They especially liked it when Morgan, a sweet, blonde little girl, gave it to them. She was very shy, so this helped her become more comfortable with talking to people. The second Christmas, we made 50 cakes because we had interacted with a lot more locals the longer we were there. The third year we made 80, and then came home from delivering them and made 20 more.

When Morgan was four and sat on Santa's lap, he asked her what she wanted for Christmas. She said, "Oh, Santa, if I could have a Christmas tree, that would be wonderful!" Santa said, "Is she for real?" I said, "Yes, we have raised her to give at Christmas, and she loves it."

With Desert Storm going on while we were in Japan, we could bake cookies and send them on a plane with a label, "To any service member." You can't do that anymore, but Morgan and I baked for weeks and weeks because it was the right thing to do. We were so blessed that Marsh didn't have to go to war. He and his command helped in other ways, and Morgan and I helped by baking cookies.

When I was little, Mom didn't bake—not at all. A couple of times, Dad went to a factory in Milwaukee where they made cookies. He would bring home a huge bag of broken cookies. It was something like a 50-pound bag, really huge. We would dip those cookies in his coffee to soften them up. Poor Dad had so many pieces of cookies in his cup that there was hardly any coffee. I wonder if he ever knew how much we appreciated those broken cookies.

One of my favorite things to do in Japan was to go out and celebrate local festivals. The parades were so colorful and festive, and everyone was smiling and having fun. We made so many friends in Japan. We had several that came to our house to learn English. They were willing to pay me, but I asked them to teach me about their culture and traditions in return as payment. Americans were continually taking advantage of the local Japanese, and it made me sick. One of my Japanese friends was in Hiroshima when the atomic bomb was dropped, and she had burns on the side of her face. I asked how could she want to be my friend, not only was I American, but my husband was in the military. She looked me in the eye and said, "Mrs. Smith-san, my country made mistakes and your country made mistakes. Hopefully, there will be nothing but friendship between us." At that time, there was a lot on the news about how terrible Japan was because they won't join us in the war in the Middle East. My Japanese friends asked why our reporters would say such things when they were honoring the treaty they signed to end WW2 stating their promise to never fight on foreign lands again. And there we were shaming them for doing the honorable thing. If there was crime or vandalism in the local area, it was almost always the American servicemembers. Please remember that when you travel to a foreign country, you are a guest in their country, and you represent our entire country, so please be respectful.

Morgan had so many ear infections as a child. I believe it had to do with her having an ultrasound so late in my pregnancy. I've seen videos of babies in the womb covering their ears when the wand was placed on the mother's tummies. When she was 26 months old, they decided to fly us to the Philippines to put tubes in her ears. By then, she had already had 24 ear infections. Marsh's immediate supervisor was a real egomaniac that loved to mess with Marsh. When he heard about Morgan being medevaced out, he sent Marsh away to school, so I had to take her to the Philippines by myself. My back was a little better by then, I was usually up two days and then in bed for a day, but I wanted Morgan's pain to stop, so off we went. Marsh made me promise not to leave the base there because of all the crime.

Well, someone at the airport stole my money. I was in another foreign country without any money to get my daughter to the hospital for her surgery. I contacted the base police, and they got me in touch with an organization that helps Air Force personnel that have problems like this. The only problem is that my husband was Navy, and I was only a DW. They told me that I needed to contact Navy Relief. It was an Air Force base, and it took seven or eight days before Navy Relief showed up. Marsh was at school in central Japan, and I had no way to contact him. I called his Command, but his supervisor had ordered all the Quarterdeck watches to send all calls from me directly to him, and not to anyone else in the Command. He told me that he wouldn't disturb Marsh at school, and then hung up on me. I was going to be in the Philippines for ten days, with no money even for food. Thank goodness, someone let me know that I could have money wired to me. I called my parents collect, and they sent me some money by Western Union. We were able to eat again and get Morgan to her surgery. When we returned, Marsh's Commanding Officer found out about all the hell I went through, and he promised that policies would change. I hope that they have.

Now that my back was doing better, we were able to get out and visit places. One of my favorites was the Showa Daibutsu (giant Buddha) in Aomori Prefecture. It is the tallest bronze seated statue of the Buddha in Japan and is so large that we are about the size of his thumbnail. Morgan was walking further and further ahead as we neared the Buddha, which was screened behind trees. I asked Marsh if he would get her because I didn't want the huge Buddha to intimidate her. Suddenly, Morgan stopped in her tracks. She turned slowly. Her eyes were huge and her mouth was wide open. I said, "Oh, no, we're too late." Suddenly Morgan came running up to us and said, "Mommy, Daddy, can I go see my friend? I haven't seen him in such a long time." I didn't know quite how to respond, so I said, "Who's your friend?" She turned and pointed to the Buddha and said, "He is." I said, "You know him?" and she responded, "Oh, yes, but we haven't seen each other for so long." I looked at Marsh, and he told her that we would be right behind her. There is a large room built under the base the Buddha sits on, and it contains statues of all the Buddhist deities, or whatever they are called.

Marsh was helping me remove my shoes before entering because this is their custom. When we got into the large, circular room divided by partitions, I got nervous because I didn't see Morgan. As we circled around the area, there she was in front of one of the gods doing a closed-eye meditation prayer kind of thing. When she finished, I asked why she chose to pray by this particular god. She pulled me as far away from the statue as possible. She whispered that he was her favorite. He is always so happy, and that makes her happy. Then she took us around and said he is the one you need to talk to if you are sick. Then she pointed at another and said if you need to know what to do, you ask him. I can't remember what else she said about the other ones; I was in such a daze. Maybe Ken was correct. Morgan may have been a Dalai Lama in a past life, or maybe a Buddhist monk, who knows. When she was about six or seven, Ken told us about a movie called *Little Buddha*[5]. He said to please watch it with Morgan. We did, and she loved it. In the movie, they had several tests for the children to find out which child was the reincarnated Dalai Lama. Morgan passed every test, and even explained to us why they did what they did. This kiddo never stops amazing me.

When we lived in Hawaii, we often visited the Byodo-In Temple. The caretaker there loved me. He hardly ever spoke a word, but I feel like he read my energy. One time, he had me sit and he rubbed his hands together and pointed at my back. I nodded yes. He then pressed his hands together and focused very hard—he was even shaking. Then he placed his hands on my forehead and back. I felt a rush of energy shoot through my spine. It was incredible. Another time, he showed us how to take a small piece of bread and put it between our thumb and forefinger. Then he showed us not to move. He whistled, and a sparrow landed on my finger and took the bread and flew off. Marsh was best at it. He reminds me of my grandfather. He is wonderful with animals, and they know that they can trust him.

Just as I loved to learn about Japanese traditions, they wanted to learn ours. When Halloween rolled around, we brought six of our Japanese friends onto base. People were so surprised when there were nine people at their door, and only little Morgan was the trick-or-treater. Some of our Japanese friends would try to look respectfully inside the homes a little to see more of how we Americans live.

While living in Japan, I was surprised at how many teenagers would approach us and ask if we liked Madonna or the Beatles. They asked why we liked to wear holes in our jeans. This was 1990-1993. The locals there went to school hours longer than American kids, and they had to go six days a week. I did volunteer work with a local school for a short time, and really enjoyed the experience. There were so many things to learn and experience, but once in a while, we had to have a taste of the U.S.A. Twice a year, we drove an hour to Hirosaki to pay $36 for six pieces of Kentucky Fried Chicken and three biscuits.

---

[5] *Little Buddha*, movie directed by Bernardo Bertolucci, and written by Rudy Wurlitzer and Mark Peploe, 1993.

When Morgan turned three, I had a couple of months where I wondered if I was doing everything wrong as a parent. I do not enjoy the "NO" stage. Every day I would get Morgan dressed, and five minutes later, she would come out of her room in her underwear. We struggled day after day. Someone recommended I beat her and show her who was boss, but I could never, ever do that. So one morning I got a brilliant idea. When I got up I went into Morgan's room in my bra and underwear. She asked me where my clothes were. I said that Mommy wants to see what Morgan likes so much about not wearing clothes. I could tell she didn't like it but didn't know how to handle it. A few hours later, I got my purse and said, "Come on, Morgan, it's time for your ballet class." She said, "Mommy, you can't go outside like that." I said, "Why not? If Morgan can do it, I can do it." She ran into her bedroom and put on some clothes, and we never had to deal with that again. Another time, we got into our van, and after Morgan got into her car seat, I didn't hear her buckle click. I said, "Are you ready?" She said, "Yes." I said, "Did you buckle up?" She said, "No." I said, "You know the rules, the van doesn't move until everyone is buckled." She said "No" again. I said, "Then we will just wait until you are ready." We waited 20 minutes in silence. Finally, I said, "Are you ready?" "No." We waited another 20 minutes. "Are you ready?" "No." We waited for another 20, and I heard the click. I said, "Are you finally ready?" She said, "Yes." I said, "Ok, you can unbuckle now. We're going back into the house. You took so long deciding if you wanted to be safe that you missed your gymnastics class." That was that; we never had to deal with that again either.

When Morgan was nine, we were at a park with her friend Nikki. I told them to please stay where I could see them. Of course, Nikki had to push the envelope. She enticed Morgan to go over by a small dam. Morgan could have said no, but she didn't. When I found them, I said in a firm voice, "If you can't follow the rules, we need to leave." It was very quiet in the car. I wanted them to think about what they had done. Finally, I told Nikki, "I'm sorry, Nikki, but I have to take you home and you are not allowed back at our house for two weeks. I do not tolerate kids breaking the few rules that I have. You guys went into a dangerous area, and I am very upset about it. And Morgan, you are grounded for a week." After we dropped Nikki off at her home, Morgan asked if she could ask a question.

I said, "Of course." She said, "What does 'grounded' mean?" It took everything I had to keep a straight face. I explained there would be no TV or friends over for a week. That night and every night the rest of the week we played games and did science experiments and other fun stuff. When the week was over Morgan asked what she needed to do so she could be grounded again.

At one point during our time in Japan, Marsh was working all the time. He had one day off a month, and most days he worked 16-to-20-hour days. His blood pressure was so low the doctor said he was almost legally dead. The reason for all these hours was Mr. Egomaniac at Marsh's work. He just loved to lord over Marsh with his power. Even though they were the same rank, he had seniority because of the number of years in service. When I needed to discuss something with Marsh that was important during that time, I would say, "Honey, I need you to concentrate, this is important, can you hear me?" He would nod, and I would continue. It was so difficult to watch Marsh go through this and not be able to do anything. Finally, I couldn't take it anymore. I couldn't watch Marsh die and not do anything. I knew Marsh would be mad, I mean really, really mad! I called his lieutenant, who was a really nice guy, and said, "I just wanted to call to say goodbye and to thank you for all you have done for our family." He asked me where I was going. I said I was leaving Marsh. He was shocked. "But you and Marsh are the happiest married couple I have ever known. Why are you leaving him?" I said, "I love him too much to watch him die." He asked me what I was talking about. I told him what the doctor said, and how many hours Marsh was working, etc. He said, "Don't go anywhere just yet, Mary Beth, let me do some investigating first... please." I said, "Ok." When Marsh came home, he was not happy about what I had done. He didn't raise his voice, but you could feel it radiate off him. He asked me why I would do that to him. I said I loved him too much to just let him die and do nothing. I asked him what happened. Mr. Egomaniac was told that he will report to an office each day until his retirement in three months. He was to speak to no one and do nothing every day for eight hours. Marsh's work went back to normal and we loved having him home again. I love my husband! Thank you, God!

There are those truly extraordinary moments in time when you look back on them, and you smile because you remember that feeling of experiencing the divinity of God. This was one of those moments. I want to bask in it for all of eternity because my entire family experienced it together. It was orchestrated by 3-year-old Morgan. We had been living in Japan for about 15 months. I could notice a difference in Morgan in Japan. It was beautiful to watch her soul come alive. To notice her witnessing and participating in her own divinity as something that was normal was so very humbling for me. It was one of those October days that feel more like winter than fall. We went to the ocean—to the beach. It was so very different from going to the beach in Hawaii. No tourists, no sunshine, no palm trees. Just starkness and cold. Huge rocks dotted along the beach as Marsh and Morgan ran ahead. I could hear their laughter being carried on the wind and into my heart. I loved witnessing their joy. They love noticing or experiencing something new together. It's like every cell in their bodies comes alive. Morgan would climb up on a rock and Marsh would catch her as she jumped into his arms and twirl her, experiencing more laughter, more joy.

I was lagging further and further behind. Not wanting to do anything that might hurt my back again, and also not wanting to break this sacred connection that my little family had in that moment. Words weren't necessary. In fact I would say words were a distraction from their experience of each other. I was so grateful for the wind carrying their laughter to me so I might join in. I noticed them so far up the beach kneeling down. I wondered what it was that caught their attention. What would Marsh be teaching her about today? A jellyfish washed ashore? A seashell and how it is formed as the sea creature grows? This man God gave me is a born teacher. He makes you feel curious about things that you didn't even know existed. He must be so curious himself to want to learn about so many different, and the way Marsh puts it, useless things. How can he call them useless?

As I get closer, I'm drawn into their excitement. Just as I expected, neither of them is talking. They are digging in the freezing cold, wet sand. Maybe they are making a sandcastle? As I am only a few yards away, I break their spell by speaking. "What are you two up to?" Morgan turned to me with so much excitement in her little body and said, "Mommy, we are digging for my buried treasure!" Just then, Marsh stops digging and winks at me several times and says,

"Yesss, Mommy, we are digging for buried treasure!" Morgan invited me to come down and join them and to help. Marsh steps in and lets Morgan know that we don't want Mommy to hurt her back again. He encourages her to continue digging. I go up close to see how big this hole actually is. Wow, it must be almost 12 inches deep. Marsh and Morgan's hands were so red from the coldness of the sand. The pile of sand next to them is getting bigger and bigger. As I settle in leaning against a rock, I ask Morgan how she knew that this is the place to dig for her buried treasure. Was there a big X on the sand? She stopped her task to think about her response, and with a scowl on her face, thought about it and finally shrugged and said, "I just knew." Those words made me smile. I know what that feels like to just know what I know. I'm so grateful God gave that gift of knowing to Morgan too. I realize He gave it to each and every one of us, but not everyone accesses it. That is the difference.

As I'm drifting off into my space that I connect to God in my head, I hear a loud "FOMP" like something had collapsed. I hurried forward, and I looked down in complete shock. Marsh and I look at each other and can't even find our words. Could it really be? Did Morgan—little 3-year-old Morgan—just find buried treasure on a cold, deserted beach? I had heard Marsh not even five minutes ago trying to prepare Morgan for the fact that maybe, just maybe they had the wrong spot, and they might not find buried treasure. I could feel him choosing his words to lessen her disappointment when the inevitable was going to happen. Those words had been wasted, because Morgan had just, in fact, found a buried treasure of sand dollars!

As I stared into this hollowed-out hole about 18 inches across, there lay hundreds and hundreds of sand dollars. There were so many of them and so many different sizes. And there was so very little sand on them. I remember being so surprised by how little sand was on top of them. Only the small amount from when the top where they had been digging had collapsed inside of this hollowed-out cove of sand dollars. Is this how sand dollars are always found? I had never heard of anyone personally who had found a sand dollar before.

Morgan was so excited about this find... this treasure. Marsh and I were still in shock. We just kept looking at each other, looking at the cove of sand dollars and looking at Morgan. I kept thinking in my head, Marsh, what just happened here? For once, it wasn't just me experiencing a miracle alone. No—we were each experiencing this miracle TOGETHER! I am not alone in this anymore. I am going to get to experience these kinds of things with Morgan again and again for the rest of our lives! Thank you, God! Thank you, God! I don't have to do this alone anymore! Thank you, God!

Morgan brought me back to the moment. The little scientist/engineer was coming out in her. How can we transport her treasure back home? We were a long way away from the car. We had no bags. Then her face lit up and she grabbed the hem of my shirt, which was enormous because I was so fat at the time. She asked me to hold my hem up, creating a big pocket to put her dollars in. That is what she kept calling them: "Her dollars." When my shirt was as full as it could be, the collar was hanging so far down and it was being stretched to its limits. None of that mattered to Morgan. We needed to transport her dollars safely and efficiently because Morgan was explaining to us that she needed to share her dollars with everyone.

The urgency in Morgan was almost desperate as she would repeat again and again that she needed to share her dollars with everyone. It felt like this was her mission in life, and it needed to be done properly, and only she knew what that meant. But Marsh and I were very good at following her directions. Marsh filled his pockets and arms with as many as Morgan could load him with and still keep her dollars safe. Morgan carried a special few in her hands. She turned to look down at the remaining sand dollars that would be left behind because we had no more hands and shirts to hold them. It felt like a private moment of gratitude, like she was thanking God for this blessed experience, or maybe she was apologizing to the sand dollars we left behind? I know that I was certainly thanking God. I felt a sadness for the sand dollars that remained on the beach. Like they were going to miss out on what Morgan was going to be doing with her dollars.

As we drove home, we had long moments of silence. I used them to relive what we had just witnessed, what we had just experienced. Thank you, God, for allowing me to live through Morgan's birth so that I could be here and experience this with her—with us! I asked Morgan what she was going to do with her dollars. She said she had to share them with everyone. She wouldn't elaborate on it, but I knew further instructions were coming. At least that's the way I usually received information.

When we got home, Morgan had to give her dollars a very special bath. It was so strange to see hundreds of sand dollars soaking in our bathtub. When Morgan decided it was time for them to come out, we laid them carefully on towels making sure the hole on the back was facing down so they could drain properly. I knew that Morgan was doing everything by guidance, and it was sacred for me to witness. While we waited for them to dry, Morgan wanted to share her story with our neighbor Katie. 2 ½-year-old Katie and her mom came over to see Morgan's treasure. As Morgan was explaining to Katie what these were, Katie's mom was looking at us with curiosity. We simply spoke the truth. Morgan found this buried treasure on the beach, and she is going to share her dollars with everyone. Morgan gave Katie the first of many dollars to be given away.

I wish you could have experienced Morgan back then. She was filled with such confidence and such knowing. Everyone gravitated to her. They had no idea why, they just wanted... needed to be in her presence. When I would take Morgan to the grocery store, I had to bring Marsh so we could have two carts. One to hold Morgan, the other to hold the groceries. So many people would stop to talk to Morgan or interact with her that it could take 30 minutes to go down one aisle. I kid you not. So Marsh would push Morgan while I shopped. Otherwise, I would be there for hours and be so distracted that I would forget half of the items I went there for. In Japan, it was even worse. Because they believed it was good luck to touch blonde hair, Morgan was overwhelmed by how many people would rub her head. She didn't consider it an honor, but a curse. She is so much like her father, she wanted to slip in unnoticed and do her thing and leave. I, on the other hand, liked to touch as many lives as I could each time I was out and about. I still do enjoy that above all things. Morgan now has this aspect also, but it has to be on her terms.

As the sand dollars dried, Morgan got out our craft box. She pulled out all the different ribbons, bells, paint and glitter that was part of "her dollars" transformation. When they were dry, Marsh, Morgan and I were going to decorate. Actually, Morgan did most of the decorating. Marsh and I held stuff and glued stuff per Morgan's directions. I was pulling out all the sand dollars that had dark blotches on them, planning on discarding them. Morgan let me know that this was unacceptable. Her dollars still had value even if they were old and faded. She was going to make them feel beautiful again. Wow, what a lesson she was teaching me. Who is the adult in this relationship? I am always willing to learn. Remember, older doesn't always mean wiser.

The next day Morgan began distributing her dollars to the people she was drawn to giving them to. I still have no idea why she chose who she chose. The decorated ones seemed to go to people she knew and loved. I had to mail both sets of grandparents theirs. Morgan made sure the ribbons looped so they could hang on a Christmas tree. My mother by then had the most sterile, unimaginative tree I had ever seen. All the bulbs were the same color and size, and the tree was flocked and looked very fake. It was not a tree filled with stories. We buy an ornament wherever we travel, and we tell our stories as we decorate our Christmas tree. It's a very special time for us. My mom's tree is special to her and her alone. Everything matched, uniform and distributed evenly. I'm sure Morgan's sand dollar went straight into the trash, but maybe not. I think Marsh's mom did the same thing. It was a childish Christmas ornament to them. How sad. But it was their dollar to use as they wished.

We kept a container of "dollars" in the car, and randomly Morgan would just hand them to her new Japanese friend (as she would call random people she met). To Morgan, anyone she met in Japan was a Japanese friend, whether they were from Japan or not. Then there were all her classmates and teachers, and Marsh's coworkers. Yes, Morgan made sure that everyone got a dollar, and we still have a small stash of them today.

Right before we left Japan, we had a couple of big earthquakes. The first was a 7.0, and the next was a 7.3 lasting three minutes. We were over at Katie's house when the 7.3 earthquake occurred. The girls were playing in the tub when the tremor started. I asked Marsh to please get Morgan NOW. Katie's mom said it's just a tremor, Mary Beth, no big deal. I said you never know when the tremor can become something bigger. Marsh had Morgan wrapped in a towel and he met me under the door jam in their hallway. The quake by then was really rocking the house. I kept saying louder and louder that I choose to have the ground below me be still. Katie's dad was having difficulty getting her out of the tub. She was being flailed from side to side and upside down, and of course, she was very slippery. We watched the pictures on the wall spin around. Things were falling, and we just held onto each other as this bazaar drama unfolded around us. How do I make this stop, I kept asking myself. Finally, it did. Thank you, God!

We went home to assess the damage to our own home. Knickknacks broken, things knocked to the floor, but nothing serious. And then I saw it... the new crack. This crack haunted me. It started at the ceiling above Morgan's window, it traveled all the way down the wall and across the floor through her closet, through the bathroom, into our closet, across our bedroom floor, and up our wall to the ceiling. I felt like that whole wall was going to go at any moment. My mother suffered from extreme anxiety, and in that moment, I understood it on a new level. For the next few days, all three of us slept on a mattress in the hallway under the door frame. We had aftershock after aftershock. A few were 6+, and most 5+. Marsh saw how nervous I was and asked me if he needed to send Morgan and me home early. We had gotten our orders to Fallon Naval Air Station in Nevada. I could no longer go into the BX and Commissary in Misawa because I was afraid that all the quakes had compromised the structures. Little did I know that this would be my future, living in fear and anxiety in every moment. I wish I had let go of my anxiety as I experienced it, life is so much easier when you do.

Soon our time in Japan came to an end. I would miss this sacred place in my heart. I was so grateful for what this country and its people had taught my family and me. Morgan's foundational years were spent in a place where they focused on "How can I serve you? How can I assist you?" And yes, Morgan is still very, very much like that today. Morgan has never, ever been a gimme-gimme person. In fact, she has difficulty being around people who only think of themselves. Neal Donald Walsch says in one of his "Conversations with God" books something like "The whole world would change if we all lived by 'My way is not the right way, it's simply a different way.'" I have seen how much better I feel about myself and others when I stop judging both them and myself. How often do we look at another only to find fault with them? When Morgan was small, I would have a contest with her. Let's see who can make someone smile first. In a country where we didn't speak much of their language, I wanted her to learn that a smile is one of the most powerful tools that ycu will ever possess. It doesn't take up a lot of storage, and you have ready access to it, and it transcends all ages, races, religions and genders. Yes, a smile means the same in any language.

Chapter 12:
Getting Ready to Retire

When we arrived in Reno, Nevada, we went through some serious culture shock. Morgan had gotten a small cut on her finger on the plane and wanted a Band-Aid. We stopped at a pharmacy and they had about 30 types of Band-Aids to choose from. It was way too much for her, so we went to lunch while Morgan thought about which Band-Aid to choose. We had lived in a place for three years, where at the BX we had two choices of shampoo, two choices of toilet paper, our milk came frozen, about ten toys that were appropriate for her age. So to suddenly be thrust into the land of plenty was very overwhelming for all of us. After lunch and Band-Aids, we needed to purchase a vehicle. We knew it had to be an automatic van for my back. I only spent about 5-10 days a year in bed by then. I was feeling pretty normal for a 260-pound woman, and I wanted to keep it that way. We got our first brand-new vehicle ever. It was a Dodge Caravan, and she became part of the family. We named our car Dora Madeline. Our next obstacle was getting insurance. Neither Marsh nor I had ever had an accident or a speeding ticket, and we had our old insurance papers from when we had lived in Hawaii and a certificate from the military stating our good driving record while in Japan. But according to every insurance company in the U.S.A., we were a high risk and should be penalized for having been a military member serving overseas. I was in tears after the first ten companies I spoke to. We could not afford to eat if this was what we were going to have to pay for insurance. Finally, I spoke to a man at Mutual of Omaha who was willing to make nothing from our policy to get us insured again. He agreed that it was ridiculous that we should be penalized for serving our country, but that was the reality at that time. For shame on you ridiculous insurance companies.

We had one more stop before we headed to our next duty station. We wanted to stop at the Toys-R-Us store to get Morgan a little something as a way to thank her for being so patient during the move and travel and everything. She was so excited. But after going down only half an aisle, Morgan had had enough. Way too many choices. She wanted to leave. So we left a Toys-R-Us with nothing because our 5-year-old daughter didn't want anything. Wow, are we ever lucky parents. Confused, but lucky.

We headed to Fallon 80 miles away from Reno. We liked to sing silly songs in the car, and tell funny stories. We were probably 60 miles into the drive when Morgan yelled, "Daddy, stop the car!" That is not like Morgan, so Marsh pulled over. He asked Morgan what was wrong. She said, "Look, Daddy, a tree!" We laughed so hard. She was correct, we had traveled miles and miles with only tumbleweeds here and there, and bare, rocky hills and flatlands, and then there was one lonely tree.

We knew that we only had one year before Marsh retired from the Navy after 20 years of service. We wanted to be in the United States when that happened, so he could look for a job and whatever else we needed to do. Calling someone from Japan had been $1 per minute. Because of the expense of long distance calls, Marsh and I had grown even closer because we had only each other to rely on. So now we needed more ready access to people in the U.S.A. First, we lived in a duplex off base, and later in a single-family house on base at the end of the runway (oh, boy, that was fun). Things were more expensive with a new vehicle and high insurance and less assistance from the military. So, I got a 6-week position at the local hospital while someone went on maternity leave. I worked as the receptionist in the Radiology department. This is where I saw babies cover their ears during ultrasounds. I enjoyed my job a lot, but it was very crowded, and I knew that it was temporary so it was difficult to settle in. When the woman I was filling in for was about to come back to work, the personal assistant to the hospital's CEO and the hospital's HR person asked if they could talk to me about staying on. We had a meeting, and they said they had received more positive feedback about me in six weeks than they ever had about any other person, and they didn't want to lose me. Would I be willing to work as the hospital receptionist/telephone operator full-time? I explained that my husband would be retiring in six months, but I would talk to him about it. Marsh's response was if it makes you happy, then I don't mind us having some extra money.

I took the position, and after being a DW (dependent wife) with no identity for three years, it was wonderful being seen, heard and appreciated again. I gave my immediate supervisor suggestions all the time. Even back then, I was being given insights. At first, he didn't appreciate it, but then he saw the change in productivity and attitudes, and realized what a gift he had in me. The employees weren't always overly friendly, but later I found out that they assumed my husband was an officer because I dressed so nicely. You see, in the military community officers and enlisted need to remain separate. My fellow employees were very embarrassed when they learned the truth.

The president of the hospital came out once to compliment me and reinforce how grateful they were to have me as part of the team. Again, the feedback was nonstop about how positive and yet professional I was. However, when he strutted into the lobby and saw me, he stopped in his tracks and sputtered and couldn't make eye contact. He asked where the woman was who usually had my position. I told him I had been in this position for a couple of months. He stalked several feet away and said to his assistant, "We can't have an obese person like her out front representing the hospital. If we have to keep her, find a closet for her somewhere." Everyone was so embarrassed by his behavior. His assistant could tell I had heard him. She said, "Having Mary Beth here has been the best thing to happen to this hospital in a long time. You need to figure out your priorities." I went home that night not knowing if I'd be back the next day because of feeling so insulted and embarrassed. I decided to stay on and show him who the bigger person was (physically, emotionally and mentally). When I left four months later, they offered to double my wages if I stayed. I told them thank you, but we needed to go where my husband could find a good job. They offered to find him a job, too. I said no thank you, and we left.

While I was doing all this working, Morgan was doing all kinds of learning. One day when I picked her up from preschool, the teachers cornered me and said, "We need to talk." Oh, no, now what. They described an activity they were working on, and Morgan yelled, "I made a mistake, I made a mistake!" The teacher went over to calm Morgan and told her that we all make mistakes and it's ok. Morgan looked at her like she was a crazy lady, and said, "Now I'm even smarter. If I never make mistakes, I can't learn from them and become even smarter." Yes, yes, yes! All this talking and teaching I had been doing with Morgan was working. She was really getting it! Another time they told me how one of the little boys was telling Morgan that she was the prettiest and smartest girl in the class. Morgan said, "Yes, but you are the best colorer in the class." They told us how she was like a ray of sunshine to everyone that got to stand in her light.

In the morning, we had our rituals after Daddy left for work on his bicycle. I would say something like, "I choose to have a really good day today." Morgan would say, "I choose to have a good day too." Then I would say, "I choose to be happy today; how about you?" Morgan would think about it and say, "I choose to be happy too." The reason for me doing this was to teach Morgan that only <u>she</u> can decide to be happy or sad. Don't give that power to someone else. Some days I would say, "I choose to be really crabby today," and she would say, "I don't. I choose to be happy." Again, I wanted her to know that not everyone is always happy and that is their choice and it's ok not to be happy. Also, it is not her responsibility to make sure everyone is happy. She can <u>try</u> to cheer them up, but the decision lies with them. So, one morning Morgan was wearing a new dress and it had a matching hat. She asked me if she could wear her new hat to school. I said, "Yes, but you cannot wear it in the classroom. Are you ok with that?" She said, "Yes." I said, "Ok, let's finish getting ready." When we got to her school, Morgan realized that she didn't have her hat. She asked if I could go home and get it. I told her that I couldn't because that would make me late for work and I could lose my job. Morgan started to cry, and then she stopped herself and said, "Silly me. I forgot that I chose to be happy today." She gave me my hug and kiss and went skipping off to have a happy day. Wow, how do I bottle this stuff? Thank you, God, for this amazing and open child!

Marsh did not do as well as Morgan and I. He felt a lot of pressure because he had no idea as to where he could get a job or how much it would pay. He was really terrified of doing a job interview. He is not good at talking about himself, much less bragging about himself. He always said he could get any job out there if I did the interview for him. Marsh asked me where I wanted to retire. He said I had followed him where ever we were sent and didn't complain (he obviously wasn't listening inside my head). Now it was my turn to decide where we would live, and he would follow my lead. I told him I had always been drawn to Colorado. I had visited Ken and Janet there, and I really like the attitude of the people, the mountains, the healthier lifestyle and how open people were to change and a different way of thinking and being. The only problem was that Ken and Janet don't live there anymore, they live in Utah now. We would have nowhere to stay while he found a job. Marsh said we could go back to Wisconsin. No—you can't make me go back there. So we talked about Utah. It was right next door to Colorado, and we could visit Colorado and figure out where we want to go next. We spoke with Ken and Janet, and they were so excited and welcoming. We started getting the Sunday paper for Salt Lake City so Marsh could look at jobs and what they pay.

One week, he said, "There you go, the Post Office is looking for ETs." I got so excited and said that it would be perfect. A government job with good benefits, and he is already an electronics tech. He very clearly stated, "I am NOT working for the post office!" I said, "At least it's a start, a foot in the door. It's just an application. If you get something better, you can just say no thank you." He was not happy about it, but he did put in the application. Several months later, they said that they were going to be doing some testing and would like him to take the test. Back then, it was a 6-to-8-hour test. Marsh again didn't want to. I said, "It's only a test, if you get another job, you can always turn down the Post Office."

Meanwhile, back in Fallon, time was ticking away before retirement. Marsh was getting more and more tense. The only thing that kept him sane was Morgan. The two of them would go digging for dinosaur remains. They even had pith helmets, which Marsh told Morgan was a requirement when digging for dinosaurs. I worried so much about snakes and scorpions. We had scorpions in our backyard, so I have no problem imagining them out in the desert. But they survived even if my nerves didn't. Again it would have been beneficial to heal this anxiety as it appeared in my life, rather than waiting until it got so huge I had no choice but to deal with it.

Marsh's mom came for a visit. Morgan loved her Grandma Abby. We decided to take her to Virginia City so she could ride a stagecoach, pan for gold, and just see an old mining town. Unfortunately, we got a flat tire on our way there. Marsh's mom was so worried. We didn't have enough food and water to survive in the desert. I had never seen Abby like this; she had always been the one with the cool head. Marsh said, don't worry Mom, we'll just change the tire and be on our way. Well, first we had to find the tire. Did we even have a spare tire? Where is a spare tire on a van? We tried ripping up the carpet in the back. Nope, that was really glued down. We tried to find a button or lever to push—no luck. Finally, he checked under the vehicle and there it was—yeah! Now how do we get it down, we had no tools. The jack must be under the tire because we couldn't find that either. Marsh tried to loosen it, but it didn't budge, so he got a rock and was whacking at it. I was laughing so hard I thought I would pee my pants. Morgan was trying to help, and Abby was practically screaming, "We're all going to die!" In that moment I was so happy. Marsh was trying to fix something, which he loves to do. Morgan was helping Daddy, which she loved to do. And I was laughing so hard, which I love to do. And I saw the absolute perfection of our family, and I felt the love and loyalty, care and joy that we all felt for one another. It was such a "life is good" moment. Marsh was laughing so hard too. He saw the humor in what was unfolding and he knew that eventually someone would come by and help us.

Finally, a Good Samaritan stopped. I bet that he was really glad that he did. Not just because of that good feeling that you get when you help another human being, but because he too laughed until he practically peed himself. What a humorous drama we presented to him. He came up with this brilliant idea once he stopped laughing enough to be able to speak. Why don't we read the manual? Oh, my gosh, Marsh and I laughed even louder. I felt like we should make pretend that we didn't know how to read so we could look a little less stupid. Oh, who cares what this stranger thinks. So, guess what? The jack was under the front hood, and it had a tool on it to crank the spare tire down. I told the guy, "Well, sure, anyone can do it when they cheat and read the manual!"

The tire was changed very quickly after that. We laughed about how this guy was going to enjoy telling the story for years to come about this young guy trying to get a tire down with a rock, and his wife laughing at him, and his mother swearing we were all going to die. Abby said, "Well, I guess our trip to Virginia City is over." I said, "Well, maybe yours is, but I plan on us going back to town and getting a new tire and heading out again." And that is exactly what we did. Abby absolutely loved Virginia City. She learned so much, and we had one of those old-time pictures taken, it was perfect. That night Abby told Marsh while I was standing there, "You know, son, I was a little worried about you marrying this city girl, but after today I'm not going to worry about you anymore. You guys are so happy and you understand each other and you're doing great."

Then several weeks before retirement Marsh broke his arm. When I asked him how it happened, he spoke in a little 3-year-old's voice and said, "I fell off my bicycle." It was so adorable. He couldn't get his dress uniform over the cast, so we weren't sure what we were going to do about his retirement ceremony. It ended up healing just in time, though, and we lived happily ever after. Until we got to Utah.

Chapter 13:
Can I Have a Do-over?

I felt Marsh, Morgan and I were living a dream life, and then Utah happened to us. Living in Utah with Ken and Janet, who are my brother and sister-in-law, was great. Morgan loved these two people so much. They were ideal for teaching her how to be sillier. Janet's beautiful gift to me at that time was how kindly she could say NO and mean it. I sat in awe as I heard her say again and again to people around her, "I'm sorry, but that doesn't work for me." Or, "I can't do that, but I hope that you can find someone who can." "Not at this time, but thank you just the same." I used to practice phrases like that in the mirror after observing and listening to Janet. No one ever felt offended or put off. It was so gracefully done because she was living her truth from a loving place. I know all of this might sound ridiculous, but I had a very difficult time saying no. People always seemed so offended when I said no. Now it is so much easier. Thank you, Janet!

About two weeks after we had arrived in Utah, we were downtown and I noticed Morgan very slowly turning around observing all the people. She touched my arm and said, "Mom, what's wrong with these people?" I said, "What do you mean?" She said, "They all look the same; they all talk the same, they feel very boring here." I looked around, and yes, I noticed mostly one skin color, and yes, everyone was speaking English. I told her, "People are drawn to different places on the planet. I guess a lot of the same type of people are drawn to Salt Lake City. That was very observant of you to notice that." She said, "I didn't know that all different kinds of people could live separately." I said, "Well, it looks like in this moment on this day, they do." I asked how she felt about that. She said, "I prefer a variety. It's what I am used to." Out of the mouths of babes.

Our first Christmas in Utah, Morgan asked when we were going to start baking chocolate cakes for the local people? Oh, boy, I hadn't thought about what we would do for our community for Christmas. I asked God to bring us something that would assist people in our community in the highest way. Two days later, I saw something in the newspaper about the homeless shelter asking people to donate sleeping bags to the homeless. My heart started racing. This is exactly the kind of thing I was looking for, but we could only afford to buy one or two. That didn't feel like enough. Then I was given more guidance. I contacted both mine and Marsh's parents and asked them if they would be interested in us purchasing a sleeping bag and donating it to the homeless shelter in their name. Everyone said that would be fine. I told Marsh I wanted him to purchase one for me instead of other gifts. He wanted me to do the same for him. Morgan asked if she could do it too. I explained to her that this meant she would only be getting presents from Santa and maybe her grandparents. She took my hand and dragged me into her bedroom. She said, "Mom, does it look like I need more presents?" Looking around Morgan's room, I realized that she was correct; she had so much already. I told her that I was so proud of her. We went to the store and bought five new sleeping bags for the coldest temperature possible. We used this as a teachable moment by talking about how difficult it must be to be homeless. Morgan said that these sleeping bags were like giving them a whole bed in one, maybe even a little home. I love the way she looks at things.

When we arrived at the homeless shelter, there were so very many people waiting for the place to open so they could go in. Marsh and I were a little uncomfortable, but not Morgan. Her angel wings were showing on that day. When we went inside and handed over the five new sleeping bags, they were shocked. They had never received brand new ones before. Morgan had made beautiful tags for each sleeping bag so whoever received them knew that Grandma and Grandpa wanted them to have this sleeping bag to keep them snuggly warm. She did that for each bag. When we were leaving, Morgan saw a man outside with no shoes on, and she freaked out. "Daddy, give him your shoes! Please, Daddy, you have more shoes at home." Marsh agreed to go home and bring back some shoes for the man. Not good enough, according to Morgan, so Marsh got in the car and gave Morgan his shoes. Morgan and I took them to this man with no shoes. The gentleman was so shocked that the tears flowed. On cold nights that winter, I always said a prayer for all those unfortunate people who were homeless to be safe and in a warm place. I hope that those sleeping bags helped those five people to feel that someone out there cared about them, even if it was only for a moment. I have had many moments like this change the way that I look at things.

Marsh was not having much luck finding a job. H.P. said he was obviously trainable, and offered him $6 an hour. He has 20 years' experience and so much schooling. This guy can even solder under a microscope, for goodness' sake. Marsh felt like he had been slapped in the face. He ended up working at Blockbuster Video in the evenings for minimum wage while he looked for better work during the day. He was more willing to do the ET postal exam after all these disappointments. While we waited for the results from the postal exam, he got a job at Radio Shack repairing mostly remote control cars. He only got paid when the customer came in and paid for the repairs, so some days he made $5 for 8 hours of work. That was when Marsh raised his voice at me for the first time ever. Of course, it was about money. He told me if we are ever going to have our own place, I have to stop spending so much. I could hear the fear in his voice. He was so despondent, and I didn't know what to do for him. He was one of the hardest workers I had ever met. He is so very honest and loyal, smart and quiet, not at all argumentative. What is wrong with these people?

Finally, after months of waiting, we heard back from the Post Office. Marsh had the second-highest score out of 426 people who took the test. I told you he was smart. Stick that in your ear, H.P. Marsh felt he had no choice but to take the job at the post office when it was offered to him. Finally, we could give Ken and Janet their space back with grateful hearts.

When Morgan started kindergarten, I wanted her to be more challenged, so we enrolled her at Montessori. Shortly after Christmas, Morgan came home from school and said she had learned something very important today. I said, "What was that?" She said, "If you are really smart and you do exactly what the teacher tells you to do, you get to sit in the corner by yourself and do worksheets. But if you're naughty and never listen to the teacher and you don't know how to read, you get to sit in a circle with everyone and play games." I was fuming! "How did that make you feel, Morgan?" She said, "Here, being smart isn't very fun." The next day I had Morgan tell the principal what she had learned. The principal was so embarrassed and she apologized. She said they would change that immediately. I said, "You don't have to bother. According to Morgan, there aren't any smart children here except her, and she is no longer your problem," and we left.

That night I had several parents call and ask if I would be willing to teach their children. We paid $400 a month for a half-day back then. One of the parents offered me the same amount to teach her child. Her daughter had been at Montessori for two years. She knew some of her ABCs, she could count to 10, but couldn't recognize any of her numbers except 1. She didn't know any phonics and couldn't read or write a word except her name. This child needed help. Maybe she had learning disabilities like me. I told her mother that I would try. At the end of a month, she could say and recognize her numbers 1-100. She could write and say her ABCs and she was getting there on her phonics. She knew easy words like 'it, up, the, at.' But Morgan was so bored. I was really helping this little girl, but at what cost to my own daughter? So the last month or two of kindergarten, Morgan went to the local public school. I figured that way she would know some kids when first grade started.

In first grade, Morgan's teacher was a dream come true. In fact, we became very good friends for many years. The class was a first and second-grade split, so Morgan did everything with the second graders. They tested her and said she couldn't move up a grade because she couldn't give out change with money. I said to give me an hour and she'll be able to, but they said that's not how it works. The problem with Utah was the way Morgan was treated by the other children. I didn't know how bad it was until it was too late and the damage had been done.

I got a job as a crossing guard for Morgan's school. That way, I could do volunteer work and be close to Morgan. I had to do something because on Morgan's first full day of school, I sat in the car and cried, and on her second day, I cried again. I wasn't ready for this yet. I wanted her to stay little. I love our kiddo so very much. I love her curiosity, I love her intelligence, I love her kind heart, and I love how respectful she is... I love her for who she is!

The guy I was a crossing guard with was 80 years old and still ran marathons. He was an ex-Marine, and it showed. He was very strict and serious... until I got my hands on him. By the end of the year, he was making pretend the stop sign was a guitar and he sang and he asked the kids what they learned today. Marsh said, "What did you do to that man, Mary Beth?" I gave him permission, just like I had my dad. He loved watching me interact with the kids. They hugged me and blew kisses to me and showed me their projects. He wanted in. What did he need to do? I told him he had to be sincere. Most kids can smell a faker from a mile away. He tried a little at a time until he found his comfort spot. I sang and waved to the drivers passing by. I wore a huge size 28 down-filled red coat so long it almost touched the ground—no one could miss me. When it rained, I had a yellow duck umbrella with a large red duck-bill. So, when I went on vacation for a couple of weeks, the school and the sheriff's department (that's who I worked for) got so many calls wondering if I was ok. That's when my boss said, "No more vacations for you!"

There was a sad side to my job, too. Because of 70% of the population belonging to a certain religion, the kids would ask me questions like, "Are you related to Joseph Smith?" I'd say, "No, no relation." The next question would be "Are you our religion?" I'd say very sweetly, "No, I'm not." Several parents started driving their children two blocks to school so I wouldn't contaminate their children.

At our apartment complex, it was the same thing; the children, and sometimes the parents, would ask our religion and then children weren't allowed to play with Morgan. Not everyone was like that, but the majority were. Our next-door neighbor was higher up in the church. His wife saw me helping so many people in our community, and we had lots of talks together. She was so very nice. During one of our many talks, she said, "It's a shame that you are not going to heaven. You are one of the most generous, kind and insightful people I have ever met. If only you belonged to our church. But since you don't, you can't go to heaven and spend all of eternity with your husband." I said, "Well, to begin with, after an entire lifetime with Marsh, maybe I won't want to spend all of eternity with him. If God wants me to be with someone else, who am I to tell God no. And as far as your heaven theory, I have some questions for you. Our neighbors behind us are baptized in your religion?" She said, "Yes." "So, they are going to Heaven?" She said, "Absolutely." I said, "He beats his children and steals from patients at a nursing home, and his wife shoplifts. But they are going to heaven?" She said, "Yes, because God is so forgiving." I said, "But I'm a good, kind person who doesn't beat her child and steal and I'm not going to heaven?" Again she said, "Yes." I said, "You can keep your God and I'll keep mine, thank you very much." That was the last time she tried to convert me.

I had another interesting interaction with this neighbor. I had been noticing more and more ants in our kitchen. I didn't want to use poison, especially with children in our home. So I asked my sister-in-law Janet for guidance on insects. She said that she talks to them and asks them to leave. I said, "Ok, I'll give it a try." I sat down on the floor in my kitchen, and I told the ants that this is my home, not their home. I said that they entered my home uninvited and that's not ok with me. I need you to leave. I will give you 48 hours to leave my home. If you don't, I will get ant traps, and you will die. The choice is yours. If you do leave, I promise to be respectful of your space outside. I will try not to step on any of you and I will respect your home outside if you respect my home inside. Three hours later, there was a single-file trail of ants walking across the floor and going out under our front door and leaving. It was so strange watching this process that looked almost like a military retreat. I thanked them and again told them that since they were honoring my wishes, I promised to respect their space outside.

A few weeks later, there was banging on my door at 2 A.M. I ran down the steps and looked out the peephole in the front door. It was my next-door neighbor. She said her son came home and found a huge ant infestation, and she wanted to warn me. Our apartments shared a concrete stoop with two steps, and it looked like it was moving. There were millions and millions of ants. I had never seen anything like it, but I noticed the concrete going into my home had not one ant. I told the neighbor that they don't seem to want to come into my home. Then I noticed that her son was pouring bleach on the ants. I bent down and told the ants, "I am not harming you. I have kept my promise. Thank you for honoring your promise also." I know this all sounds very strange and foreign, but it is the truth, and it taught me how connected we all are.

We had a new family in our apartment complex, a mother and her 13-year-old daughter. The mother was blind. They had been homeless for a couple of years. They finally got help, and they had this apartment, but no furnishings or clothes or food. I put a big container out at the apartment complex office for people to donate to them, but then the good people from the church found out and put a stop to it; "If they want help, they need to get it from their church." I thought churches were supposed to be inclusive, but there in Utah, my experience was they were very exclusive. So, I did it on my own as much as I could.

I had the daughter babysit for Morgan a couple of times. I always walked her to her door afterward. The second time she babysat, she asked if we could sit on the park bench because she wanted to tell me something. She wanted me to know that most nights, she stands outside our apartment and watches us. She said that sometimes she makes pretend that she belongs in our family. She loves how we jump on the furniture and swing Morgan in blankets and launch her onto the couch, how we are always singing and laughing. She apologized for intruding on our privacy. I told her that she should never apologize for having a wish or a dream. Sometimes that's all we have to keep us going.

I told her that next time, I hoped that she would knock on the door and come in and join us. She said she can't because she is dirty. I asked her what that meant. She said her dad had molested her all the time when she was little. When her mom found out about it, she felt so bad that she tried to shoot herself. She missed, kinda, so now she has no eyeballs. Her dad went to prison, and she and her mom became homeless. So everything bad happens to her because she is so dirty from her dad. I hugged her and said, "You couldn't be more wrong. If anyone is bad and dirty, it would be your dad. I'm so glad that he is in prison so you could be safe again. The rest of the bad stuff came from a place of sadness. It's not your fault; trust me." She said, "That's easy for you to say, you've got the perfect family." I said, "Yes, I have my perfect family now, but I had a relative that sexually abused me when I was little also. I know what I am talking about. You deserve your happily-ever-after just like me. But you have to believe that you deserve it." I hope that her life got better as time went on.

Once, while we were at Ken and Janet's home, and I was telling a story. I was all animated standing there in the middle of the living room, and my arms were gesturing parts of the story when Ken stopped me. He laughed and said, "Can I have the short version?" I was so stunned by his words. For someone who was working towards enlightenment, he really could be a jerk sometimes. I stopped talking and said it wasn't important. That night I told myself again and again so I wouldn't forget, "Stop telling my siblings my stories. They don't care. They don't want to hear it. What you have to say is of no importance to any of them. Who you are is insignificant to them. What you have experienced or learned is not what they want to hear. So please, please, please shut up, so that I can stop feeling hurt and disappointed by them."

So now to the heart-wrenching bit about what happened to Morgan. From a parent's perspective... she was bullied. Not in the way that most of us think of bullying. She was not called names, she was not beaten up. No. Morgan was shunned. These good, supposedly Christ-like Christian children learned well from their elders. They are the superior religion. They are above everyone else. Let me tell you right here and now, this behavior has absolutely nothing to do with Christ or God. Jesus would never ever treat another human being with anything less than love and respect. End of statement. But there in Utah, she was not allowed to play with the other children, for she might contaminate them. Yeah, right—I call bullshit! She would contaminate them with kindness, compassion, and a greater understanding of how to be a good person. It's a shame she didn't contaminate them, maybe they would have become better human beings. These children didn't want her sitting by them, eating with them, or joining them at recess. Morgan would come home and ask why we can't be their religion. I told her that you should not become a religion because of pressures, but because you are called to it.

How much of the prayers that we utter week after week are not what we truly believe? My conversations with God are a relationship. I have taken out the middleman. I feel that religions can be very, very beneficial to people who don't know how to do that themselves. Or people that like the camaraderie that they experience with a group of like-minded individuals. I am so very grateful that my mother had the Catholic Church in her life. It was something that she could count on. The rules and regulations gave her a sense of rightness and belonging to something bigger than herself. She said the rosary almost every night for decades and it brought her peace, and I am grateful for that. Whatever connects you to your God and brings you peace and teaches you to be a higher version of yourself, I am all for it. But I get frustrated when people think a label or a ceremony is a direct connection to God. In my opinion, it is <u>NOT</u>!

I made Marsh seek a position outside of Utah so we could get Morgan out of there as soon as possible. Our little girl was so altered that she now behaved like a victim. She no longer trusted herself. She lost her vibrancy unless she was with people she could fully trust. She looked to others to figure out what she should do next, instead of trusting her own inner guidance. She no longer looked people in the eye. She no longer seemed to know what she knew. But there were three things that Morgan still trusted. She trusted her mom, she trusted her dad, and she trusted her intelligence. Morgan knew that she was smart, and I believe that has helped her to keep her sanity in a world where being fair and kind are a detriment.

For the record, I want you to know that I have great respect for many of the people who belong to that religion. In fact, I'm having lunch with a very good friend tomorrow who belongs to that very religion. My favorite neighbors are that religion. I love how family-oriented that religion is. I believe that many people in the Salt Lake City area of that religion have just gotten off balance. Their power has gone to their heads instead of their hearts. Love, compassion, and tolerance is the way—always, and in all ways!

During our stay in Utah, I noticed a new pattern. I love noticing patterns and learning from them. I look for patterns in everything. As we are speaking of being Christ-like, I noticed how so many people were talking Jesus, Jesus, Jesus, but very few were talking about God, not just in Utah, but anywhere. Why is that, I asked myself? Then I started asking other people that I respected. Why do so many believe in Jesus more than God? Because that is what it felt like to me. The answer to my question that resonated with me the most was that Jesus died for our sins, and because he was a human walking this earth trying to be the very best person he could be, and so people can relate to him more. They can try to be like him. I get that, and I highly respect that. But my past experience taught me that when I tried to be like someone else, I always fell short. I learned that when I imitate others, I was not being the highest version of who I came here to be. I like to use them as an example, a guide, but I felt that God put me here to be Mary Beth. I cannot be Jesus, because I'm not Jesus. But I can be kind and accepting like Jesus. I can be tolerant and respectful like Jesus. I can be Love—pure, simple Love like Jesus. But I need to do that as Mary Beth, right? What do I do with this Jesus thing and why can I not let it go? I was really, really confused. I asked God for guidance on this. I wanted to understand. And then one day I got my answer in a most unexpected way.

Marsh and I had dropped off Morgan to spend a couple of hours with Ken and Janet while we went to a movie that was not a cartoon. We were walking across the parking lot when I felt a tap on my right shoulder. I turned around, and there was no one there. I scowled and continued walking when I felt the tap again, but it was harder. Again I turned around—no one there. Marsh was looking at me with a questioning look. I shrugged and took his hand and continued on. The tap was so strong the third time that I turned and said very loudly, "What! What do you want?" No one was there. Absolutely no one. And then I heard, "I want to be your friend." I said, "I don't know how to do that." I have absolutely no idea how I knew it was Jesus that was talking to me, but I did. I knew what I knew. He said, "The same way you would any other friend. When you have a great day, what do you do with a friend?" I said, "I would call them up and tell them every detail so that they could experience it as fully as they possibly can without having been there." He said, "Exactly. That's what I want you to do with me. And when you have something challenging happen in your life, what do you do with a friend?" I said, "I call and cry on their shoulder. I have a full-fledged pity party." I was asked, "And how does doing those things make you feel?" My response after a moment of contemplation was, "I feel heard, and my burden feels less and depending on the friend... I feel loved. When that happens, whatever was bothering me feels lighter, less overwhelming." "Exactly," was what he said to me. "And that is the kind of relationship I want to have with you. When you have something wonderful and exciting, I would love for you to talk to me about it. When something is bothering you, or if you are in pain or suffering, I want to be that shoulder you cry on. Can you do that?" "I don't know, to be honest with you." He said, "Being honest with me is the only way I want you to be. It's normal and ok to doubt and to hesitate. I'm asking you to step out of your place of comfort into the unknown. That can be scary." I agreed. "I still don't know where to put you in my life." I loved his response so much. He said, "I want to walk beside you. Not in front of you, not behind you, but beside you! I have been hanging on that cross for a very, very long time. It is difficult to have a relationship with someone when they only see you up there—hanging on a cross. I want to come down off that cross and walk beside you. Mary Beth, can I do that with you? Can I be your friend, Mary Beth?" I said, "I would like that," and I cried.

I learned from my therapist Robert that the Catholic churches have Jesus hanging on the cross, but there are other Christian religions that only have a bare cross. This reminds their congregations that Jesus has risen, and they should celebrate and rejoice, while we Catholics keep Him hanging on the cross suffering, with no relief in sight. Will that poor man ever be allowed off of that cross?

In the meantime, can you imagine what my confused Marsh must have been experiencing? There I was in a parking lot having a conversation with absolutely no one. And in that moment, he was being the person God promised me... he was loving me no matter what! He doesn't always understand me. He doesn't always want to understand me. But he always loves me.

And now I know how to do this Jesus thing. I walk beside him as we talk of crisis and pain, joy and happiness. Sometimes we talk about the weather because that's what friends do. Thank you, God, for bringing my new friend into my life and all the incredible friends he has introduced me to since then, especially Sananda.

Chapter 14: Welcome to Colorado

New place, new space in my head. With all of this moving I have done, I have learned a very big lesson. If you have not resolved your issues before you move, you will simply bring your issues along with you. So many of us think that if I live somewhere different, my life will be different. That can only happen if you have become different. You have to let go of your old patterns, your old beliefs that carry over into every aspect of your life. This is not my belief, simply an example: when we move I don't want to get involved with the neighbors (pattern) because then they might expect something from me (belief). Yes, in a new place, things will feel different for a while, and then you will start noticing that people are treating you the same as they did in the last place that you lived. That is because you brought your beliefs with you. Just like those women that keep saying this guy is different from the last 20 guys I've dated, only to find out that he is very much like the last 20 guys. You brought your old patterns and beliefs with you into this relationship. Usually, that belief is "I am a victim, or I don't deserve," or even just coming from a place of doubt or needing someone to fulfill them. So, as we moved into Colorado, I arrived with a different attitude, and with different beliefs.

Colorado was the first time ever in my life where I chose where we lived. Before it was where my parents chose to live, or Marsh chose to live, or the military chose for us to live. This is the only time I chose to live in a certain place, and it showed. I was empowered by this move, not a victim of this move. I learned that many people on a spiritual path had chosen Colorado, only to have the area drain them, and they must leave after a few years. This is true of Hawaii, also. Both areas hold a very intense energy that either assists you or drains you. I was surprised to learn that an area or a state holds either Male energy or Female energy. You need to decide if you do better in the male frequency or a female frequency. Once you realize this, you can find your "happy place" much easier, or you can understand why you felt so suppressed or uncomfortable in an area. I cannot tell you what each state is, male or female, because I have not lived in every state. To me, Colorado feels like female energy.

Marsh was working up in Wyoming and driving to Colorado so I could live where I dreamed of living. We drove through different parts of Colorado trying to find the right fit. When we arrived in our town, all three of us said this is it! One of the most important things for us in choosing where we lived was Morgan's education. She was a highly intelligent young lady, and she needed to be somewhere that she felt nurtured, stimulated intellectually and encouraged so she can achieve her true potential. There were times that Morgan begged me to let her be homeschooled. That is a great option for some, but Morgan is not a good self-starter. She used to need someone to give her direction and a deadline. By the end of second grade, Morgan was doing binary math. I had no idea what that was. Thank goodness Marsh did and was able to help her if she needed help, and of course, then Morgan taught me. How can I homeschool a child that was smarter than me? This is a lie. Morgan is intelligent, but so am I, just in different ways. Eventually, we found the I.B. program (International Baccalaureate) for her. It was a perfect fit. In I.B., all classes are advanced, while in A.P., only a specific class is advanced. So in A.P., a student enhances what they are already good at. In i.B., they want to create a well-rounded person. They have to work even harder at subjects that they are not necessarily the best at, along with doing volunteer work in their community and doing an independent project that can last two years. Yes,

I.B. was a perfect fit for Morgan, except now she was no longer the smartest person in the room sometimes. At times that was difficult, but she is resourceful and adaptable and chose to learn from her peers instead of resenting them.

We asked Morgan's first-grade teacher to help us find a school in Colorado that would be a good fit, but that didn't turn out very well. Because Morgan is very creative, she chose a more touchy-feely school, and we listened. There are no mistakes, and I feel this experience helped Morgan realize with every fiber of her being that her education is a priority in her life (and it still is). Every morning, the school (the whole school) got together to discuss things. It could be world events, local events, and how they felt about things. Then they went back to their classes and talked about their feelings some more. Morgan said that finally, at 10 A.M. they started doing some learning. I tried to explain that we can learn from our feelings, but Morgan wasn't buying it. They finally worked for 45 minutes and then had recess. Morgan was going bonkers inside. There were a few in her class of 13 that couldn't read. In math, they were tracing their numbers. I kept asking when they were going to do some real learning. The teacher said she needed to assess where each child was at before she knows what she should teach and how. After a couple of months, she finally realized that Morgan and Harriet were so much more advanced than the rest, so they were given a topic to research in the library. I didn't realize that it was ALL day, every day that these two were sent to the library to research... China. In 2nd grade! Not doing any spelling, not doing any math, not doing any reading. There were days when they were completely forgotten about and even missed lunch. During Christmas break, Morgan informed me that she couldn't go back to that school because if she did, she would eventually become stupid, and she is not stupid. Again I had to have a talk with the school so that they could improve. We spent Christmas break finding a school that was a better fit. That's when we found the IB program.

The blessing in that experience was that Morgan and Harriet remained friends through high school. Harriet stayed at that school and seemed to like it, but we moved on. At least twice a month, either Harriet would do a sleepover at our house, or Morgan would have a sleepover at Harriet's. I always tried to do fun activities for the girls. I usually had a scavenger hunt where the clues were numbers that they had to decipher into letters to figure out what it said. Sometimes they did a performance for Marsh and I using a big box of dress-up clothes. My favorite was when they set up their beanie babies in different parts of the house to represent their habitat. Then they sold tickets for 10 cents to take us on a tour. They had all the forest or tree climbers by my plants, water animals in the bathroom, etc. They would teach us what the different animals ate and what they were good at and if they hunted and what they hunted, and what their habitat was like. When I asked Morgan what they did at Harriet's when she did a sleepover, it was something like alphabetizing the VHS tapes.

A favorite activity Morgan and I did each year was we made homemade Valentine's Day cards for everyone in her class, and for people that touched Morgan's life. We spent weeks working on them, and the kids really, really loved and appreciated them. She would personalize them to each child. Morgan would say that this boy loves fishing, then we would have a fish with a string coming from its mouth saying, "I'm hooked on you." I really miss doing those kinds of things with Morgan, but I am so grateful that I took the time and did it with her. She now does knitted knockers for women who have had mastectomies. She makes reusable gift bags out of fabric. She knits hats for babies in neonatal ICU just like when she was in as a newborn. And she knitted hats for the cancer center during my treatments. Where did all of this come from? Well, most of it came from Morgan, but it started because her mom showed her how much more special it is when it is handmade and comes from the heart. I have taught my child again and again the importance of touching someone's life in a positive way.

For Morgan's 8th birthday, we did a homemade carnival, and we invited 35 kids. It was her very favorite birthday, and it was the least expensive birthday party, and we did it as a family. For over a month, we came up with creative ways to make a carnival. Then we cut and painted until our masterpiece was complete. We had a game of tossing ping-pong balls into different-sized decorated buckets. Rubber duckies were floating in the tub. A mermaid on a partition that you were able to fish behind and hook a prize. Beanbag toss that we sewed ourselves. I went to clown school when I was 19 (it was a gift from my sister Christine), so two neighbor girls and I dressed up as clowns. I did magic and balloon animals, and it was so much fun. When we are the example of creativity to our children, we teach them so much more than we can possibly comprehend. Anyone can order something off the internet, but when was the last time you made something together as a family?

While Morgan and I were having all this fun, I bet you are wondering where Marsh was. He was working midnights and driving an hour each way. He was always sleeping. And if Marsh wasn't sleeping, he was on the computer. He did take Morgan out on their adventures, and their favorite was river rafting. Marsh bought a nice raft at a local outdoor camping and sports store. Every time they went, it was nonstop excitement and sometimes even danger. The raft's name was Patches because... you guessed it, it had so many patches on it. I would drop them off upriver and meet them further downriver because this was when I was too fat to do much. Besides, doing outdoor activities really wasn't my thing. One time Morgan had a guy friend join them. After I left to go downriver to the pickup point, Morgan discovered a hole in the raft, and Marsh discovered that they had no oars. This guy couldn't believe they were still going. Morgan rode with her thumb over the hole, and they paddled with their hands. This was about eight years into their rafting adventures on the river, so they pretty much knew what to expect. You should always expect the unexpected. Sometimes when I'd pick them up the raft hardly had any air in it, but their smiles were very inflated.

Marsh working midnights was difficult on all of us. We had to keep the house quiet all the time, and he was so exhausted that he had so little left to give Morgan and I. I was constantly badgering Marsh about why he doesn't love me. Again, it was my perception, my beliefs that led me to believe that. As I learned more and more about my spirituality, my God connection, I started to realize that I had enormous expectations for Marsh. It was his job to make me happy. And if I wasn't happy, it meant Marsh had failed, and he didn't love me enough, and a whole bunch of lies I told myself so I wouldn't have to be responsible for my life or my happiness, and I could continually blame others for my misery. I have since learned that I don't want anyone else to be responsible for my happiness or for my life because no one can know what I need and think and feel except me. When I take on the responsibility of my life, it empowers me and my life flows so much more. And as a bonus, when I stopped placing all these expectations on Marsh and our marriage, everything changed. I became more independent and I enjoyed my own company more and more. That doesn't mean I didn't still enjoy doing things with Marsh. Not at all. Our time together became more about us, instead of me. I also found I wanted to be happier because I enjoyed being with myself when I was happy.

Chapter 15:
What Are You Weighting For

On my 36th birthday, I weighed 289 pounds. On that day I looked in the mirror and I didn't recognize myself. Who was this obese woman looking back at me? That is what the doctor called me, "Morbidly Obese." What a horrible thing to call another human being—even if it was the truth. Every time we got pictures developed, I was shocked that there were no pictures of me. I know I was there, why didn't anyone take my picture? And then my hubby would point at the pictures and say—that's you and that's you and that's you. I would think in my head, that can't be me--she is so fat. I don't look even close to that fat! Well, guess what? It was me and I was that fat.

So I had a heart-to-heart talk with God the morning of my 36th birthday. This woman that I see in the mirror is not me. I don't recognize her as the beautiful and amazing woman that I am. The beautiful and amazing woman that I was born to be. No—I am not ok with this anymore! And I started to make some demands. I want to be thin again. I want to lose weight safely and have a doctor be part of the process. I don't want it to cost a lot of money. I want to be healthy doing it. I want who I am inside to show on the outside, and I want it NOW! And then I cried. It felt like so much was being lifted from my shoulders, from my heart, from my being. I didn't know when or how, but I knew that God had heard me (I know what I know—end of statement). That night as I was flipping through channels, on 20/20[6] or 60 Minutes[7], I don't know which, there was a woman about my age. She weighed what I weighed. She had a young daughter just like me. And there she was describing my life, and I cried. She talked about how difficult it was to get on the floor to play with her daughter (just like me). She talked about how she couldn't play chase or go down the slide (just like me). She talked about how she felt like a failure every day (just like me). And how she felt her family deserved better (just like me). Then she talked about this surgery she had to lose weight and how her whole life had changed. I saw footage of her chasing after her daughter, and of her race walking. She talked about how much more energy she had and how good she felt. I couldn't believe the difference in only six months. I wanted in—where do I sign! Miracles really do happen. I was so excited and grateful to be given this information. I asked God to send me the right surgeon and to keep me safe. That night before I went to bed, I thanked God for giving me the answer to my prayer.

The next morning I called a Physician referral line and was referred to a surgical group that specializes in this type of surgery. I took a very deep breath, let it out slowly and reminded myself that I live a very guided life, and I trust the guidance that I am given. I then dialed the number, and when a pleasant voice answered, I told her what I was looking for. She looked at the schedule, and they just had a cancelation for that day with Dr. O, would that work? Yes, yes, yes!

For some strange reason, I never spoke to my husband about any of this. It was like I was in a dream and was just moving forward one step at a time until I couldn't anymore. So on January 6th, I met Dr. O, and suddenly things were falling into place. He asked me about diets I've tried and failed. Health problems I had. What my family life is like. What I wanted from the surgery. He really listened to me and heard me on so many levels; he even understood me, which is difficult to do when you have never experienced obesity. I asked him, "When can we start—where do I sign?" He laughed at me and said, "Oh, no, that's not how I do things.

[6] American television program, 20/20, American Broadcasting Company (ABC), 1978-2002.
[7] American television program, 60 Minutes, Columbia Broadcasting System (CBS), 1968-present.

I want you to go home and talk to your family. This surgery is life-changing and it will affect everyone in your family. I want you to do your research and think long and hard about it. I don't want to hear from you for at least a week." I couldn't believe that this doctor was turning down an opportunity to make some excellent money. Then I remembered that I had asked God for this and it was Good!

Marsh woke up (remember, he worked midnights), and we talked about the surgery. I was talking a million miles an hour, telling him about the mirror, the TV show, my prayer, the doctor appointment. He could tell I wanted this so very much, but he was scared. How can he be honest with me and not break my heart? He asked me how I can expect him to be excited about me having a non-essential, elective surgery when I almost died during surgery, and he almost died after having surgery. He just couldn't do it. He promised me that we would go for walks each day and eat healthier meals and in no time I would see and feel a difference. And most importantly, we would do it together. How can I say no to that? He loved me and cared about me so much that he just wanted to keep me safe and with him. So I agreed and tried to let it go.

Always in the back of my mind was this statement of "But God gave this to me, and God doesn't want me to die any more than Marsh wants me to die." After about six months of waiting and gaining another ten pounds and not going on a single walk together, I decided it was time to have another talk with God about what to do. Ok, God, I want to have this weight loss surgery. I understand Marsh's fears, but it feels like the right thing to do in my heart. So please, God, if you agree that it's the right thing for me to do, and I'm going to be safe and healthy, please bring me three signs. Well, we were in West Virginia visiting his family, so I figured it was going to take a while, but it didn't. I picked up the phone to make a call, and his family had a party line and guess what they were talking about. Yep, bypass surgery. I giggled and hung up right away. Then one of his brother's ex-girlfriends came over and as we were talking, she asked if I had ever heard of anyone having surgery to lose weight. I don't remember what the third one was, but now that I had my answer from God, I had to have a heart to heart talk with my hubby. I told Marsh that I really value his opinion and that I am so grateful that my health is so important to him. But he isn't the one sitting on the couch staring out the window watching others living life to the fullest. He doesn't know what it's like to get stuck on a slide and your little girl is trying to help you get unstuck while everyone is staring. You aren't the one that can't go to certain restaurants because they don't have chairs I can fit in, and many other things that only another obese person can understand. I told him this is my body and my life and I want to live it more fully. I want to participate in our daughter's life, not just watch from the sidelines.

So, on Sept 25th, I had vertical gastric banding surgery performed by the gifted Dr. O. There was only one scary moment, and that was when they gave me morphine for pain after the surgery through my IV drip, and my arteries would collapse every time (Spirit was trying to protect me). Then finally, some of the morphine got into my system, and it was not good. I just remember thinking that I was going to die. People were running around in a panic, and Marsh was very, very scared. But, thank you, God, only a little got into my system and I made it through. After that, Marsh slept in the car for five nights. He came up at 3 A.M. to help me get to the bathroom, and he took care of me. You see, the nursing staff didn't understand my medical history of having a bad back, so they wanted me to do more than I was physically able to. So Marsh stepped in and saved the day. He took care of me and stood by me even when he was not sure that this surgery had been a good decision. Now that is love. Real day-to-day in-the-trenches-with-you love—no matter what! Thank you, God, for this perfect man for me.

Now that I have had the surgery, this is what unfolded next. The weight was falling off faster than it ever had before, but I was so concerned because I was eating so little. Then some wise person (my sister Christine) told me that what I was eating was what a thin, healthy woman would eat in a day, 4-6 small meals so my body could work more efficiently. What a concept! The first time I went into the normal Misses sizes at the store, I actually felt fear. This was a place where only the chosen get to shop. What do I want? There were so many more choices and colors, and the tops weren't all shaped like trash bags. Again, I had to go into the dressing room to cry because I couldn't believe how wonderful this life was that I was living.

One of my funny stories about losing weight is that we would go for walks to get out of the house and get some exercise. I would fling my leg up because it was so light, and I was used to massive, heavy legs that were hard to move. I really looked ridiculous. We would just laugh about it. Then I lost enough weight that my inner thighs no longer kept my legs apart, and I kept tripping myself. So I had to relearn how to walk. I started with my knees wide apart like I was bowlegged. I would laugh so hard that tears would flow. I was finally able to laugh at myself, instead of finding fault with myself. Hallelujah! That was when I knew that I had turned a corner, and I never wanted to go back to that old way of being ever again.

Another time, I was in the tub taking a bath, and I screamed. My family came running in to see what was wrong. I said, "Look—water." At first, they didn't understand what I meant. Then I showed them that there was water alongside my legs. For years I had been wedged into the tub, and I had forgotten what that felt like to be able to move and splash. I felt a little bit guilty because I used so much more water now. Before, it was just a few inches of water, and when my body mass got in the water, it was up to the overflow drain.

Yes, I had many adjustments to make, but the one that surprised me the most was the fact that many people reject their new body. Each person is different, but I spent some time with a therapist that specializes in people dealing with eating issues. When she was talking to me about this, it triggered something inside of me. When something triggers me, I choose to take a moment to figure out why. That means I close my eyes and simply focus on the thought or concept that triggered me and then wait for guidance. In this instance, I didn't want to reject my new body. I had rejected enough of me in the past, but I no longer live from that space or belief. So what could I do? How could I see my body as beautiful and perfect in this moment? And when I ask a question, I usually get an answer from Spirit, and often it is not what I expected. This one was no different.

I was told to stand naked in front of a full-length mirror and talk to my body in a loving but honest way throughout this weight loss journey. Well, the profound effect this had on me went beyond what I could possibly conceive. Of course, in the beginning, all I saw was my imperfections. Clumps of cellulite, wrinkles and saggy skin were all that I saw. But as I continued to repeat this exercise in getting to know my body, I began to see the perfection in every aspect of my body. Eventually, I saw these things called ribs, and they made me giggle. I saw how my breasts have always been lower than other women's, but they were my own beautiful breasts, and they were shrinking more and more every day. I could see my eyes in ways that I never noticed before. I started to understand the statement that your eyes are the window to your soul. I saw something in my eyes—a spark—and I wanted to connect to it deeper, so I started talking to myself in the mirror. Sometimes it was a conversation where she (the image in the mirror) was the old, damaged me and I was telling her the truth about all those lies. Sometimes she (the image in the mirror) was the wise, spiritual one telling me how magnificent and beautiful I am. I still practice this exercise 22 years later, and it is so healing for me.

Taking the time to talk to your body and learning to love every bit of it can be so beneficial. Have a relationship with your body on a whole new level, and you will find that when something is wrong with your body, you are going to know it way before the doctors because you and your body are one now. I know that sounds silly—of course I am one with my body, we go everywhere together. Yes, but do you talk to each other? Do you have an open and honest dialog? Not saying what you want to hear, but instead, you speak and hear the truth. And as you continue to do this, you can start having these conversations with the little girl or boy you used to be. Give the child you used to be, permission to say and feel all that it needs to say and feel about their experiences. To say that this is healing is an understatement. Think of the words that you always wanted your mother or father to say to you. Now look at yourself in the mirror and say them to yourself. And most importantly—really mean them. Only say the truth to yourself. There is no reason to lie here. Being honest with yourself gives you a greater respect for yourself and more trust in yourself. What you will notice from this experience is that you will start speaking the truth to others. Which evolves into others being more truthful with you. And when that happens, your whole life will never be the same again. Thank you, God!

A few years ago, one of my brothers got sick, and it was life-threatening. We had a family group text, and it was very active during that time. I kept trying to hold back what I was seeing happening in his body and around his body. My family might reject me if they knew the truth about what I see and hear. They might never want to speak to me again. So I just generalized things and softened everything. But it took so much longer to say, and it wasn't complete, and it felt wrong. Well, it felt wrong because it was wrong. It was time for me to stop pretending that I'm something other than who I am. So I spoke from a place of total honesty, and there were times that things got pretty quiet on the group text. I could see where blood was pooling, or where nerves were pinched off and needed a new route to reach other parts of his body. Whatever it was. Then I would ask the family to visualize or pray, or whatever they felt comfortable with.

My adorable sister Charlotte in her beautiful honesty, would ask questions like, how do you know that, Mary? Where does this come from? Like I told you readers in the beginning, sometimes I can see things in people's bodies. The more I trust it, the more that I can see. Sometimes I hear things from Spirit. The more I trust it, the more I hear. I say spirit a lot. The reason why I say spirit is because to take the time to ask who it is that is talking to me kind of distracts me and shifts the connection. Sometimes I get so wrapped up in who it is because the human ego comes into play. So I just label any information that comes through as spirit. It can be God, it can be Mother Mary, it can be Jesus, it can be Buddha, it can be angels, it can be any ascended master from the heavenly realms. Also, sometimes it's loved ones who have passed. Those I know right away because I know their energy. For instance, my grandfather on my dad's side was a horse whisperer. Actually, to be more accurate, he was an animal and nature whisperer. He connected to anything that was more of nature. Animals, rocks, plants, they spoke to him in a way others couldn't understand. He never talked like this or about this while he was living, but he talks about it with me now. My family knows this about him, but they only know the surface stuff. Grandpa could talk in his mind to animals and nature things, and they spoke back to him. So when I do healing work with family members, Grandpa is the first one to show up. So now you understand a little bit more about who I am and what this "spirit" thing is all about. Trust me, there is so much more to it and I want to share it all with you because we are all one.

As I lost weight, I began to change. I had so much more confidence. I had so much to say, so much to share. I was seeing things with new eyes and my vision was very clear. I had an audience too, which really helped. The surgical group that did my vertical gastric banding had a support group, and back then, we talked about important things like, be careful when you drink alcohol because a couple of sips can affect you more now than a whole drink did before your surgery. Sometimes you just need to ask someone if something is going to be permanent, or will it change again. Having others that were going through the same thing, or had gone through it already, was so beneficial. I had a new tribe that held a wealth of knowledge. What I had to say was having a profound effect on others, and the honest way it was being delivered seemed to help also. People were surprised when I would say things like, I needed to have the light on when my husband and I make love. Not because I want him to see and appreciate my new and improved body, but because my body feels different and connecting with him feels different and sometimes it was so different that I felt like I was having an affair. So I would keep the lights on so I can see his beautiful blue eyes and know that it is truly him loving me, and me loving him. Wow—talk about being open and honest. And my wonderful, sweet, shy husband allows me to be me. He allows me to express myself as I need to express myself. He doesn't always like it, but he always allows it!

So people started noticing how articulate I was; how I had a unique way of expressing myself and my experiences. So the hospital newspaper contacted me. They wanted to interview me and hear the story about my weight loss journey. Eventually, I was even interviewed by *Women's Day* or *Women's Circle* magazine. I apologize that I don't remember which one it was, but the magazine is in a box in the basement somewhere, and a lot has happened in the past twenty years. I spoke on a stage to people wanting to know about my experience with weight loss surgery. I spoke to a group of student nurses once, and I know there are no stupid questions, but... one future nurse said, "Fat people don't like to be touched, right?" Boy, did I set her straight. Obese people have the same sense of touch that skinny people have. In fact, maybe we have more because we have a lot more skin to be touched. As an obese person, we tend to feel alienated from society, so when someone touches us, it touches our heart too, because many obese people (me included) believe that we are ugly, and people don't touch or even bother with ugly things. Though we need to remember that what is true for some, isn't true for everyone. Obese people have their own language and understandings, just like any other group of addicts, because food is, or can be an addiction. Many obese people will tell you that food is their best friend. It doesn't judge me, it's always there for me, and it even understands my needs. I'm not saying this is right or even healthy; it's simply "our" truth, as we believe it. The difference in having a food addiction versus ANY other addiction, for instance smoking, is that you can live without ever smoking again, but with a food addiction a person still has to continue eating to live. So it's a very different experience.

At some point, I did a TV commercial for the hospital where I had my surgery. I was featured in advertisements on bus stop benches and billboards. I would never have done any of this unless I believed in it. My final "showcase" (I guess you would call it) was when *Discovery Health* channel did a series called "I Lost It." It showcased different people and the different ways they lost weight, telling their own unique stories and celebrating our successes and our failures. It was very exciting and exhausting. They ended up filming for 20 hours to do a 12-minute episode. They had people who did Weight Watchers, exercising, weightlifting, all kinds of stories and choices. The thing I liked most about it was that it gave overweight people hope, and also options. After watching it, you had a better understanding that we each need to lose weight in the way that works best for our lifestyle, our mentality, our abilities, beliefs, and most importantly our willingness. I also personally feel we need to do it when we are ready. It has been my experience that if you do it before you are ready, you will fail every time. Just like writing this book. Whenever people heard my stories, they would say, "You need to write a book. Your stories are so inspiring, and the way you look at things is so different." But I wasn't ready to write this book—until now.

An interesting thing happened during the filming of "I Lost It." My shy, quiet, and loving family had to tell their stories. In fact, the filming crew wouldn't even allow me to be in the same room during that part, but I was at the top of the stairs listening and crying. I didn't realize that I had never heard my husband's side of the story regarding our daughter's birth. It was all about me and the baby. My eyes were opened, and I loved him even more. I didn't know how he or Morgan felt about my obesity. The person interviewing Marsh seemed to expect him to say things like he was embarrassed to be seen in public with me, or that this obese woman was not the woman he married. Instead, what they got was, "Have you met my wife? She's amazing! So she put on a little weight, who cares." From Morgan, it was simple and direct. She said, "I didn't know anything different. To me, it was just normal."

Once, when we lived in Utah, Morgan was playing at the park, and I was watching from a nearby bench. A little boy came up to her and said, "Your mom is fat." Morgan turned around and looked at me like she had never really seen me or scrutinized me before. She turned back to the little boy and said, "Yes, she is. And she is really nice. Would you like to meet her?" He shrugged and said, "OK," and Morgan proceeded with the introduction. Why aren't more adults like that? Why aren't more children like that? Why do we teach our children that finding fault with others gives them superiority? It doesn't. It only makes them judgmental and sad—along with the person that they are judging.

Having this experience of weight loss was so life-changing for me on so many levels. I started the journey weighing 300+ pounds. I got down to 150 pounds. You do the math. I lost half of me! I lost an entire person! I always told people that I released the part of me that I didn't like very much, and in many respects, that is absolutely true. The happier, more vibrant me came out to play. What I learned much later was that she didn't come out because of the weight loss. She came out because I allowed her to come out. I allowed myself to finally be ME, and it was GOOD! Thank you, God!

I would like to share a few more things that I have learned. When we change our words, it can change the entire frequency of what is being said. I'm going to make two simple statements, and I want you to feel the difference in the frequency between them.

#1: I lost 150 pounds.

#2: I release 150 pounds from my body.

Can you feel the difference? I sure can. I have a long way to go, but word by word, I am getting there. When we say "I lost something," there is an aspect of ourselves that feels we need to find what we lost. So we find our weight and put it back on, and often with a few extra bonus pounds. But when we release the weight, it feels much lighter to me, and I can almost see it being given to God. I release this burden and give it to God. I choose choice #2, please. It is almost 22 years to the day since I had my vertical gastric banding surgery, and I weigh 187 pounds; I wear a size 14, and I still talk to myself and my body in the mirror. Talk to your body, and just as important—listen to your body. Start the conversation now. You don't have to stand naked in front of the mirror if you don't feel comfortable, but that's kinda the point. Time to get out of our comfort zone and become something else, something more.

Are you ready for one other thing that I learned from Spirit on this journey? Well, of course you are—that's why you were drawn to this book. Spirit taught me that wait and weight are somewhat interchangeable. The way that Spirit explained it to me is, when we humans have a certain mindset (our mind is set in a certain way), when we are waiting for our life, waiting for something to happen in our life, waiting for something to come to us, we put weight on our body. Again, holy crap, mind-blowing idea for me. Look back at your life, and if you have the same "mindset" as me, this could be seen as truth for you too. When I look back and see that the times I was not living in the present and was focused on the future, I would put on weight. For example, when I graduate and move out of the house, my life will get better (20-lb. gain). When I finally meet Mr. Right, I won't be lonely anymore (10-lb. gain). When I finally get to be a mom, I can finally allow all that knowledge and wisdom out (80-lb. gain). Boy, look at how many times I say "finally." That says I don't feel I can allow myself to be that yet—but someday I will allow it. Well, guess what—I call bullshit! I'm sorry if that language offends you, but I found that if the language is stronger, it goes deeper and has more of an impact. Again, I'm going to make two statements and I want you to feel how different the frequency or energy is between them, and yet they are saying similar things.

#1: That is a lie, and you should be more honest with yourself.

#2: I call bullshit.

When I call bullshit, I am telling myself... I know you're telling me a lie, and I'm not going to let you get away with it. In case you didn't notice, this tool would have been so beneficial at the beginning of my life. I believed so many lies, and I'm calling them all out now and calling BULLSHIT!

Are you waiting for your life to happen? Are you noticing a weight gain as you are waiting? I tell you there is no time like the present to start living your life. What are you waiting for (or what are you weighting for) and why? Don't waste anymore of your life. That is what we are doing when we are always waiting. We are wasting our time and wasting our lives. If that serves you then continue what you are doing. If it doesn't serve you then there is no time like the present to start changing.

Chapter 16:
My Light Is Shining Brighter

About that same time, I got another surprise from Spirit; I started to channel. In 1997 my spirit guide Charles came forward and introduced himself to me. As you can tell, there were moments before this that I would hear things or see things, but I never knew when it was going to happen and how long it would last. Once Charles came forward, my channeling could go on all day and all night. I eventually had to put down some rules. When I went to bed, Charles needed to respect my need for sleep. I found when some spiritual beings came through to communicate with me, that I would get nauseous or very spinny. So, for several years, any spiritual being that wanted to talk to me had to go through Charles. Marsh was not happy at all with this new development. He asked me very nicely to please stop doing this because it made him very uncomfortable. I thought about it for a while, then informed him that this is a gift from God. God would not give me this gift if it was bad. If I have to choose between God and you, guess who I'm going to choose. Or I can choose both of you, and we can live happily ever after. At first, I was all over the place learning how to do this channeling consistently and accurately. I learned it was beneficial to talk to Charles about what my expectations were. For instance, I stated right from the start that I'm going to trust the first thing

I get as far as information. I learned there needed to be trust between me and my spirit guide. In the beginning, I found speaking out loud helped because I always have so much chatter going on in my head, and I wasn't good at noticing the spiritual information because back then to me it was all just chatter. I guess that is why it took me so long to learn how to "channel." I learned the difference between what I wanted Spirit to say and what they really were saying.

A crucial part of the trusting aspect came from my grandpa on my dad's side. He had passed away when I was five or six. He was able to communicate with animals. I told myself that it's in my DNA, and that made it easier for me to trust. Anyone and everyone can channel. We have all had those moments when we heard something in our head, or had a feeling or knowing, and were surprised by it. Before I "officially" started channeling, meaning when I actually knew what I was hearing and we were able to communicate back and forth, there were some funny moments that I have to share with you. My first thought about this gift was that I can't channel... I'm not vegetarian. I don't compost, I don't chant, I don't like the smell of incense, how can I be chosen to channel? Well, I wasn't "chosen," I had asked. God is waiting for us to ask and to trust. I had watched Sylvia Brown on TV and asked God to be able to do that too. I always thought Sylvia was kind of abrupt. I now know that she was speaking from a place of knowing, and it's just so factual. I also can occasionally come across as abrupt, but it is not my intention.

After my family (as in Marsh and Morgan) got used to Charles, we had a lot of fun with him. I especially loved it when he did something to keep us safe like a guardian angel. One time, we had taken Morgan and Harriet to an amusement park, and when it was time to go home, Charles told me that we needed to wait a minimum of five minutes. I told Marsh, and he shut off the car. I heard Harriet whisper to Morgan, "What are we waiting for?" I was ready to step in if Morgan needed me to, but she handled it beautifully. She said, "I believe we're waiting for most of the crowd to disperse." When we left ten minutes later, there was a 5-car pileup ten miles down the road, and I heard Marsh say, "Thank you, Charles." And he gave me an apologetic look, like, "I'm sorry I ever said I didn't want this." Thank you, Charles! Thank you, God!

Because Colorado, in my opinion, was very progressive in regards to energy work and healings and things like that, I wanted to take some classes to learn how to do this healing with energy. I was already doing it sometimes and had "cured" my hypothyroidism with God's assistance. Also, in 1994 I had noticed a lump in my breast and had surgery to remove it. About five years later, I had found another one, and I had made an appointment to see a surgeon. The night before the appointment, I was doing a meditation when a light came from above and shot into my breast and gave me quite a jolt. I saw that the lump was broken into pieces. I asked for another jolt to break it up even more, and I received what I had asked for. The weird thing that so often happens with Spirit is that I will be so in the moment that afterward I can't remember what happened or what was said by Spirit unless something triggers it, and this is especially true when I channel for others. I know this sounds strange, but it's true. The memory trigger this time was my appointment with the surgeon. I was lying on the exam table while she felt for the lump, but she couldn't find it. She had me sit up, and she tried again but could not find it. She asked me to show her where it was, and I couldn't find it either. She took a mammo, and it was gone! As we walked back to the car afterward, I was telling Morgan about it, and I was so excited that the lump was gone! Morgan said matter-of-factly, "Mom, that's just what you do."

I had assisted others several times with healings, but it felt like it was hit or miss, so I signed up for a class to learn how to read energy and learn how to work with it. I was so very excited. When I arrived early for the class, the teacher asked me what I was doing there. I said, "I am here to learn how to work with energy." She giggled and asked if I was sure. I said, "Yes, why?" She said that she could tell that I was already doing work at a Master's level. I said, "You must have me confused with someone else," but she said, "No, your energy is right in front of me." I said, "Sometimes I can experience some extraordinary things, but I'm very inconsistent." She said, "Ok, welcome. I'm going to need to pair you with the right person for this class. I don't want to hold you back at all." She chose my partner, and I really enjoyed working with her. One time, as I was lying on the table while my partner was scanning my body, I noticed something above me. As I focused my attention there, the image became clearer and clearer until I gasped.

Tears poured from my eyes as I saw the most beautiful woman all soft and sparkly floating above me. The teacher asked me if I was ok. I said, "Can you see her?" and I pointed above me. The teacher said "yes." I said, "Isn't she incredible? Have you ever seen anything so beautiful?" She asked, "Don't you know who that is?" I said, "No." She said, "That's you, Mary Beth. It's your higher self, and yes, you are very beautiful." I have no idea what happened for the rest of the class. I was living in a dream world and I never wanted to wake up. I have found it to be beneficial when you notice an energy like I had noticed above me, all you need to do is be very present with that energy. That means you focus all your attention there and then you will notice more and eventually it will become clearer. Don't force it, don't have an agenda, just let it unfold. It could be a voice, a vision or just feeling emotions. The more you practice and trust this the more it becomes a way of life for you.

After we had been in Colorado a couple of years, I had symptoms of M.S. so the doctors did a brain scan. The doctor asked me what injury I had sustained when I was younger that caused this dead spot on my brain. What dead spot? What are you talking about? He showed me a dark gray-black spot about the size of a nickel. He said I must have really gotten hit in the head hard. I had no idea. When I got home, I called my mom to ask her about it. "Oh, that must have been when Grant tripped you when you were little. You fell and hit your head on the buffet table. You were out for a pretty long time." I asked what the doctor had said about it. She said, "We didn't take you to the doctor. I called your father, and he brought one of the ambulance workers home with him. By the time they got to the house, you were awake again. They checked you out and said you seemed to be ok, so we just left it." I said, "Well, I just had an MRI and it shows I have a dead spot on my brain." She made some comment about how that would explain a lot. I said, "No, Mom, I have a dead spot on my brain and you did nothing about it. I can't believe this." A few years later I had another MRI, and that same doctor (a neurologist) said, "That's strange." I said, "What?" He said, "If you look at this area here, you can see that there had been damage done to the brain. It seems to have made a barrier and rebuilt itself." I told him that the last time I had seen him he had informed me I had a dead spot. He said, "Not anymore. It seems to have regenerated the tissue." I was so ecstatic, and I had never even worked on it.

When I was six months old, Connie, Grant, and I had bronchitis really bad. Connie and Grant went to the hospital and were in oxygen tents. Mom said my eyes were swollen shut for three days, and yet again, they didn't bother to take me to the doctor. Why? Was my mother half hoping that I would die? I don't know why my mother didn't like me. I was six months old. What could I have done to have made her not like me already at six months old? Then I realized what I had done... I was born. She didn't want another child. She didn't need another child. What would it have felt like to be wanted, to be loved? Well, at least my child was wanted and loved every moment of every day. Even when she frustrates me, she is loved.

Well, I wasn't the only one having brain scans. Morgan had one when she was in 5th grade. She was experiencing double vision and dizziness. I was a nervous wreck. I called Mom and told her what was going on. She said, "You always overreact. Why do you have to be so dramatic?" "How can you say that? What if Morgan has a brain tumor?" Then Mom went on to tell me about something adorable that Anna did. She said, "I know that everyone thinks I'm being ridiculous because all I talk about is Anna, Anna, Anna. But all of you kids need to understand that she is my only real grandchild." And that's when I lost it. I said, "I knew I must have been adopted." Mom laughed, "Yeah, we needed another child as much as we needed a hole in the head. Trust me, you were not adopted." My reply was, "Then how can Anna be your only grandchild?" She said, "I know my grandchildren are all important to me. But Anna is my only biological grandchild." I said, "And what is Morgan?" Mom thought about it for a while and said, "Oh, yeah, and Morgan too." I said, "Never mind, Mom, I'd rather you had no connection to my child. You don't deserve to be her grandmother. I have to go." And I hung up. My mother didn't call me for over six months, and she didn't even notice that I hadn't called her either. Mom never asked how Morgan's MRI turned out or if she was feeling better. That's when I decided that I needed to break ties with Mom for at least a year or two. Once I decided I didn't want to talk to her, she called about three times a week. I had no desire to waste my time with someone that obviously did not care about me or my family.

What brought me back in contact with my mom was, my dad had another heart attack in a Dairy Queen. Connie, Anna, Connie's daughter, and Mom were there, I believe. Connie kept encouraging the EMTs to save him because he was one of their own. They ended up zapping Dad 25 times to keep bringing him back. By the time Marsh, Morgan and I arrived from Colorado it was about 1 A.M. Dad was in ICU. Connie was a mess. She told us how she kept talking very determinedly to the EMTs, and they did save Dad. But there lay Dad on a ventilator. Connie said that they don't expect him to make it through the night, and she was so grateful I had gotten there in time. Marsh and Morgan said hi to my dad and then left for the night. I wanted to stay with him and help him in any way that I could. I looked at this man who was my father. A man that I had always wanted to have a deeper relationship with. Dad was always so strong, so very, very strong. Not only physically strong but strong with determination. I started to see things and understand things about Dad. Just as I had learned when I was 16, no one had ever given my father permission to just be loving. He always had to be strong. Strong enough to take care of nine children. Strong enough to go into burning buildings. Strong enough to never give up, even as the love of his life lay dying in a hospital bed. He had to be strong. I saw my grandfather appear on Dad's right side. I thought that he was here to welcome Dad home. Then I saw Dad's first wife Rose on his left. Grandma was behind Grandpa.

Dad's eyes opened. I greeted him and said, "Boy, Dad, when you do something, you really go all out." I told him I loved him, and he squeezed my hand. Tears were flowing from his eyes. I thanked him for being my father. Another squeeze of my hand. I told him, "I know that you feel that you weren't the best father, but you did get better and better at it. That is what matters, Dad. I think we are here to become the best person we can be." Another squeeze. I said, "You have quite a bit of company here. Do you see them, Dad? Your dad and mom are here on your right." I pointed to them. Dad shook his head. The ventilator prevented him from being able to speak. Then his eyes got wide like he could suddenly see them (this is that focusing aspect I spoke about a couple of pages back). I then said, "And here is your Rose on your left." The tears really flowed then, as he sobbed. I said, "It looks like it is time for you to go." He shook his head violently. I said, "Dad, do you see the angel? Do you feel that amazing peace?" Again he shook his head violently. What was going on? Dad was supposed to feel at peace. I asked him again if he was ready to go. Again NO. I thought about it. I looked at Grandpa, and he nodded at me in encouragement. I said, "OK, Dad. Maybe Grandma and Grandpa and Rose are here to help you."

"Dad, you've always said that you didn't want to live if you were not fully there. I can see that there has been some damage to your brain. How about we start there?" He nodded. I said, "Please just relax and allow God to come in and heal you." He nodded and closed his eyes. I focused on his brain. I saw what looked like burned and frayed connectors. I'm not a medical person; I'm just describing what I saw. It doesn't always make sense. As I focused everything I had in me, I saw beautiful swirls of light come down from above. They were such vivid colors. Like neon lights, only softer and yet brighter. I watched as the light swirled in, through and around Dad's brain. I knew that the different colors were doing different things. I knew that every single aspect of this had an intention. I didn't need to know or define any of it; I only had to hold the intention of love, healing, and oneness. I chose to encourage the light as I watched it swirl and dance in the most graceful way. Every movement was purposeful. My thoughts needed to remain filled with purpose and intent. Slowly, so very slowly, the lights started to fade, and then they were gone. Dad opened his eyes and he smiled as best he could with a huge tube in his mouth. His eyes were twinkling. I said, "How are you doing, Dad?" He nodded vigorously. I said, "I know, I have felt the light in my own body and it is beyond words, isn't it?" Another nod and tears.

I said, "Ok, now that everything seems to be in order with your brain, how about we fix that heart of yours?" His eyes got big, and another nod, nod, nod. "Ok. Please relax again, Dad. Allow God to fill your heart with his healing light. Allow God's love for you to fill your heart." I could hear Dad's thoughts that he didn't feel he deserved God's love. I said, "Dad, that's not where you need to go at this time. God does love you, whether you believe you deserve it or not. Can you allow him to love you even if you feel you don't deserve it?" He nodded.

I watched as the lights appeared again, but not nearly as strong. I let them start their dance in Dad's heart. When I spoke again, the lights faded a bit. I said, "Did you feel that in your heart, Dad?" He nodded. I said, "That is God's love. God is filling your heart with his love for you. Can you please open up to receiving more? If you really do want to stay and not die, if you really do want to be healed, this is the only way I know to do it, Dad. You have to be willing. You have to allow God in all the way. Trust me, Dad, there is nothing in there that God doesn't already know about." He nodded, and Dad struck his chest out so far. He looked like he was waiting for God to pin a medal on his chest. It was so very beautiful to experience this with my daddy. To finally allow someone in my family to see who I am. To see what I do. I said, "Now close your eyes, relax and enjoy the ride." The colors were more vibrant. The dancing and swirling began, and I held my love for this man who was my father as God my Father healed him. I watched as every nook and cranny was being taken care of. Again I saw burn marks. I saw weakness, I saw disease all fall away as it was being transformed into something so vibrant and strong. I remember thinking, "Now that is the kind of heart that belongs in my daddy!" This took a long time. There was a lifetime of hate, anger, fear, doubt, and resentment to heal. But heal it He did. I watched as the light and color receded. Dad opened his eyes and released more tears. I said, "I know. It's pretty remarkable, isn't it, Daddy?" He nodded. "Would you like to rest for a little bit?" I saw fear in his eyes. I said, "No, Daddy, I'm not going anywhere. I will be right here for as long as you need me."

"You have been through a lot tonight, and if you want to rest, you can. Eventually, I would like to work on your lungs so we can get you off that ventilator." I heard his thoughts again that he really wanted to continue. I laughed, "So you don't like having that huge thing in your mouth and throat?" He shook his head no. A nurse came in to check on Dad. I know that Spirit was assisting in making sure that we were not interrupted. Divine timing was unfolding before us.

When she left, I told Daddy that I kinda like spending this time with him and getting to do all the talking. He squeezed my hand and then pulled it to his heart. "Ok, here we go, Daddy. Relax and allow, you know how this works by now." He closed his eyes; the lights and colors came in. Some went into his mouth and down his throat, some went directly into his chest, and some went in from his back. I understood that they were filling him with the breath of life. There was more happening here than just fixing his lungs. Just as working on his heart and his brain were more than just taking care of his physical body. I wondered how much of this Dad understood. Suddenly alarms started blaring. The healing light receded. The nurse came rushing in. She was checking the ventilator and said that he seems to be breathing more on his own. That's a good sign. I laughed and said, "Did you hear that, Daddy? You SEEM to be breathing more on your own. Can you imagine that?" and I winked at him with one of my awkward, exaggerated winks that I usually only give my hubby to make him laugh. Dad nodded. The nurse turned down how much the ventilator was assisting him (at least that's what I think she did).

She left the room, and we continued our work. I really prefer to call it play. When you watch the dance and feel the energy of the experience, it feels strange to call it work. The whole experience seems so playful to me. Maybe that is why sometimes this works and sometimes it doesn't. Could it be because sometimes I feel so desperate and pushy? That makes sense. Nothing about this should be forced. It's not a force so much as a flow.

Again the machine was going off. The nurse decided to call respiratory therapy in. Guess what they decided? Yep, Dad was having to work too hard fighting the ventilator, so they took it out. I had to leave the room as they did it. The sun was starting to rise, but I didn't feel tired at all. When I came back in, Dad seemed a little more tired. I said, "Why don't you rest, Dad. I'll stay here and watch over you." He hugged me and said, "I love you so much, Mary Beth." I said, "I love you too, Daddy."

At 7 A.M. Connie called the hospital to see if Dad was still with us. The nurse said that yes, he's sitting up in his chair eating breakfast. When Connie arrived, she came up to me and hugged me. She said, "I know what you did." I was so shocked by her words. Did she really know what God and I did? Was my big secret out? We have never ever spoken about it. Never in the decades since that day has she asked me questions about it, or told me what she thought happened. I have been too afraid of my family rejecting me to ask. But no more.

Unfortunately, within two days of Dad's healing, he didn't remember any of it. He didn't even remember that we had been there. When I spoke to him on the phone after we got back home, he said how great it was that Christine's family came from Tennessee, and Charlotte came from out of country. I spoke up and said, "And Mary Beth's family came from Colorado." He said, "I'm sorry you and your family couldn't make it." I said, "Dad, we were there a couple of days." He asked Mom over his shoulder. She said that yes, we had been there, but that we hadn't stayed long. So Dad said thanks for coming. Another ache in my heart (which I choose to let go of). I have learned it was to teach me to give freely without needing any recognition in return. Not an easy one for me when it comes to my family.

Chapter 17: A Special Relationship

I have the complete and humbling honor to have a wonderful niece on Marsh's side of the family. Her name is Rochelle, and she radiates love and kindness. Whenever we are in Rochelle's presence, I see her watching Marsh, Morgan, and I. The first time I met Rochelle, she was 1 ½ years old. Marsh's sister Kacy lived in Illinois with her husband and Rochelle. While we were visiting in Wisconsin, we stopped at Kacy's to visit. Even back then, Rochelle just stared wide-eyed at me. We had a heart connection, and she sees such amazingness in me, and I must admit that means so much to me. Rochelle just wants to spend every moment she can learning from me. I absolutely love being around people that want to learn from me. I know that sounds egotistical, but God put me here to teach others another way of being. So when I get the opportunity to do what I came here to do, I'm in my sacred space. The first time I met Rochelle, I was singing and dancing and playing with her, and she kept looking at her mom like, is this ok? That evening when she took her bath, I was sprinkling her with long balloon animal balloons straight out of the bag. She was smiling so big and my heart was so full of happiness. I absolutely love Rochelle!

The second time I met Rochelle, her mom was pregnant, and our time together was so short. The third time, we met in West Virginia because they had moved back there. Rochelle and her brother Andy were in the backseat with Morgan, and we were going on an adventure. They stared at us, I think because I was so loud, or maybe because of what they had been told about us? We sang songs, and because Marsh hadn't been in West Virginia for so long, he kept making wrong turns. He would yell, "What kind of turn are we going to make?" and Morgan and I would yell, "U-turn!" and then we would all laugh. By the 3rd or 4th U-turn, Rochelle and Andy were joining in. Once back at the house, we swung them in blankets and flung them onto the bed. We took them to Dairy Queen, and little Andy wanted a banana split. He had never had one, so I described it to him. His mom said, "No, it's too much." I told her, "We only get to spoil our niece and nephew every three years, please let us do this." Kacy finally gave in. Andy had about five spoonfuls and decided he didn't like banana splits. Kacy felt bad about the waste, but I told her it's never a waste if you learn from it. "So, Andy, are you ever going to order a banana split again?" He stated a definite "NO." I said, "See, Kacy, lesson learned. Andy never has to waste another moment dreaming of banana splits."

The reason I'm telling you so much about my sweet Rochelle is that when she was a teenager and we were visiting again, we were at Marsh's sister Mandy's house. Marsh and the kids wanted to go swimming in the river behind the house. This was before my weight loss surgery, so I didn't go in, and Rochelle decided to stay with me. She asked me if she could sit by me and ask me something. I said of course. She paused like she really wanted to get this right. Then she said, "How can I have a good marriage like you and Uncle Marsh?" Wow, this was huge for me. No relative had ever acknowledged that Marsh and I had a good marriage, except Grandma Abby that one time in Nevada. In fact, when Marsh and I were first married and Morgan was young, Connie and Christine were standing right next to me when Connie said, "I could never be married to a guy like Marsh." Christine said, "Me either." As I held back the tears, I thought about it and responded, "Well, of course, you guys couldn't be married to a guy like Marsh. He is kind, generous and he puts Morgan and me first. There is nothing he wouldn't do for Morgan or me. You two only want to date and marry guys who are nothing like that."

Once, when Morgan was little and we were visiting Wisconsin, my mother asked Marsh, "When are you going to smarten up and divorce Mary Beth? You could do so much better than her." Marsh was so shocked that a mother could say such a thing about her own daughter. In that moment, I think he had a better understanding of what my life with her was like. He looked her in the eyes so she knew how serious he was and he said, "I'm the lucky one that she chose me to be her husband. I don't deserve her, but I'm so grateful every day. She is a great wife and mother."

During another trip to Wisconsin, Marsh wasn't with Morgan and me. On our first night there, Morgan was sleeping, and Mom said, "You really missed all of the excitement here." I said, "Why, what happened?" She said, "When Connie had Anna." I said, "I thought it wasn't that difficult of a birth other than the hemorrhoids." She said, "You weren't here, you have no idea how bad it was. I hope that she never has to go through that again." I said, "What was so bad about it? Why didn't anyone tell me?" She started to cry, "Oh, Mary Beth, there are no words to describe the pain that she was in. She had to walk around with a pillow, and using the bathroom was just awful!" I said, "Oh, so we are talking about hemorrhoids. Mom, I know that it was bad, but it could have been much worse, she could have almost died." She said, "What Connie went through was weeks of torture; yours was done in a couple of hours." "Are you saying that Connie having hemorrhoids is more horrific than my almost dying?" She said, "Well, yes. She cried when she had to use the toilet." "Ok, Mom, this is it. For once in your life you are going to admit that having a 5% chance of living is more critical than hemorrhoids. Mary Beth's delivery was scarier than Connie's." She said, "Wah, wah, wah, poor Mary Beth and her pity party." I said, "No, Mom. Right here and now you are going to admit that dying tops hemorrhoids." "Of course, Mary Beth, boo-hoo-hoo, you always have to be the center of attention. You weren't here, you don't understand."

"Yes, I do! You went down to Tennessee for Anna's birth, but no one bothered to fly to Hawaii and help me out. Hell, no one even called. For five days they said I wasn't going to live. I was seizing all over the place. My baby was in ICU for 20 days. But you are right, hemorrhoids are so much more critical." I went into the bedroom Morgan and I were staying in and I threw all our stuff into our luggage. I took our bags and threw them on the front lawn. Mom was screaming, "What are you doing?" I said, "I'm doing what I should have done years ago. I can never compete with perfect Connie. I am done. Say goodbye to your granddaughter, you don't deserve the title of grandmother to her." She screamed, "Dad, make her stop!" Dad came out and said, "What am I supposed to do about it? She's an adult, she can do what she wants." So I carried my sleeping child to the car and left. I called Marsh collect from a payphone crying, and he said he was proud of me and that I did the right thing. Morgan and I slept in the car that night, and then stayed at Christine's house for the rest of the trip. Every three years we paid thousands of dollars to be treated like this... why?

So, finally back to my sweet Rochelle, who wanted to know how she can have a marriage like mine. I told her that to me, having laughter in a marriage was the most important thing. I gave her examples of how Marsh and I laughed at ourselves or at the things that happened to us. One time, while living in Hawaii, I called Marsh at work and I said, "Honey, if I burned down the apartment, would you still love me?" He said, "Oh, my gosh, what happened?" I said, "The apartment is fine, but would you still love me?" He said, "Of course." Then I said, "Honey, if I totaled the car, would you still love me?" He yelled, "What happened... are you ok?" I said, "I'm just fine, but would you still love me?" He said, "Yes." "If I destroyed your favorite clothes in the washer, would you still love me?" He said, "Yes, so what really happened?" I told him I had broken a vase of his. He said, "That's all?" I said, "Yes. It's no big deal now that you haven't lost your home, your car and your clothes!" We both laughed.

Another time, I had gotten new glass cooking pans. I put oil on the stove to pop popcorn. Pouring the oil reminded me that I needed to use the bathroom real quick. The bathroom is literally four feet away. Boy, did that oil heat up fast— I had flames coming from the pan. I was going to put a lid on it, but there was a lip in the pan, and the flames would have come shooting out the side. I remembered my dad, the fireman, had taught me to pour baking soda on a grease fire, so I did. Well, the fire diminished for a moment and then it was back, so I called 911. They said, "Fire, police and ambulance, can I send an ambulance?" I said, "Not yet. I have a grease fire, how do I put it out?" I was told to dump flour on it. "My dad, who's a fireman, always said baking soda, but it didn't work." He said, "You need to use a lot of it." I thanked him, and dumped ten pounds of flour on the fire. It worked wonderfully. But I left it so Marsh could see what happened. I wanted to prepare him first, but he opened up the door to the kitchen before I could say anything, and he said, "What the heck?" I said, "Hi, honey, welcome home!" He said, "What happened?" I said, "You know those new glass pans we got? Well, they heat up oil really fast." I told him the story, and we both laughed. There was flour everywhere. He was so grateful that I was safe.

I wanted Rochelle to understand that it's how my husband treats me when he is frustrated or upset that helped me to know that Marsh and I were a good fit. I told her that Uncle Marsh has never belittled me, which is so important to me. He puts my needs before his own. He respects me, and I have great respect for him also. I watched him with children to see if he would be a good father. Make sure you have the same values. But really, to me having laughter in our marriage was the most important thing, and I didn't understand at first why that was so important because I had never seen it in a marriage until my own. It was Spirit at work again.

I explained that anyone can make a birthday or an anniversary special, but can they make the day-to-day living special? That is the kind of wife I want to be and the kind of husband I wanted. I tell Marsh all the time how much I appreciate how hard he works for us. I thank him for all the little things he does instead of just expecting him to do them. I treat him the way that I want to be treated. Don't put expectations on him or yourself that are unrealistic—it sets you both up for failure every time. Does this help you at all? We hugged, and that was such a special moment for me. Another important thing Marsh taught me that I later shared with Rochelle is that you can never take back words. You can apologize, but they can never be unsaid. Marsh said right from the start of our relationship that he likes to wait until he is calm before we talk about something that upset either one of us. It has served us well for 34 years.

Chapter 18: Our First Home

Marsh and I began talking about buying our first home. This was such a dream come true for me. Marsh let me know that his family had never owned a home until he had left for the Navy and his mom had remarried. Looking at homes is so much fun for me. Can I see my family in this living room? Does this tub feel comfortable on my neck? Would I enjoy long soaks in it? Does the kitchen have enough counter space to hold all my cookie sheets? What about the bedrooms and closets? Looking at houses and seeing their potential means so much to me. I guess that's why I enjoyed working at Real Estate companies. I've done it twice. There is a feeling of pride having the honor of being part of that process even if it's only as their receptionist. So, we finally found a tri-level in a nice neighborhood that we could afford. It was perfect for us. Morgan had her own bath with a shower, and Marsh and I had a huge room with a full bath.

Marsh and Morgan loved to tease each other about silly things. The bottom level of the house had a great room we used for Marsh's computer and Morgan's toys, games and books. Marsh would put tape on the floor down the center of the room and tell Morgan she couldn't cross the line. Morgan would move the tape so Marsh couldn't get in or out of the room. There was so much laughter in each and every room. Even when our offer had first been accepted on the house, we were caught dancing on the kitchen counters by another agent and his clients. I said, "Sorry, you're too late, it's all ours!" I loved our neighborhood, too. We had a park one block away. We had really nice neighbors on both sides of us with no barking dogs. It wasn't close enough for Morgan to walk to and from school, but I didn't mind. I learned that if you drove Morgan home from school, you got to really hear about her day. When she took the bus, she was all talked out by the time she got home, and I only heard the surface stuff.

The neighbor to our right worked at a property management company. After living there a couple of years, our neighbor asked me if I'd be willing to clean for them a couple of days a week. I thought it would be nice to help out financially now that Morgan was in school. Well, as soon as I start at any job, they see all kinds of possibilities for me, and this job was no exception. The owner started noticing that a place would be rented shortly after I cleaned it. She asked me what I was doing to create this. I explained that I would bless the houses and apartments as I cleaned them. I would ask God to bring the right person or family for this house. I asked that every person that entered this home felt welcomed and appreciated. I asked that both the home and people be kept safe from harm. As I cleaned the kitchen, I would ask to have healthy meals prepared here and for an abundance of food. In the dining room, I would ask for honest conversations where everyone felt heard. In the bathroom, I asked that the people living there be allowed to release anything their body no longer needed down the toilet, and that it would bless Mother Earth. In the shower and tub, they would feel their bodies cleansed and release all that was not serving them. In the bedrooms, I asked that whoever slept here would have their bodies healed as they slept and they would wake up feeling refreshed.

One morning the owner asked me to give a certain home a good cleaning because it had been vacant a long time. I thought, boy, this is going to be an easy day. I started on the main floor and just did touchups and got through it pretty fast. Next, I got to the basement and my work went into a snail's pace. The energy of the space felt so thick, and the floor plan was very bizarre. I kept looking over my shoulder like someone was watching me. There were a lot of rooms, and I almost felt lost. Every single room had wires hanging out of the wall up near the ceiling. Boy, these people are really into surround sound! But I don't think it's safe to have live wires hanging down in every room. I cried as I was working. What was going on here? I called in angels and ascended masters like Mother Mary and Jesus to help. I was shaking as I cleaned the bathroom. I came back to the main floor and took a break, drank some water, had some lunch and was finally feeling strong enough to do the upstairs.

As I went up the steps, I could barely stand. What the heck was going on! I ended up crawling up the last five steps. I gave myself a pep talk. "Come on, Mary Beth, three bedrooms and two baths and you can get out of here!" First bedroom looked fine, the second bedroom fine, I just want to get out of here. Main bath upstairs I saw shadows behind me when I looked in the mirror. Move faster, Mary Beth, just move faster. As I entered the master bedroom, I went into a complete panic. There was a huge red stain on the floor. Why didn't they have it professionally cleaned? I need to let the office know. As I cleaned, I experienced paranoia all around me. When I went into the master bath, the floodgates of fear opened up. Again, I was crawling. Finally my spirit guide Charles came through and said that there was a very negative vortex in this bathroom, and it would be beneficial to close it. I said, "I don't even know what a vortex is, so how can I close it?" He said, "Call on anyone and everyone you know of in the heavenly realm and ask them to assist you." As I did, I noticed something like a funnel in the floor. Again this is me focusing all of my attention on some energy and then getting clarity. This is why I could eventually see this funnel-like vortex. I was hanging on to the jetted tub and crying like crazy. I prayed and prayed. It looked like blood was on the tiles. What the crap am I doing here? Suddenly things felt calmer because of the assistance I was receiving from on high.

I crawled out of there and crawled down the steps. It felt so good to get out of the house and into my car, but I wasn't safe enough to drive. I waited 10 or 15 minutes, and suddenly my whole system relaxed. I noticed that I didn't have my purse. I hadn't taken it into the house, so it must still be at the office. I didn't care, I wasn't going to the office. I need to go home. Charles, my spirit guide, said I had to go to the office. It was very important. I said NO! We argued all the way... to the office. The owner looked at me and knew something was up. I said, "What the hell happened in that house!" She tried to act all innocent and said, "What do you mean? What happened?" I told her about feeling watched and unsafe in the basement, and she said that a long time ago child pornography took place in the basement, and there had been cameras everywhere. I asked how she could send me in there without any warning. I had felt so scared and violated.

I said, "And why haven't you gotten the carpet cleaned in the master bedroom? There is a huge red stain." She said that the carpet was replaced, and it's not stained. She asked me where I saw it. I said between the door to the master bedroom and the door to the bath. She said that was where the guy who perpetrated the crimes was shot. Holy crap, no wonder why it felt so horrible in there. She apologized to me. She had felt that I had abilities, but did not realize I was so sensitive. I now understand why Spirit wanted me to go to the office. I thought I was going crazy. Nothing had made sense that day. But talking to the owner and hearing what had happened many years ago helped, especially after I explained what I had experienced, and I realized I wasn't losing it. I was so afraid of being judged as looney. Instead, I found out I was right on in what I had experienced and what had happened years ago. Thank you, God, for the guidance and for keeping me safe. I called the next day and asked if I could take my husband back to that house with me so I could bless it in a different way now that I know what happened there. She said yes. I was terrified to go back, but I wanted to face my fears. Marsh told me there was no way that he was going to let me go into that house again alone. He and I went into this house together. I think he better understands when I talk about energy now because he kept saying how strange and uncomfortable it felt in the house (Marsh was feeling the energy of it). He wouldn't let me leave his side, and I was so very grateful. Bless this house and those poor, innocent children who had suffered. Please, God, no more abuse of the innocent children. No more!

My spirit guide said that the angels and spiritual beings had been working assisting with the energy of this home since I was there yesterday because I had asked them to. WE HAVE TO ASK IN ORDER TO RECEIVE! I went downstairs and commanded that any energy and/or beings connected with the atrocities that occurred here be removed at once. Clear, clear, clear any and all energy less than Love from this space. I waited until it felt like it had been lifted. What that feels like for me is tension leaving my body like a sigh or a relaxing of my muscles. I asked that anyone that was ever abused here be healed and that their burdens be lifted. Bless them on their path in the most sacred way.

I asked for the main floor and the upstairs to be cleansed and purified from any and every negative thought, feeling or action that had occurred there. As we finally went upstairs, I couldn't believe this was the same house. The energy was so much calmer. I had no issues at all going up these steps, and there was absolutely no stain on the carpet. This is crazy! I feel so ridiculous. Then Charles spoke up and said, "Don't. You did a great job yesterday. Feel how different everything feels today. This is wonderful, and we are so proud of you and grateful. You could have walked away, but you didn't." I said, "Really, I could have walked away? I wish I had." He said, "No, what was accomplished here yesterday and today is good. We are so grateful to you." I told Spirit that I do not want to experience such negative vortexes again, please.

Several years later, we lived in a house with a very fun ghost. I named him Sam because that was the name that came to me when I met him. The way I understood it, he was the farmer that had owned all this land that the neighborhood was built on. He devoted his life to his land, and he was making sure everyone was respecting his land. I don't think Marsh and Morgan really believed me until I told them that Sam loves electronics. I told them he likes to just randomly show up and push buttons. I told him (just like I told the ants in Utah) that I will respect this house and land, but you must respect our wishes too. After the first time he turned on the TV at 3 A.M. I stated, "No playing with our electronics once we go to sleep." You could be making dinner and the microwave would turn on. As you shut that off, the CD player would start playing. This did not happen all the time, only a couple of times a week. Then one day, Marsh was home alone playing on the computer and a VHS tape popped out of the VCR across the room, went back in, and then out again. Marsh said, "Hi, Sam." Morgan loved it when Sam would visit while she was home. I think that we were his favorite house because we always acknowledged him and were not afraid of him. During the Christmas season that year, we were walking in the neighborhood and Morgan (who sees patterns too) noticed that on every other house the top right string of lights on the peak of the garages weren't lit. It went on for two blocks. Morgan pointed it out to us and we all laughed... "Sam!" Morgan did not want to move out of that house unless we took Sam with us. I told her that as much as I would like that, Sam wants to stay with his land. She understood, but was disappointed.

I have helped people do blessings on their homes over the years, especially when they are selling a home. I was never taught any of this, I just noticed a difference when I stated what I want vs. when I did nothing. We can't expect something to change if we are not willing to ask for the change. We need to participate in our own lives. We also need to participate in CHANGING our lives. There is a huge difference between when I am living my life with intention, rather than when I am just reacting to my life and feeling like I spend my day just dealing with one crisis after another. The difference is amazing when I am living my life from a place of intention, where I can constantly say that I live a guided life, and I'm going to trust my guidance. I choose to touch as many lives as possible today in a wonderful, happy way. Or whatever I choose as my intention. Trust me, I've done both, and I prefer to participate in my life and have an active role in what I create. It helps to take one moment at a time. Instead of looking at how many things I didn't do very well, I tell myself I caught myself slipping into judgment four times today and corrected it right away. That may not be much, but it's better than zero. Soon I'm up to 20 a day. What can I say, I'm a work in progress, and I am progressing beautifully!

While living in this home with Sam the ghost, I went into some pretty serious depression, and it really affected Morgan. I didn't know this until many years later when my sister Christine informed me. For me, depression is God's way of getting my attention. I can't do anything or really be anything for anyone during my bouts of depression. It's time for me to be totally selfish and take care of myself by going inside and connecting with God. I cry and sob a lot. I have huge pity parties. I blame everyone for everything bad that has ever happened to me. I feel so much hatred and resentment. I wallow in it and wallow in it until I am spent. I sleep a lot. And the moment love comes in... I have <u>clarity</u>. Suddenly, I have a greater understanding of my role in all of this. I had to cry and cry to let <u>it</u> all go. Until I am able to let it all go, there is no room for clarity and God's light. I am so full of pain, resentment and fear that there is no room for compassion and understanding.

So, my understanding for <u>myself</u> is that I'm given the experience of depression to see and understand better what it is that I am holding inside. To see what I <u>believe</u> about myself. To see what I <u>believe </u>about others. As I allow myself to think and feel all of it without holding back, I feel a release. It comes in layers. Crying – pain – yelling = Release. Crying – pain – yelling = Release. Crying – pain – yelling = Release, and then eventually my clarity. Was it really as bad in reality as it was in my head? So often we tend to make things worse with our thoughts in our head. How many times did I allow my thoughts to take me to a horrible place? <u>I ALLOWED!</u> I DID NOT STAND UP FOR MYSELF AND SAY "NO MORE!" or even just stop them. I'm not saying I allowed the abuse, I'm saying I allowed my negative thoughts to continue and fester.

I tried to do this process many times during this time in my life, but Morgan needed me to be a mom, groceries needed to be bought, responsibilities were all around me. So, I never really got to the clarity part, and my depression lasted a very long time. I wouldn't allow myself to give myself what I needed. It felt like such extreme lows. It had nothing to do with Morgan. It had nothing to do with Marsh. I hope that less and less people suffer from depression because they take the time to go inside and have honest conversations with themselves, or God or whoever they are comfortable with. It is beneficial to work through our stuff continually and then let it go so that our mind and body become more empty so we can fill ourselves with joy and love and light, instead of hatred, anger, and judgment.

I always thought that if I lost my excess weight, my life would be magical. Well, thin people have problems too. I remember when I weighed 300 pounds hearing skinny women talk about how bloated they felt. How they had gained 5 pounds and none of their clothes fit. I rolled my eyes at them and felt <u>no</u> compassion for them. When I later lost the weight and wore a size 8, there were times I felt bloated and didn't like the way my clothes fit. In that moment, I apologized to every skinny woman that I had experienced no compassion for before. I realized that every person has a right to feel good about their body in whatever way that means to them. I have no right to tell someone what they should look like. Only they get to make that decision.

After I had lost my weight, and Morgan and I went home to Wisconsin for the first time, the shock on everyone's face was so interesting to experience. I would say that half of my family criticized me and said I had lost too much weight and I looked sickly. I remember saying to one of my sisters, "Well, you didn't like the way I looked when I was fat, why would I expect you to be ok with the way I look when I am thinner." Why does anyone think that they have a right to tell someone what they should weigh? If someone asks their opinion, then yes. I had people I hardly knew telling me I should lose another ten pounds. I had people who had condemned my weight for 20 years tell me I needed to put another ten pounds back on. I loved the way that I looked, and if you don't like it then don't look at me.

One of my nieces was adorable at Christmas that year. She couldn't stop staring at me. They all recognized my voice, but I didn't look like the relative they remembered. Sometimes, people would walk around me like they didn't want to catch whatever disease I obviously had. I was so surprised that people weren't as supportive as I thought they would be. What a Silly Willy I am. When have they ever been supportive and what have I ever done to change that? Again, I had expectations. When you have expectations, you set yourself up for disappointment. Things tend to play out better in our heads than in real life. I find it's better to flow with life and allow things to unfold. Plan ahead, yes. But also allow things to shift and change along the way.

This experience reminded me of when I had lived in Hawaii and Japan. I expected my family to ask a ton of questions about the people and what I did and what I saw. That wasn't my experience. Why were none of them curious about what it was like to live a military life? Or to live in a foreign country where they speak a different language? Why didn't they want to learn and grow and expand their understanding of the world, or even just my world? I felt everyone thought I was bragging. No—it's called sharing my life with you. Shut up, Mary Beth! No one is interested in you. Watching football on TV is more interesting than a snow sculpture festival in Hachinohe. Why couldn't I remember this?

Now that my siblings are older, they are traveling more and like to share pictures and stories with each other. I'm grateful that they get to be seen and heard. I now understand through my spiritual growth that we must experience something first, then understand it and then gain wisdom from it. So until they actually left their corner of the world, they could not understand what it is like to experience another culture or lifestyle, nor did they want to. Now they understand better and have greater wisdom and want to share. Yeah! Amen! Thank you, God!

On our way home from visiting my family in Wisconsin that year after releasing the weight, Morgan and I had to leave two days early because a huge snowstorm was coming in. We made it to Iowa near the Nebraska border and stopped for the night. The next morning, I watched the weather channel and it looked like we were going to go through some mild snow, but not a huge storm until the evening. I never considered the temperature. Morgan and I headed out. By the second bridge we had gone over, I could feel the ice, and there were patches of fog. I needed to find the next exit and get off the interstate. I felt panic in my gut. My arms felt so tense. I was trying to seem calm so I didn't worry Morgan.

We came over a hill, and the road was pure ice. The car in front of me hit its brakes, I hit mine, we started to do a donut and got hit head on. Everything was in slow motion. We were now sideways on I-80. I watched as a big, white Bronco-looking vehicle was heading right at Morgan. I threw as much of my body over Morgan's as I possibly could while wearing a seatbelt. When I looked up, we were facing the right way, but cars were skidding all around us trying to avoid us and all the other crashed vehicles. A car hit us from behind and we went off into a huge, wide median. Morgan yelled, "Make it stop, Mommy! Make it stop!" I felt so helpless. A person pulled in behind us to see if we were ok. I said, "Yes, just shook up." She said, "Then I'm going to get out of here." I said, "That's a good idea."

I suddenly noticed there were angels surrounding our van (again I noticed this because I focused on it). I asked Morgan if she could see all of the angels standing shoulder to shoulder surrounding our van. "We are safe, Morgan." About 10-20 yards in front of us, a state trooper was pulled over. He was standing in his open door talking on his CB when his eyes got wide and he started running backwards trying to get away as a vehicle smashed into his car and continued to move it, move it, move it. Thank you, God, he was ok and didn't get hurt. Finally, we could breathe again. Only, I saw on the other side of the road there were several cars in the ditch, and there was a woman standing behind her car on the side of the road. I'm yelling, "Get in your car, get in your car!" I told Morgan, "Look at me, don't look over there, look at me!" I didn't want Morgan to see this woman getting hit by a car spinning out of control on this ice rink called a road. Then I watched as a semi came through swerving and skidding until it jack-knifed and stopped, but it was across both lanes. I said, "Please, God..."—too late. A car slid under the semi and it took off the top of the car. I was grateful that Morgan didn't see that. Please, please, God, help us on this cold, icy road. Send more angels to protect all of us and keep us safe.

Then I noticed everything had stopped. What had happened? I found out later that a semi on top of the hill went into the middle of the two lanes so no one could pass him and go down the hill of ice. He saved so many people that day. He was one of many angels God sent to us that day. We stayed in our van, waiting for help. I noticed that the longer we waited, the more my neck hurt. I need to get it checked out. As Morgan and I sat there in our beautiful, damaged van named Dora Madeline (that was like a family member to us), I started to laugh. There in all the heating vents, the dashboard and the console were cookies and lemon bars all over the place. Because we had left Wisconsin early, I hadn't delivered all the cookies I had made for people, so we had them in the van. When we got hit from behind, it must have thrown open the containers, and we had probably 100 cookies around us. I turned to Morgan and said, "Well, at least we won't starve. Look at all these cookies, baby girl." We laughed. That laughter was so healing for me. To find anything to laugh at during so much damage and fear, was a true gift from God. Thank you, God!

I knew that Morgan tends to do best when she has a job or purpose. I also know that she likes to have a plan in place, so I talked to her about some of the things that were probably going to happen so she would be prepared. I told her that Mommy has hurt her neck, and just to be safe, we are going to get it checked out. So we will be going in an ambulance together to the hospital and have an x-ray of Mommy's neck. I need you to help me by keeping Mommy's purse with you at all times. Can you do that, Morgan? She thought a moment and said yes. By then, a state trooper came by my window to see if anyone was hurt. I told him that my neck ached, but it was not an emergency. It was getting pretty cold in the van because the engine was no longer working because the radiator was gone. It was 11 degrees below zero. I asked Morgan if she could please very carefully climb into the back and get us some clothes or blankets to cover up with, if we had any. I wish I had thought to take some clothes with us for the next day, I guess I was a little distracted.

When my ambulance arrived, I was so grateful. These men and women were all volunteers and boy, was I happy to see them. The gurney that I was put on had so much metal, I was shivering like crazy. Morgan was such a trooper. She hung on to my purse like it was her lifeline. Every time someone spoke to her, she would look at me, like "Is it ok for me to talk to this stranger?" And I would give her a nod of encouragement.

They took me in for an x-ray, and when I came out, Morgan was talking so fast because she was so excited. When Morgan figures something out all by herself, she always gets hyper-excited. She said, "Mom, I learned something very important today." I said, "What was that, baby girl?" She said, "I know that I'm not supposed to talk to strangers, but today I learned that there are times you have to break the rules to help someone." I said, "You are totally correct about that, Morgan." She said that they had needed her to help fill out some of my medical information, and she knew most of it. She didn't know my social security number yet, but most of the rest of the questions she was able to answer. On that day, my baby girl seemed to have grown up on so many levels. She had witnessed uncontrollable chaos, and she did better than I thought she would. Later in her early 20s, Morgan was in an accident. She was fine, but her car was a goner. The state trooper and the insurance guy both said how mature and articulate Morgan was. They were so impressed. So maybe this accident we had when she was 10 was beneficial in teaching Morgan how to keep a cool head during a crisis?

The doctor in the emergency room gave me a neck brace and some, I believe, muscle relaxants. I was released and told to keep the brace on 24/7 and check with my doctor when I got home. I asked a really nice nurse that Morgan had made friends with, "Now what do we do? Is there a hotel around here?" She got on the phone to a hotel nearby that had a couple of rooms with a Jacuzzi, and she got a room for us. A maintenance guy was just clocking out, and he offered to drive us there. I couldn't believe I was getting in a car with a stranger, especially with my daughter. But like Morgan says, sometimes you have to break the rules to allow someone to help you, or you to help them.

When we got to the hotel, I told the women at the desk the short version of what had happened with our day. We got a Jacuzzi room, and I couldn't wait to get into it. I was frozen and sore and hungry. I asked if there was a convenience store close by because some food would help. She said, "Leave it to me. You just go take care of yourself and that sweet little girl of yours." An hour later, she arrived with a pizza that someone staying at the hotel had bought for us after hearing me tell my story. God was really, really going all out at providing us with angels to help us out. Thank you, God!

After a long conversation with Marsh trying to figure out how I was going to pay for the hotel room and someone to drive us 300 miles to the airport, along with two airline tickets, Marsh managed to get everything figured out. He sure knows how to take care of us. You could hear in his voice how helpless he felt. He couldn't drive to get us because of the weather. He just needed us home and safe.

As I soaked in the Jacuzzi, which was in the same room with the beds and TV, I looked at Morgan, and it really hit me for the first time that Morgan and I both could have died today. How do I hold this child in my protective arm for the rest of our lives? I cried as I watched her in her innocence watching TV. Does she realize what happened today? Please, God, give me the strength to do what needs to be done tomorrow. Guide our amazing paths like you did today. No, please make it better than today. Please bring kind, generous people on our paths as we walk every step with you! Thank you, God.

The lady at the front desk found someone willing to take us to our van in a lot about 40 miles away and then drive us 300 miles to the airport. I told him all I could give him was $100. He said that would be fine. Morgan and I were shocked when we saw Dora Madeline, our van. There was not a single scratch or dent in the back of the van. I just burst out crying when I saw that, and then on

Morgan's side of the van, same thing, not a scratch. I said, "See, Morgan, I told you that angels were surrounding us. They didn't even let that big, white Bronco-type vehicle hit you, and yet we were bumped and bashed around. Not a scratch." I wish I had pictures. As I showed the young man helping us what suitcases we needed, he loaded them in his car. Morgan and I thanked our van for keeping us so safe, and for giving her life for us. I know that may sound silly to you, but that is what it felt like. She was the very best vehicle, and we still miss her. When we got home, I don't know if Marsh realized how much he hovered over us. How different his life would be today if things had turned out differently that day. Thank you, thank you, God and all of you angels that came on our path that freezing cold day. I am so very grateful!

Chapter 19: Shift Happens

Our egos are very loud and in our face telling us lies. Like for me, it was that I am unlovable and worthless. I am a victim and will always be a victim. Everyone does stuff to me, and I have no say over my life. All of that is ego and lies. It has nothing to do with <u>truth</u> and nothing to do with <u>God</u>. There are several steps that we can take to shift our lives. One of them is to stop believing those lies that our ego keeps running in the back of our minds. Telling us we will never amount to anything, that we'll never be happy, that we'll always have to fight and struggle to get ahead. So long as you believe that crap, then it will be your truth. One of the lies that we can buy into is no pain, no gain. Why would I buy into that? I call BULLSHIT! I can gain so much without pain. I can gain knowledge, I can gain truth, I can gain respect. And none of that needs to be through pain. I know that you are thinking that this is related to working out. Well, guess what, if you take that on as your belief, it will affect all aspects of your life. Is that what you want? Do you really want to live from a place of struggle and pain? I can learn how to walk through the painful moments of my life to see the lies in that experience. Only then can I move beyond it to a place of peace.

When I allow someone else to decide if I can ever be happy or successful, I give away my power, my life, and my free will. Why would I do that?

Because they know more than me? I don't think so! I am the greatest authority on me that there is walking this Earth in human form at this time. Why would I believe someone else's lies and make them my own? That is what I'm talking about when I say I know what I know. I know that I am highly intelligent. I'm <u>not</u> ignorant like I was told constantly as a child. I have some learning disabilities that I am loving free and they don't affect my life as much as they used to except when I have to do multiple things, I get flustered (I'm working on this also). That does not mean I'm not intelligent. I find it beneficial to look at my beliefs and patterns and separate the truth from the lies. From there, I decide if <u>I want</u> to continue believing that or not. If not, I let it go by showing myself I don't believe that anymore, and each time it comes up, I call it out as a lie and let it go again and again until it no longer comes up anymore. Morgan has helped me so much with the lie that I'm stupid. Now when it comes up for me, I just laugh and say that's ridiculous! Sometimes I wonder how that thought can even still exist in my head because it hasn't been my belief for a very long time. But old patterns that are repeated multiple times daily for 40 or 50 years can take a while to release, or it can be instantaneous. The choice is ours.

To me, one of the greatest things that we can do to shift our life into a place of awesomeness is living in a state of utter and complete gratitude. We have so much to be grateful for in every moment. When I was lying in bed with my hurt back my favorite activity was finding endless things to be grateful for, including having a hurt back. If I hadn't experienced having a hurt back, how long would it have taken for me to have a greater connection to God and all that is? Would I have ever experienced it? In addition, I have greater compassion for anyone having to stay in bed or having back issues. I am definitely growing towards being able to experience more compassion and love without having to experience something traumatic to get me there.

Another thing we can do to shift our lives is to be honest. For me, I needed to start by being honest with myself. When I look in the mirror and want to say, "Wow, I'm fat," instead I say things more honestly, like "I still have excess weight on my body, but this is only temporary. I am 110 pounds less than I used to be, and that is fantastic." Notice that I only state my truth. Instead of focusing on <u>I'm</u>

<u>fat</u>, I am more honest and say, "Yes, I still have excess weight, but it is temporary." I only say that if I believe that it's true. My "being" needs to know that it can trust my words. Then as I shift my old recordings, my "being" believes me. Old recordings are the words that repeatedly loop in the back of your mind. When you are quiet, you can hear the dialog going continuously. My "being" is my emotional, my physical, mental and spiritual aspects of me. As we connect more with Spirit, as our frequency raises all these aspects merge and become one "being."

As I start shifting to being honest with myself, I notice I started dealing with others more honestly, and then eventually, my words become more honest. How often do we tell people who we love most, what they want to hear, instead of the truth? I'm going to let you in on a secret. A lie, is a lie, is a lie. There is no fib or white lie or stretching the truth. As you connect to God more and more, you can feel so deeply inside of you how off you feel when you tell a lie. There is only a lie and the truth, end of statement. Does that mean I go around being really mean and offensive with everyone and call it God's work? NO, absolutely not. I have learned to soften my words to say things like, are you sure you want my opinion? It might not be what you want to hear, and I don't want you to feel bad. I will always be honest with you in the highest way I can.

Morgan has learned to say, "Mom, I don't want your opinion, I just want to be able to vent." I tell her, "I can do that, vent away." I know that means she just needs a sounding board. As she vents, sometimes things become clearer, and she then is strong enough and will ask my opinion. She knows from experience that Mom is going to tell her the truth if she asks for it. There are times I start telling her the truth, and I can tell from her energy and/or posturing that it is getting too real, and I will soften my words, or stop to give her time to take in this information. When it comes from a place of love and not from a place of I-am-a-know-it-all ego, then it can be received in such an incredible way. Just like how Janet taught me how to say "no" from such a loving and honest place.

Another way I am enjoying shifting is by taking the advice of my therapist Robert that I have already included it in this book, but it bears repeating. What is the kindest thing I can do in this moment? Robert's wording is, what is the next right thing? I use both of them so that I can continually improve, to become the grandest vision of who I can be in this moment. I find this to be so much easier for me because I don't have to shift my past stuff, just do the next right thing in this one moment. And then try to do it again in the following moment. My sister Christine started this new thing of putting stickers on envelopes and cards she sends. Well, take it a step further and put it on the bills you send. I know you probably don't do paper bills anymore. I do get some from the landscape people and doctor's offices. Can you just see the smile on their face when they see it covered in stickers? It shifts the whole energy of a bill, don't you think? What about helping someone load their groceries into their car, or return their cart.

I have a habit of going ahead of people through doors. I don't mean to, it's just a habit. It's not a horrible thing, but it's also not the kindest thing that I can do. Every time I catch myself doing it, I feel a shift in my being just like I experience when I lie. I try to correct my errors, and it usually looks like an awkward dance. I just laugh it off and say I intend to do better next time. I must admit I am not at my best when I am distracted. That's not an excuse, just something I've observed.

That leads me into another thing we can shift, to bring our lives more into alignment is to be in a place of observation. It is my opinion that as we become more spiritually evolved beings, we let go of living from a place of judgment and duality and shift to a place of observation. I have not mastered it, but when I am in that space, it is heaven on earth! For those who are saying, wait a minute, what is this duality thing now? Let me help you. Duality is right and wrong, good and bad, higher and lower. I think of it as any time we judge that something is better or worse. When I talk about raising to a higher frequency, we instantly go to a place of higher-is-better. When we let go of judgment and duality that statement shifts to "I changed frequency." It doesn't need to be higher or lower, it is simply a change, a shift. In this book I use a lot of duality as a learning tool so that I can get my point across. As we evolve, we don't need to be the best or believe that someone else is better than us, we simply are. They simply are. We are different. We are supposed to be different.

When we are ready, we let go of the competition and simply allow everything that is, to be what it is. We shift to a place of observation so much easier and without judgment when we simply allow and observe. I know that this may be kind of out there for some of you. I simply want to plant the seed of this, so when it is something you experience, you can take that experience and enhance it to be even more (which is a duality word). I love it when I can say to myself, "Now that I have experienced that, I choose to shift the energy to a new experience beyond this one." And then I wait and observe what unfolds next.

As I observe, at first I notice that I am judging each observation. I just let the judgments go one by one and move back into a place of observation. One of the things that helps me is to say, "Isn't that interesting?" It helps me keep the judgments out of my thoughts and words. The interesting thing about saying "Isn't that interesting" is I do find many aspects of what I am observing very, very interesting. I guess you could say it's the power of suggestion, but for me it is so much more than that.

Here is an example. I'm observing my neighbor painting his house. He is up near the top of a peak. I observe that he is really having to stretch to reach. I notice I'm about to go into a place of judging what I think he should do. I stop myself and say, "That is an interesting way of painting. I have never seen that before. How interesting he chose that technique," and I walked away. I can choose not to judge, or I can stand in judgment, the choice is mine in every moment.

Now consider what this would look like if we took this observation even further than our day-to-day lives, but what we are experiencing in our communities—our country and even the planet as a whole! I'm not saying you shouldn't get involved in changing things. Not at all. However, I have noticed when I look at situations around me from an observation point of view, I have a clearer understanding of my role in the situation. Then I can assist from a place of love and trust, instead of, if they are wrong and I am right.

Our planet is going through some great changes. On the outside, it looks like everything is in terrible shape. There are so many people who were not standing up and saying "no more." That it took absolute shake-you-out-of-your-stupor to get them involved and saying NO MORE! How many mass shootings do we need before we say no more? Well, we are in the process of finding that out. How radical does the weather need to change before we admit our mistakes and change our behavior and we say NO MORE? We are finding that out too. How many people need to get sick before we stop putting junk in our food and air? We are finding out in this moment. We are being pushed to the point that those that couldn't be bothered five years ago are standing up and saying NO MORE. Thank you, God. We have been asking for change and we were heard.

I know that the words I wrote above are probably pushing some people's buttons. If you look back at our history, it's usually only when people are pushed to their limits that they stand up and say no more. And then change happens. Can you imagine the change we could experience if we didn't need to have horrific things happen to get us moving in a more positive direction? What if we decided to create change from a place of love instead of fear? Would the change be any less valuable or maybe even more valuable? What if we started showing God that we are actively changing our lives and the planet from a place of love and empowerment? Then we don't need to have the bitter, sometimes hate-filled experiences to make us stand up and make a change. We could even do it lying down in meditation. How much of your day is spent being enraged? How is that going for you? How happy are you?

What if for a moment we stop the insanity and remember that we are a child of God? What would that feel like to know with every fiber of your being that an aspect of God lives in you? Would you do more from a place of love and gratitude? If we are an aspect of God, why would we choose to experience so many doubts and limits? Because we believe the doubts and the limits more than we believe we are an aspect of God! Well, then, I would like you to know that an aspect of God resides in you. And an aspect of you resides in God. Here comes some good old human guilt... do you think God is happy that an aspect of you resides within Him? Of course he is!

What if we take the worst thing that is happening in our life at this time and say, "I came here to experience this." How does that feel? Does it take the burden from you that says I have to fix this or be different? Does it make you want to pause and come from a place of curiosity and observation and say... "So what am I learning from it?" To me those words assist in making my experience less "fatal" and more "ok—now what?" Can you feel the difference?

What if we stopped believing that we can't and started believing we can. What would be the things you would do with the ability of I can... Well, why aren't you, then?

What if you could remember what you were like on the other side, before you became a human in this lifetime? What do you imagine you were like? Would you treat yourself better, or believe in yourself more, if you knew you had been an Angel or an Ascended Master? Would you treat others better if you knew you were so full of light and love on the other side? Well, you are.

We are all made up of energy. What if we were able to remember how to work with energy to shift things? How would you shift your life? How would you shift the planet? When I work with light in someone's body that's what I am doing. I'm shifting energy.

How often do our old thoughts, those old recordings that are on a continual loop in our head, tell us of our limitations? What if we changed those recordings to ones that remind us we are limitless? Now take it further, what if we believed we were limitless? How much of the old recordings are actually part of what we believe? If we don't believe them anymore, why would we allow them "free air time"? Let's change the channel, change the frequency to what we do believe or what we choose to change our beliefs to be and give <u>them</u> the "free air time" in our heads. Or we can just be in our moment.

How often are you stretching the truth to have it suit your needs? A truth is a truth. A lie is a lie. How many lies do you tell yourself each day? How often do you say something and then pause because it's an old pattern? It's not who you are anymore, nor is it who you want to be. Last August, I went to a spiritual conference with Marsh and my brother Ken and his wife Janet. One day as we were finding our seats, I made a snide comment to my brother that stopped me in my tracks, and I said, "Wow, where did that come from?" Janet said, "Yes, I could tell the moment it came out of your mouth you regretted it." Ken loves being the goofy one in our family, but that doesn't mean it's ok to do those old family patterns of belittling. It just does not work for me anymore. Nor is it who I want to be!

Who we have become is based on what we were taught. But is what we were taught what we wanted to learn? I did not want to learn that some people are better or worse than others. They aren't, they are simply different. We all have gifts and talents. We have choices and options that we don't even realize. We can choose to change, by changing our thoughts one thought at a time. I can't understand why I keep thinking someone else is so much more than me. Maybe they are in some aspects and less than me in others. But to think that is to live in a place of competition. Not what I choose anymore.

What would happen if we chose differently? Would the earth stop spinning? Would people stop wanting to be with us? What are we afraid will happen if we change? When do we stop living our lies and start living our truths? That can truly happen right here, right now, by changing one thought. Correcting one lie at a time and replacing it with what you choose to be your truth, and then be that truth. Let others continue with their truths. We can't change others, we can only change ourselves. It is our responsibility to live our lives as truthful as we possibly can. These old lies don't serve us anymore. Actually, they never did!

When we say a statement like "I can't believe how stupid I am," we are taking on the belief that we actually are stupid every time we say it. You can say that you are just kidding, but the words still carry a frequency. What if we change it to "Well, that was a silly thing to do." The second one is less offensive to me. Also, we change from labeling I am stupid, to that (not me) is silly. Not that I mind being silly, but I do mind being stupid. Can you feel the difference in the words?

Here's another story about Marsh because he loves me sharing all his secrets. He has a really bad gag reflex. He has felt so uncomfortable and embarrassed about going to the dentist and them having to stop working on him because he keeps gagging. One dentist he went to would continually leave the room in frustration. I am so impressed that Marsh continued going back, or maybe I'm not. Why continue submitting yourself to anything less than love and respect? Anyway, Marsh found sedation dentistry has been beneficial for him to the point where he stopped getting so upset with himself and shifted his belief about going to the dentist. As he shifted, he created a new experience to the point of finding an incredible hygienist that figured out that if she can keep everything, like the mirror, suction and instruments away from his tongue, he doesn't experience gagging. So as he shifted, his experience shifted. Good job, Hunny-Bunny!

One last thing I have found beneficial is to surrender. Even saying the word shifts me to a place of less pressure. As I surrender my thoughts, that means I am willing to have my thoughts change to something different. And if those aren't what I want to create, I surrender my thoughts again. How do I know something is the best for me if I don't surrender it to see if something else might work out more beneficial for me? I also like to surrender who I am, or who I believe I am, so that I am able to bring forth a new belief of who I am. Or better yet, surrender all the labels and beliefs! Try just lying down and saying "I surrender," and if you truly mean it, you will notice something shift and say "I surrender that too." By the time I leave my bed, I feel so much lighter and more at peace. Give it a try, what have you got to lose except stress and frustration, and who wouldn't benefit from less stress and frustration?

Chapter 20: Is Our Foundation Stable Enough to Support Us?

The beginning of our life creates our foundation. It is what we learned about ourselves, others and our world as we perceive it through the eyes of a child. As children, we think people who are bigger than us or older than us are smarter than us. By now, you hopefully know that isn't always true. I work and play at trying to remember what it was like to believe with everything I am, like I did when I was a child. To have that trust that when your dad throws you into the air, he's going to catch you. Yes, I want that!

As we stumble and fall, as we make mistakes and see our heroes make mistakes, we start doubting everything. We start wondering if any of it is true. Is any of it real! The problem is we aren't always asking the right questions to the right people. At school, when we worked on fire safety, they always told us to have a plan of escape in case of a fire. I remember going home and asking my dad who was a firefighter, what I should do if the house catches on fire. His wise life experience answer was... get out of the house. It was a smart answer, but after that, I felt a little less safe about my dad saving me. Why? Because he didn't give me a hero's response.

We put people on pedestals only to have them come crashing down later. None of these people asked to be placed on a pedestal. We put them there of our own free will. I think that is why so many relationships fail. As soon as we meet Mr. Right, we put him up on a pedestal. He's perfect in every way. Marsh hated, I mean really hated it when I called him perfect. Then I realized that those words created too high of an expectation for him to have to live up to. So I shifted it to "You are the perfect Marsh. No one can be Marsh like you can." He was ok with that. Those are expectations he can live up to. Why do we even have expectations? How do they really assist us? I have been trying to let go of these too. Some are certainly easier than others. I've been noticing that the people many respect most at this time on the planet are the people who get away with something—why? Is it because we wish we could get away with something ourselves? Is that really who you want to be? Is that an aspect of God?

With my child, I know it's crazy to say this because it's not the norm in our society, but I hoped she would encounter enough obstacles to give her confidence that she could overcome obstacles when she needs to, by using her intelligence and abilities (and she does that constantly). I wanted her to have to work towards something instead of having everything always fall in her lap. So she would feel a greater sense of accomplishment at the end of the day and the end of this lifetime. Yep, she has that, too. I wanted her to see the impact her decisions have on not only her life but her family, her school, her company, her community and the world. Yes, yes, and yes, she has all of those too. Now, because I am her mom, I do not own her, I am simply her teacher for a while. What did I teach her today? Was I a good teacher, or a lazy teacher? Did I instill values that I will be proud of for the rest of my life? Or did I teach her how to take shortcuts and get away with something? That doesn't mean I don't appreciate all the easy flow moments in her life. Those are beyond awesome! Yes, I take the responsibility of being a parent very seriously. This is not a doll that we set in front of a TV, tablet, phone or computer because we can't be bothered. How often do we use the excuse of "I had a rough day and need some time to myself"? One of my pet peeves is when parents say, "I don't want to hear it." When that child grows to a teenager and an adult and they have so many secrets and don't involve you in their lives, just remember they are giving you what you asked for. "You don't have to hear it," any of it. Be careful what you ask for.

I apologize to my daughter if any of the things I taught you were not what you wanted to learn. I taught you what I wish someone had taught me when I was young. But you are not me. Your needs are different from what my needs were back then. Know that I am totally ok if you want to let go of all your old stuff and even everything I taught you, and create new possibilities. I did my best with the knowledge and experiences I had, and I know sometimes I fell short of the mark, but I'm ok with that because it helped you to see how human I am.

This brings me back to my own childhood experiences. No one, not one of my family members, knew anything about my healing abilities or talking to spirits in my head (and in my closet) except my mother. And she didn't want to know. She forbade me to talk about it with anyone. If I did, I would bring shame on my family. I also know that I probably would have been teased mercilessly about it and I would have been a big joke. My abilities would have been a joke. My abilities are too sacred to me, so I could not allow that. Because of my strong connection to spirit, I lived in my head, and it made so much more sense than my "real" life, so those recordings that loop in your head, multiply them 100 fold and that's what I experienced. That is why I have lived in the past so much and why it has been difficult for me to let all those old recordings and beliefs go sometimes. I repeated and repeated and repeated things so I wouldn't slip up. "Don't say anything, Mary Beth, no one wants to hear what you think. Don't be you. Be anyone else but don't be you. You are a mistake. Your birth was the worst thing to have ever happened to this family, maybe even the whole planet. Have you ever done anything right? Why do you even bother?" I had millions of them. I am probably down to 10,000 now. I know they are lies, but they are my lies and they were what I could count on to survive my childhood. If I let them go, who will I be? I know the answer to that one. I will be… happy.

My kind, loving husband has stuck with me through all this as I process and let go, process and let go. If I had talked all this God stuff when Marsh and I were first together, he would have run the other way. I probably would have run away too if the roles had been reversed. Back then, I didn't know it was God, or

Spirit, talking to me in my head. I thought it was my imagination. The way Marsh explains his connection to God is, "I don't know how to not believe in God." But having God be involved in everything I do, and having Spirits talking to me, and all the other things I am, and I am experiencing, was more than Marsh bargained for. And yet his love is so steady and true. He protects me with a fierceness I can't even describe. I AM SAFE WITH MARSH! I AM HOME WITH MARSH!

As we speak of my foundation, the two people that had the biggest influence in my life as a child was my mother and Connie (who was 2 ½ years older than me). You know what my relationship with my mother was like. Now let me share more about what my relationship with Connie was like. Connie was my idol. I worshipped her. I wanted to be her. Connie is so much fun and everyone loves her.

When I was young, Connie thought it would be fun to light candles under my bed. I HATE FIRE! Connie loves fire. Our dad was a firefighter. This was a story right out of the book of stupid things people do. Of course, Connie was on the side of the bed by the door in case anything happened. At the end of her fire show, she plucked one of my hairs out and said, "If you tell Mom or Dad, this is what I'll do to you," and she put that hair into the flame and it fizzled so fast. She said, "I'll set your hair on fire." Connie loves that story. I don't love that story. It reminds me of how much my safety was dismissed. What I wanted didn't matter. And another reason why I was so afraid of fire.

The two elements that made up my foundation were abuse and neglect. Abuse and neglect were my constant companions. The louder and more obnoxious you were in this family, the more you were respected. Christine is the exception to that rule, she is the oldest. I was not willing to be abusive to be loved, so I didn't fit in. I could be sarcastic, but not abusive.

An asset of having Connie in my life was that she had a gift of understanding and interpreting our mom for me. She was very good at getting what she wanted by using her understanding of Mom. I, on the other hand, doubted myself and my worthiness too much. Connie would say things like, "You need to understand, Mary, that Mom was the youngest and was doted on by her brothers and sisters." Or, "Where Mom is coming from when she says stuff like that is her religious beliefs." Those few words would help me to make sense of something that made no sense at all. I can't stress enough how every moment of my childhood I was trying to figure out "why." If I could understand why people did what they did, maybe I would stop making so many mistakes... stop being a mistake.

When I was seven or eight, Connie, Mom and I went shopping for school clothes. Which is strange because we wore uniforms. I was trying not to want anything, I really was, but I love clothes. I love putting outfits together, and I think I'm pretty good at it. As I became an adult, Connie and Mom were always asking me to help them decide what to wear. So there I was, trying not to look at things, trying not to desire anything, trying to remember that I don't matter. That my needs and desires don't matter. And then I saw it. A green jumper with a bow on it. It was nothing extravagant, just a simple green jumper with a bow on it, but it called to me. I picked it up and put it back at least ten times before I convinced myself that maybe this time my mom would say yes. So I asked Mom if I could get this dress for church. I thought the church part might help my cause. Mom barely glanced at it and said you don't need it. I put it back. I slipped under the circular clothes rack and had a nice, quiet cry, always making sure that I didn't draw attention to myself. Make yourself small, Mary Beth. Maybe if you make yourself small enough, you can disappear. So I went inside myself where I lived. And in that silence inside of me, I got an idea.

I grabbed the jumper several sizes bigger, and I went to Connie and said, "Connie, isn't this pretty? I think it would look really nice on you. You should ask Mom if you could have it." She said, "I don't know." I said, "Go try it on before you decide, and then let Mom see it." Yes, this is called manipulation. I'm not proud of it, but I was trying to learn how to navigate my life. She did, and Mom loved it, and Connie got it. I knew it would take years, but eventually, I would get to wear that jumper.

As young teenagers, Connie and I babysat. She was not as busy babysitting as I was, because I loved kids. I liked to make up games with them, play make pretend and even board games. I was not a big TV watcher until the kids were in bed, because I really enjoyed being present with children. Connie, on the other hand, didn't want to have kids and had no patience with them. One time, Connie called me on a Saturday afternoon and said, "You better get over here, or I am dropping these kids from the second-story window and it will be your fault if you don't hurry up and get here." Yes, folks, guilt was alive and well and living in my house as a child. So I hopped on a bike and rode several miles to get there. I got the two boys to play a game with me while Connie tried to clean up some of the mess. One of the boys had decided to feed the fish baby powder and dumped the entire container in the tank. He decided it was too much, and Connie discovered him standing in the tank about to vacuum the powder out. Oh, my gosh, that was scary, and what a mess. The older boy had locked himself in the bathroom reading, or should I say looking at, his dad's adult magazines.

One summer, Connie was invited to go up to Door County, Wisconsin, for a vacation with a family she babysat for. She was to watch the kids when the parents wanted alone time. Connie had such an incredible time. It must have been wonderful to see how some families had vacations. During the trip, Connie cut the bottom of her foot while swimming in Lake Michigan. Later as infection set in, Connie became very, very sick. Mom spent most of her time up at the hospital. One time, she came home and told us all to pray. We all knelt before a statue of Mother Mary and prayed for a very long time. I asked Mom if I could go to the hospital to see Connie. The answer was no. When Dad came home, I asked him and he said yes, but I would have to just sit there and be quiet. This was very serious and he won't allow any shenanigans.

As I walked into Connie's hospital room, I was overcome by fear. Her head was moving back and forth, and her teeth were chattering so loud that I was afraid they would break. Her whole body was shaking. I was listening to Mom explain to Dad what was going on. Her fever was so high that they had her on an ice bed. There was a pad under her that moved freezing cold water through it to help cool her body temperature. She had an IV in her arm, and as I focused on the needle and the tubing and the bottles of fluid, I could feel that these were good things. I didn't know why, I just knew that they were helping her. I remember thanking them for helping my sister. When no one was paying attention I felt the mat under

Connie's body, I understood that it was too concentrated. It needed to surround her. In my mind a really strange thing happened. I saw that the core of her body was hot, and that the back of her body on the mat was freezing cold, and that they were fighting each other. Suddenly, a shift happened. I saw the mat and her sheet become one. The mat and sheet on top of her began drawing the heat out of her body and her core was calming down. I watched this happen for a very long time, and I knew she was getting better even if no one else saw it. Notice how again things shifted because I was focusing and watching new possibilities unfold.

I just needed not to tell anyone ever what I saw and felt. When I left, I whispered to Connie that she was going to be ok and that I loved her. I didn't understand at the time that it would have been beneficial to concentrate on her foot, which was the source of the problem. We should always focus energy on the source of a problem. It assists in clearing it so much faster and more thoroughly, and it shows us so much more of the information needed to shift the energy. At least this is what has assisted me. I didn't know any of this back then. When I got home, I went to bed in Connie's bed so I could be close to her energy. I cried and thanked God for helping my sister and for showing me that she was going to be ok.

In seventh or eighth grade, Connie and her best friend liked to pull a big entryway rug halfway out the door each day as they left the building after school. When she told me about it, my first thought was "poor Smitty." He was our custodian and quite old and beloved, and he would have to maneuver that big rug by himself each day. Why? Our dad worked as a custodian after he retired from the fire department, and I would hate to have someone treat him like that. I don't understand why people do stuff that can cause others hardship or even just inconvenience, simply for a laugh. Is that funny? I know that they were only 12 or 13 years old, and most people would say that they were just being kids. I'm not perfect, I did stupid stuff too. A friend talked me into throwing eggs at cars one time. Why? Another time in high school I toilet papered a coworker's house. I still feel bad about it 40 years later. Time to let that one go. Yes, we do stupid stuff as kids, but are we still doing stupid stuff as adults because no one taught us differently, or because we got away with it. I realize now that I didn't show much

179

malice to others back then because I was too busy hating myself. Why? I wasn't a horrible person, I was just very confused... lost. Bad behavior was rewarded in my family and good behavior ignored. I remember Dad waking me up to rip newspapers to toilet paper a teacher's yard. Why? They had the gall to say that one of my brothers wasn't perfect... well, he wasn't. What kind of example did that set for me as a small child?

So, I have had a difficult time understanding why so many things bothered me and made me feel unsafe when Mom and Connie made me feel like it was normal. Guess what? It's not normal and it was not ok. I deserved to feel safe. I deserved to be treated with kindness and respect. And I will accept nothing less! My existence matters, and if you have a problem with that, take it up with God. Thank you, God, for keeping me safe enough to live through my younger years.

When I told Connie that I was having a baby, her response was "Better you than me." She knew that having a baby was the most important thing to me, and yet she couldn't be happy for me. When we bought our first house, her response was "Why would you do that, now you have to do all the maintenance yourself." She obviously could not be happy for me. When she had a baby, I spent hundreds of dollars mailing her boxes of clothes, and one box she didn't even bother going to the post office to pick up. I let her know I wanted the clothes back when she was done with them, so I could save them for Morgan's children. Connie sold them at a yard sale. I said No More, and her daughter didn't get any more clothes. When she bought a house I sent a housewarming present. It isn't difficult to be kind. You just need to decide that is who you want to be.

Like I told you earlier, I was always trying to imitate Connie, so in school, when she loved drama, I decided to do drama. The only play she was ever in was a children's play where she roller-skated across the stage with branches in her hair. And of course, she used my roller-skates and lost them. I was pretty good at drama. I got Top Female Drama Student two out of three years. I usually played batty old ladies. I loved it because I got to be someone else for a while. When I was Mrs. Gibbs in *Our Town* by Thornton Wilde[8], I got so deeply into character

---

[8] Thorton Wilder, *Our Town*, 1938.

that it felt like it was at least two hours afterward before Mary Beth reappeared. I had a gentleman come up to talk to me after one of my performances. He said, "I have seen this play at every level from Broadway, off-Broadway, Community theatre and high school, and yours was the best Mrs. Gibbs I have ever seen. You moved me to tears and I want to thank you for that."

Another reason I enjoyed drama was that then I didn't have to take an English class. I got physically sick when I had to read in class because it was so embarrassing. I read so slowly and I didn't understand the flow of a sentence or paragraph. Everyone would laugh at me. I felt so very stupid. Then in 10th grade, my high school decided to do some testing on me because I had never finished a test in any of my classes. What they found was, I was reading at a 5th-grade reading level but my comprehension was a sophomore in college, so they couldn't put me in special education classes.

When Connie started driving, it was "Look out, world, here she comes!" One time, Connie was blasting her horn out front. I looked out the window, and she was going up the next-door neighbor's driveway, across our front lawn, down our driveway into the street and back up the neighbor's driveway. The whole while she is blasting the horn. I told whoever was at home with me to come check it out, and we went outside to find out what was going on. It ended up she had no brakes and was trying to slow the car down or run out of gas, whichever came first. It wouldn't take long because Connie was constantly on empty. I remember her calling Dad at 2 A.M. because she ran out of gas. I asked her why she didn't fill up before she went out. She told me that Dad likes to help out, it makes him feel useful. Does she really believe that? I felt it made him feel used and taken advantage of.

Then there was the time her defroster didn't work. I mean not at all. This was Wisconsin in the middle of the winter. She was driving a girlfriend and me to school. She could not see out the front windshield, so we had the side windows down with our heads sticking out trying to navigate. Left-hand turns were ok, but when she had a right turn, she said, "I know it's around here somewhere," and she just turned right into a parked car. I couldn't believe she had just done that. It was strange watching Connie because she took these kinds of things in stride, almost like it was the most normal thing.

I didn't like the thought of all the responsibility that comes with driving, so I waited till age 19 to get my license. Shortly after getting my license, I borrowed Connie's car so I could go visit a friend in Madison. On the way home, Connie's muffler came loose and was dragging on the ground. I pulled over, and again wanting to be like Connie, said, "What would Connie do?" So I wrapped some wire clothes hangers I found in the back seat around the muffler and then tied them to a belt that I held onto out the window as I drove, to keep the muffler off the ground the entire drive home. My hand was numb by the time I got home. Connie experienced stuff like that all the time. I must admit that she is so resourceful, and goes with the flow more than anyone I know.

As we grew to adults, Connie's need for me to serve her grew. She would call Mom and ask her to have me bring her a new pair of pantyhose because hers had a run. Her work was in another city and about 30 minutes away. She never paid for the gas or the new pantyhose, it was just expected. I did stuff like this for her at least once a week. On and on went the behavior that truly made no sense to me. When we lived together in Tennessee, if a guy spent the night with Connie, I would sometimes find him in my room in the middle of the night. I would tell whoever it was to get the hell out of my room. When I would tell Connie, she would say they were probably looking for the bathroom. Did she really believe that, or did my feeling safe in my own home not matter? When I stayed with her and her boyfriend later on in life, during my visit from Hawaii, her boyfriend would come into my room naked every morning. Connie said, "Well, of course he does, he keeps his clothes in that room." Like it was what everyone does. Again, not safe. Then the night before her wedding, her future husband wanted something to happen between us. ARE YOU KIDDING ME? YOU ARE ABOUT TO MARRY MY SISTER. When I told Connie, she said, "Oh, he was drunk." Thank you, God, Connie eventually divorced him.

Spirit says that it's important to understand that when a person uses excuses to dismiss what is really happening, they are living from a place of avoidance. If they (or you) live from a place of making excuses, it's so that we don't have to look at, or deal with the truth of what we are avoiding in our lives. By doing this we all are missing incredible opportunities for growth. It's also important for us to understand that this is their issue and we need not take it on as our own (like I did). When we notice the pattern of making excuses constantly in our life, we can ask the question... "What am I avoiding being willing to look at?" Often people who use excuses a lot get very irritated when others use excuses with them. This is a mirroring situation . They are being given an opportunity to see their own truth about avoidance.

As a person observes this pattern without making anyone wrong they can gain an understanding or truth, and from there they can gain wisdom. Again it is our experience of something that gives us an opportunity to see things differently. When we do this from a place of honesty instead of judgment (they or I did something wrong) we begin to understand what it really is and can learn from it (gain wisdom). From there we can change our experience with that person or ourselves.

I do not share these stories about Connie to shame her. No, not at all! I tell these stories about my experiences with Connie when I was young so you understand why I did not feel safe and protected. When I hear these stories now, I understand why God needed to bring Marsh into my life. Why more than anything else I needed someone to assist me in _feeling_ safe. Then eventually, I could _know_ that I am safe. Only then could I be safe enough to stop needing to be in protection mode and move to a place of being a more true expression of who I am at my core. Also this was obviously something that I worked on again and again over the years until it no longer was painful for me, it was only the past.

My sister Connie is one of the most fun people you will ever meet. Her wit is so spontaneous. She missed her calling as a comedian. She has spent her whole life laughing at the ridiculous stuff that happens to her all the time. I am in awe of her resilience and tenacity. She simply was not someone that could put my needs before her own, even though she was the big sister. My love for her and the gift that she is in my life are so very important to me.

Chapter 21:
Morgan the Science Nerd!

Science, did someone say science? My kiddo Morgan is a science nerd. She loves anything to do with science. I think she feels like me, as far as, in a world that makes no sense, you need to find the thing that helps you to make sense of it all. For me, it is my spirituality. For Morgan it was science. It speaks her language. In high school, she had a teacher who had taken our gifted science nerds to Nationals for Science Bowl, Science Olympiad, and Ocean Bowl. He did this year after year. It was so wonderful watching Morgan blossom in her expression of herself. It was difficult for me because it wasn't something I could join in on. Marsh and I couldn't even watch from the sidelines. She would go into a room with others, be judged and come out. I've never really gotten to watch Morgan do her thing.

This teacher enjoyed Morgan and appreciated all she did for him, but I felt he never really saw the gifts that Morgan had, but another science man certainly took notice. The summer after 10th grade, Morgan spent a couple of weeks with Uncle Ken and Aunt Janet in Utah. During game night while Morgan was there, Aunt Janet introduced Morgan to her friend who had a passion for science also. She perked up and asked this guy if he was a science nerd too. He said yes, and they chit-chatted, then Morgan asked if she could ask him a question.

He said yes, expecting it to be ridiculously simple, when Morgan said something like… "If indirect inhibitors could act on other molecules elsewhere in the body to some different effect?" she blew him away.

She called me after he left and said, "Mom, can I work in a lab next summer with a friend of Aunt Janet's?" I didn't know how to respond. Who is he? What lab? What does this lab do? How long would you be doing it? Is this a job? The list goes on and on. She told me about their encounter and his surprise at her questions. He asked her how old she was. She said she had just finished 10th grade. Then he asked if she would be interested in working in his lab next summer. It ended up that he was in charge of a lab at the University of Utah, and they were working on the AIDS virus. This was an incredible opportunity, but… but… it's the AIDS virus. I'm supposed to keep her safe. What should I do? I spoke to Aunt Janet's friend, and he was wonderful at answering my questions. So the summer between 11th and 12th grade our Morgan worked on the AIDS virus at the University of Utah. It was a huge experience in Morgan's life. The first three weeks in the lab, no one knew of Morgan's existence. Not only was she not a graduate student, she wasn't even an undergrad. As time went on, she got comfortable enough in the lab to ask more and more questions, and she began to think of more "what if" questions. Because she didn't have a preformed idea of how things were supposed to be, she was able to think outside the box.

I was going crazy being so far away from Morgan. I had no clue as to how she was really doing. When we would talk, I could feel the eye-rolling going on at the other end of the phone. When I would ask Janet, she would say things like, "She seems to be doing well." Or, "She seems to be enjoying it." On the few occasions I could get her to open up, she talked in science jargon and I had no idea if what she was saying was good or bad. I did learn that near the end of her ten weeks, the grad students were inviting her to learn about their aspects of the project. Again, I think they were impressed with her level of comprehension and where she could take things. I have always felt Morgan can see further into something if she trusts herself and the information she gets.

So as we are talking about her actual work in the lab, she would always generalize everything. I still have no clue what she did there. I decided to call her supervisor at the end of the summer and ask him some questions. He said, "Didn't Morgan tell you?" My response was, "She's a teenager," and he instantly understood where I was coming from. So he said, go ahead, what are your questions? I asked if she was respectful. Did she show up on time? Did she get along with others? Did she do a good job? He said, "Yes, Morgan is a very articulate and conscientious young woman. She was very respectful and curious. That curiosity was a great asset to our lab. Morgan advanced us two years beyond where we thought we would be in the project in her ten weeks with us. She has an insightful way of looking at things, and where she takes them is incredible. Morgan went beyond what I was hoping she could do and I really hope that I have the privilege of working with her again in the future." She did so well that he offered her own graduate level assignment as an incoming freshman. That was huge! Wow! I ran and told Morgan what he said, and she very calmly said, "That's great." I'm jumping up and down inside, and wanting to call anyone and everyone that I know. I did call Ken and Janet to tell them and to thank them for their willingness to allow Morgan to stay with them all summer. They have been and continue to be huge Morgan supporters.

Morgan decided she wanted to go to the University to Utah instead of Colorado State University, which would have been so much less expensive. But Morgan was going to have to pay back the student loans eventually, so it was her call. We managed to get her a private dorm room—thank you, God. Morgan is not a partier, and I wanted her to have her own space to retreat to when and if she needed it. That, I think, worked out very well for her. At orientation, they had parents and students go their separate ways. We parents were told something very interesting. They said that when your kids graduate, encourage them to get their own place and their own life. This is the first generation that actually likes their parents. Unfortunately, parents are doing everything for their children. So these kids will have no problem staying home and having Mom and Dad handle everything and pay for everything for them into their 40s. That's not a good idea. So encourage your children to be responsible for their own life and you will both win. I thought that was really interesting.

I loved sending Morgan care boxes with all kinds of food and jokes and gift cards. It was so very difficult letting Morgan go, but I was so glad she was doing what made sense to her and what made her happy. Of course, our conversations were not as detailed as I had hoped. I would call Janet and ask her how she thought Morgan was doing. She thought that she was doing pretty well. There were definitely some adjustments that needed to happen. Morgan mentioned a guy for a while and I had red flags. This guy felt like the smooth talker that didn't mean any of it. Thank goodness it didn't last long.

Then one evening I got a very strange call from Morgan. She said, "I'm in the stairwell heading up to my room." She was whispering like she was afraid someone might hear. I said, "Do you want to call me back when you get to your room?" She jumped at me saying, "No, don't hang up. I need you to talk to me." I said, "Morgan, do you feel threatened?" "No." "Is someone bothering you?" Again, "No." I knew something was wrong. I also could tell Morgan wasn't ready to talk about it. So I tried to lighten the mood to get her more comfortable. I asked about her favorite class, which was Dance. She started to lighten up and then said, "Oh, no, there are people coming." I said, "Do you know these people?" She said, "I don't think so." She was so paranoid. What the hell was going on? When she got to her room and locked the door, she made some excuse to hang up. I tried to keep her on the phone, but she wasn't going to let me. After we hung up, I called Janet. I needed her and Ken to go and check on Morgan. I needed to know what was going on. Janet reminded me that "Morgan won't talk until she is ready. But Morgan is resourceful and she knows that we are here for her." Crap, crap, crap! What should I do? Marsh was concerned too, but he hadn't heard the paranoia in her voice.

The next time I spoke with Morgan, she didn't want to talk about it and was vague about everything. Now I understand better how teenagers drive their parents nuts. I had to wait for that moment when Morgan was ready to talk. Finally when Morgan came home at Christmas, she opened up to me. It took a while, but eventually, when I talked to her about what she would need when she went back to school, she spoke up. "I'm not going back to Utah." "Why not? What's going on?" She said, "Something happened, and I don't want you to freak out about it." I took a deep breath and let it out slowly. "I will try not to freak out. Now tell me what happened." She said, "Something is wrong with me medically and it's affecting my mental capabilities." "Ok, what does that mean?" She explained that one morning while taking her shower, she must have passed out. When she came to, she was hanging by her hair from the hot and cold water knobs. She has no idea how long she had been unconscious. I kept telling myself not to freak out... keep it together, or Morgan is going to clam up. But this is my baby girl and something is wrong with her!! Breathe.

"Holy crap, Morgan, that must have been terrifying! Did it only happen that one time?" She said, "Yes, but my cognitive thinking has been off." "Ok, well, hopefully that's not too bad because I don't even know what cognitive thinking is." She explained that sometimes she would come out of a class and not know where she was or how to get home. She explained some different scenarios where she just couldn't figure things out. She would just sit down and wait until her mind cleared up enough that she could figure out what she needed to do. I wanted to ask her a bunch of "why didn't you..." questions, but I didn't want her to feel she did anything wrong. I said that I guess we'll be making some doctor appointments to figure this all out. As we were waiting for the day of her doctor's appointment, I was calling our insurance company. Is Morgan still covered under our insurance if she's not enrolled in school? No. Shit. But she can't even figure out how to get home. What can we do? Our only real option was to keep signing her up for classes that she can't even go to, just so she can be covered. Who knows what kind of tests this was going to take and how long before we had a diagnosis. What if she needs surgery?

Morgan's regular doctor is an internal medicine doctor. She wanted Morgan to see a neurologist. After his examination, he wanted Morgan to have a CT of the brain. Things looked normal. Let's do an EEG. And then it was a sleep-deprived EEG. We were referred from one doctor to another, to another. Her episodes were so sporadic we didn't know what to do. Most specialists would say that since she wasn't showing symptoms at the time, there wasn't much they could do. Some would offer medication, but when Morgan would ask what it was for and what the side-effects were, she would realize from their answers that they had no clue what was wrong. She wasn't willing to risk the side-effects for something that even the doctors didn't think would help. Finally, her doctor suggested a tilt table test.

They wanted me to wait outside while they did the test. I told them that I had worked in hospitals, and I was used to seeing all kinds of things. Well, nothing prepares a mom for that moment when her child's heart stops beating. I lunged forward as one of the techs says her heart has stopped. Then Spirit stops me and says, let them do what they need to do. For nine seconds, Morgan's heart had paused. They lowered the table and it started again. From this test result we had a diagnosis. Morgan had something called neurocardiogenic syncope. Basically it means that her brain and her heart aren't communicating properly. When she stands up, instead of her brain telling her heart to speed up, it tells her heart to slow down.

The good news is that it usually only lasts about two years. It usually happens to young women during puberty. By the time we had gotten this diagnosis, Morgan was 21. There's no medication or surgery to help her. We just needed to be patient and wait and see. Morgan said, "Well, that explains part of her symptoms, but what about the cognitive thinking?" Her neurologist just kept redoing the same test. We were done with him. All these doctors, when they first met Morgan, would get excited about the challenge she presented. Then after some tests, they would say, "I can't help you," or "Come back in six months." Her seizure neurologist said she was definitely having a certain type of seizures. I would tell her how I would be talking to Morgan and she would just stare out into space, and you could tell the moment she was back. After running her tests to confirm her diagnosis, she said, "No, it is not seizures, I can't help her."

They did a neuro-psych test on Morgan. It was an all-day test of questions. In the end, they said there were aspects of the test that she scored higher than anyone who has ever taken the test. There were other parts that she only got a 42. I asked if they could figure out what part of the brain she was using during the part of the test that she got a 42 and go from there? Nope, that's not how this test is done. Well, that certainly didn't help us. Morgan really enjoyed the test and being tested. Sometimes when she is in her element, she gets this sparkle that lights up her whole being. This test did that for her. It had been so long since I had seen it, I had wondered if it was a thing of the past. She really liked the guy who administered the test. She said one section was definitions. The word was 'pragmatic.' Morgan's answer was 'washing machine.' He said, "Come on, Morgan, you know this... pragmatic." "Washing machine." She said, "I know it's not the answer, but it's all I've got."

At the end of four years, Morgan was doing well enough that this brilliant young woman was finally able to take a CNA class and pass it. Now she can work in a nursing home. At first, I was very sad that this was all Morgan could handle. I worried for her future. But like with everything in life, first we experience, then we understand, then we have wisdom. Morgan needed to start slowly with less stress and then figure out what and where she needed to do some tweaking. Morgan loved working in the nursing home. She felt like she understood how some of these patients felt, not being able to find their words or remember things. She enjoyed joining them in their world, instead of insisting that they leave their reality and join her out here. Because of that, she was able to calm them down quickly and effortlessly most times. What a gift she was to each and every life she touched there. When one of their patients passed away, Morgan encouraged staff members to go to her funeral wearing bright red lipstick. This patient had loved her bright red lipstick, and everyone from friends and family to the nursing home staff knew that. At the funeral, the family was so touched. They said, "You obviously knew our mom, and we are so grateful for all the care you gave her."

I bet there are many of you wondering why I didn't do the healing work like I had done with my dad. There is no easy answer here. Maybe the work I was doing on Morgan was helping to a certain extent, and that's why the doctors weren't able to find much. Maybe this was what Morgan came here to experience, and if so, God's will overrides my will every time. Another aspect is when you have an emotional attachment to the outcome, you are not as clear of a channel. I definitely had an emotional attachment to the outcome. This is my baby girl we are talking about here. As hard as I tried to detach, I couldn't stay there.

During those four years, Morgan had 14 specialists. Many she refused to go back to because they admitted they didn't know how to help her. Some she was uncomfortable with because they would patronize her by patting her on the head and say come back in six months. Morgan would say, "Why, what is your plan in six months?" When they would say they could repeat the same tests, it just made no sense to her. So she was enrolled in colleges with a zero GPA because she couldn't attend classes, but she needed the insurance. When the university threw her out because of her low grades, she went to the community college until they wouldn't allow her back either. Morgan had $30,000 in student loans and no degree. She was making $10 an hour. We had so many doctor bills that I took on a second job, and six months later, Marsh took on a second job with me cleaning offices in the evening. I let Morgan know that Daddy and I could very easily have filed for bankruptcy. We definitely have reason enough to do that, but we signed our name saying we promise to pay these bills and we will because that is the way we were raised and the way we raised you. This was our choice, not everyone is like Marsh and I and that's ok.

While cleaning offices, I met a new friend. I saw her each night Monday through Friday, as I cleaned her office building during the time that Morgan was sick. She was very friendly, but I was a bit overwhelmed at the time. I was friendly, too, but somewhat reserved. She was very good at asking questions, and soon we found we were both working on our spirituality. Sometimes Charles would give me some words to assist her, but I didn't want to make the mistakes I had made in past friendships so I held back a lot of what I was getting. I have finally figured out that if I have someone in my life, I need them to be interested and interesting, otherwise I am bored. Finally, after many months, I agreed to let Joleen come to my home for a session with Charles and Spirit. I don't enjoy doing sessions, so this was uncomfortable for me.

Right from the start, Joleen came with a list of questions, a pen and paper to write notes, and an open mind to receive as much information as she could. Because I saw so much of myself in Joleen's energy, she was an absolute joy to play with. My day job was roughly 60 hours a week with prep work, and I worked cleaning offices in the evenings, so the only drawback with Joleen was that she wanted more time than I was able to give her. However, unlike others I had friendships with, Joleen was not pushy and just enjoyed what I was able to give her. In the beginning, her questions would get sidetracked by more questions about my answers. This beautiful young woman was absolutely perfect for my energy. She would ask me things like what is energy. Every time we spoke, we would take it a little further and a little further. She learned how everything is made up of energy, so as you connect to that truth, you can then start working with the energy to shift it.

Learning that words are made up of energy, we can learn to shift our thoughts and words and then we shift our lives. It was a blast and an honor to watch Joleen as she was really getting it and transforming her life and the way she saw things. We had both bought into that victim crap as children, so as Spirit worked with Joleen they were working with me also. I learned an important element while working with her, which was that if I close my eyes as I channel, I can focus better and not get distracted by the person's reactions written on their face. I know it sounds crazy but that was life-changing for me. It's amazing how one little shift can change everything.

Another thing that was so wonderful to witness is how in the beginning of doing spiritual work together, all of her questions were about things out there, relationships, jobs, family, where to live. As time went on, it became how to raise her frequency and connect as One. I felt so proud of her as I watched her change and grow. One of the things that helped Joleen to shift so fast and so far was that after she would get the information, she would go to work on implementing it and seeing where it would take her. Then she would work on taking it even further.

Joleen is an excellent channeler now, though I don't know if she has ever used her abilities to channel for another person other than me. I'm sure she has, because once you open and allow, the information just flows for you and the people you are assisting. The way I taught her to channel is to settle into a quiet and safe place. Ask Spirit to join you as you quiet your thoughts. Let Spirit know that you are going to <u>trust</u> the first thing that comes to you. If you don't trust, there will be no connection and so don't waste your time. When you are ready, ask your question. Then wait to hear the answer. At first you might just have a feeling. That's fine, it's a starting point. Continue to ask questions and then softening yourself enough that Spirit can get through. Wait and listen for a response. Be very patient with yourself. As time goes on, you learn to feel the difference in frequency or energy of ego, vs the truth. You need to be willing to hear the truth, not what you or the person you are channeling for want the truth to be (that's ego). Thank you, God, for the Gift of Joleen. What a blessing she and her questions were in my life.

Chapter 22: My Dream Home Turns into a Reality

For seven years I told everyone that understood that I have visions, that I was going to live in a yellow Victorian house with a wrap-around porch. After several months of searching for the right home, it just showed up in a stack of listings our real estate agent had given us to consider. He was so frustrated with me. We would go and look at a house two or three times and then I would say never mind, and we'd start all over again. Finally he got to the point where he'd hand me 10 or 15 listings. I'd go to sit outside them to decide if I wanted to bother with a showing. Then one day there it was—my yellow Victorian with a wrap-around porch. As a bonus, it was new construction. I like new construction because I can feel the energy of the people who have lived in a house previously. If there was a lot of conflict, that could disrupt my flow there. I didn't understand this until my late forties, but I sure experienced it. This house was about $20,000 more than we were approved for. So we needed to figure out how to make it work financially. We ended up with an adjustable rate mortgage.

As we were moving in, I realized an important thing. In all the times I had visualized a yellow Victorian house, I had never gone inside it to visualize its interior. I have hopefully learned from that mistake. Morgan asked me where she should put the sheets and towels as we were unpacking. I said, "The linen closet, of course." She said, "Where is it?" I said, "In the hallway." She said, "I can't find it." I looked at what I thought was a linen closet, but it was the laundry hookup. I looked in our bath—nothing. I looked in Morgan's bath—nothing. We had a coat closet down on the main floor by the ½-bath, but that was it. I sat on the steps wondering, who would build a house without a linen closet? New houses do not have medicine cabinets... why? It ended up that I had a love-hate relationship with this house. The things I loved, I really loved. The things I hated, I really hated (more duality).

The guy who built the house was not a person of integrity. We found out that every few years, he closed his business and started a new one because his reputation had gotten so bad. He didn't pay his contractors until they sued him for the money. How can such practices be legal? Within a couple of months, we had water damage from an unglued furnace vent pipe. The banister broke the first time Marsh and Morgan chased each other up the steps. And after about six months of struggling financially, we had to put my dream/nightmare home back on the market.

At that time, I found out we had paid $15-20,000 too much for the house, and between the realtor's fee and what we needed to sell the house for, we couldn't sell it. I felt so very guilty. Marsh did this for me and now look at the pickle I got us into. I kept asking God what this was all about. I needed to get a job and fast. I looked in the paper, and the jobs I was qualified for are always very limited with my learning disabilities. The computer is very confusing to me, I can never remember what does what. Poor Marsh and Morgan try again and again to teach me with no luck. I've learned computers don't carry a frequency like humans, so I can't "read" them. So even though I am an excellent receptionist, they all require computer work now. Cleaning toilets was all I felt qualified for. I felt myself slip into depression again. Old recordings playing louder and louder. I can't believe I thought I deserved something so beautiful. Now look at what I have done to my family. How are we going to make it? All I ever earn is minimum wage. I have no skills. I'm not worth shit! I am so sorry I am dragging Marsh down with me. I really am worthless. I moved into the closet for a while. I don't deserve anything better. When will I finally get it—I don't deserve happiness. I am the scum of the earth! I don't deserve to live! Marsh and Morgan would be better off without me.

Marsh and Morgan let me wallow for almost a week, and then Marsh wrapped me in love and said, "Honey, we are going to get through this, we always do." We have found the more he allows me, or gives me permission to be exactly where I am, feeling exactly what I am feeling, the faster I will shift. But sometimes I get into a stuck place where I just keep replaying the past without moving forward. That's when Marsh needs to step in and just love me through it. He doesn't even realize what he is doing. He is just following his instincts.

The next time I checked the newspaper, there was a position working in a daycare. Wow, I can definitely do that! I am wonderful with children. So I had Morgan help me with my resume. I turned it in and they called me for an interview. I was so excited about this interview. This is one of those I know what I know times. When I walked in all full of smiles, there before me were the ten board members, and you could tell they had all been crying. I mean really, really crying about something. I took a deep breath and said this could be a tough crowd, but I've got this. Well, by the end of the interview they were laughing and smiling and happy as could be. I told them that I would really like to work with the babies. They hired me on the spot. I found out later that the reason they had all been crying was because a board member had just informed all of them that she had terminal cancer. My interview was a balm to their sorrow.

I loved my boss, and she really wanted me to be happy. My room had ten babies, me, and the woman in charge of our room. She didn't seem to like children, especially babies, and she was the one showing me how they do things. Well, to those of you who have children in daycare or are looking for a daycare, here are some helpful hints. If a certain provider is always finding excuses to go to the kitchen, the office, the bathroom, the storage area, etc., that person does not want to be there with the children. Your child will feel it too, and they will be more clingy when they get home because they didn't get much attention during the day. Also, watch how much time the providers spend on the floor interacting with the children. That's where the magic happens!

This job was so easy for me, except for my coworker. She was always going to other rooms to drop something off. Or running to the office. You get the idea. One time, my supervisor came by, and I was sitting on the floor crying. I had a sleeping baby in each arm, sleeping babies in both crooks of my legs, and a baby leaning against me sleeping, and I was so afraid he was going to fall and get hurt so I was leaning forward to keep him in place. My legs were numb and I needed to use the bathroom. When my boss saw I was crying, she jumped the gate into the room. She asked me where my partner was. I said, "She went to the bathroom over 45 minutes ago and I was afraid to move and wake the babies, and then more kept climbing on and falling asleep, and I can't feel my legs. Please help me."

The next day my "partner" was moved to a different room closer to the office. I got a very young girl as my partner, and we did so much better. I always had things to complain about (usually the parents), but overall I really loved caring for my babies. I did so much more talking to them, encouraging them to crawl, reading to them. I was bringing in my own toys and books because nearly everything in the room was broken, and that made me so sad. And the books had to be kept out of the babies' reach. That made no sense to me, so I got cardboard books and vinyl books for them. I was always taking them for walks in a 4-baby stroller. My babies were flourishing and engaged, and the parents were really responding, though there's always one or two that like to complain. I get it, because as you can tell I was not afraid to speak up for my child, but some of this stuff was wearing on me. The rules kept changing as to what is allowed and what isn't. We were periodically inspected by the state, and they made sure it was while I was working. The inspector said that I should be training the whole daycare on how to do things. Yes, folks, I was in my element. But then came a new rule, I was told I am not allowed to kiss the babies. I tried, I really did, but I'm always kissing the tops of their heads. I kept getting into trouble for it, so I had to quit. Babies need to feel loved, end of statement! I am here to love all babies in a sacred way, end of statement! The parents were so upset. Several begged me to take care of their child at their home or at mine. I explained that my daughter was 16 and I didn't have any baby things anymore. And as far as working at someone else's home... I didn't want to do their cooking and cleaning, etc. It just felt off.

During the time I worked at the daycare, we were able to refinance the house so our payments were less, and Marsh had transferred and was working in town during the day. Yes, things were finally taking a turn for the better, other than I was having some issues with our neighbors. When we hired our landscape company, they said we needed to have a survey done, especially in the back where there was a drainage ditch. In doing so, we found that the neighbors on our right had put their fence 19 inches onto our property. I asked Marsh to go with me to talk to them because the husband was a big, scary guy. He and his wife would be drunk out on the patio by 10:30 in the morning.

When we told him about the fence, he got really angry and threatened to sue us. He gave me his attorney's card and said I needed to run everything through him. One day our landscaper, the surveyor and the neighbor were in our backyard and things were really getting heated. I was feeling a lot of fear, so I called Marsh and asked him to come home because I didn't feel safe. Of course, by the time he arrived, things were calmer. We ended up having to hire an attorney to get them to move their fence. They tried all kinds of stuff to try to intimidate us, but wrong is wrong. They ended up suing their own landscape company and got them to move the fence.

After that, I felt uncomfortable being in my own yard or sitting on my own porch until their house went into foreclosure and they moved out. Then the neighbor at our back corner asked our landscaper what we were going to do back there by his property. Our landscaper said, "Nothing, really." So this guy starts digging fence post holes on our property. I had to go out and talk to him, too. I showed him where the stakes for the property lines were and told him that he couldn't cross the property line when digging or planting. He kept saying, "But you're not doing anything back here." I said, "It doesn't matter, it's our property, not yours." Marsh and I went to get some bright pink string to mark the property line because Spirit had said that he wasn't going to listen. Sure enough, the next day he watched me take Marsh to work and he started digging post holes on our property again. When I got home and saw this, I took my phone out and said, "Ok, I'm dialing 911 if you do not get off my property." Again, he said, "But you're not going to do anything back here." I could not believe this guy ran his own business. I calmly explained the law to him and then said, "Well, since you're just going to have grass in your backyard, you don't mind me putting a swing set in your yard." He took offense to that and said of course I couldn't, that's his yard. I said, "Exactly, and this is my yard. I really look forward to seeing what your yard is going to look like when it is all done, on your side of this string." He didn't talk to me much over the next eight years.

When I got into the house shaking, I heard my spirit guide say, "Well, it looks like you are doing better with having boundaries, now aren't you?" I started laughing so hard. I said, "Yes, I think that I have really gotten that one. So tell me, is my third neighbor bordering us going to mess with us too?" I just heard my spirit guide laugh. I guess as long as I continue to have boundaries and stick to them, I won't need that lesson anymore.

The reason why I told you that story was so you could see the pattern I was experiencing in my life and why. I needed to learn to say, "I won't allow you to cross this line, and I will use the tools that I have access to, to make sure that you honor my boundaries." It was so beautiful to look at in hindsight, but not fun during all that drama. I was very proud of myself for learning how to stand up for something besides Morgan. This ended up being a very expensive lesson, but worth it in the long run.

Chapter 23:
The Baby Whisperer Arrives

Six months after leaving the daycare I had worked at, one of the moms called me asking me if I could take care of her daughter. She was potty trained at one year old, but the daycare would not take the children to the bathroom until they were 18 months old. Would I be willing to take care of Sarah (not her real name)for six months so that she could continue with her potty training? Ok, well, what do I say? I don't have any toys or a crib or anything. She said that was ok. Sarah slept with her mom in her bed, and her dad was not in the picture. I told her I needed to talk with Marsh and Morgan. She was willing to pay me what she had paid the daycare. When I talked to Marsh, he said I should do what would make me happy. Like I've said before, Marsh is so supportive of me. Morgan said, "Mom, I know how much you love babies. If you are drawn to it, you should go for it."

Marsh and I were not going to kid ourselves, I was going to spend every dollar I made buying things for Sarah and me to do. I started with some books and puzzles (my favorites), and I lucked out because it was Sarah's favorites too. She took naps with me holding her, and I spent that time in my head with God. This was so very wonderful because Sarah was very much like Morgan was at that age... smart and curious. We went to the pool, and our town had a farm we liked to visit. There was only one real drawback to all this—Sarah was not potty trained. As Morgan put it, she had peed in almost every room in our house, and on many of its surfaces, too. She maybe used the toilet correctly one time each day, so my brand-new Victorian house was getting pretty stained.

I changed my spiritual room (the formal dining room) into a daycare room to minimize the staining of the carpet. Pretty soon, we had a little table and chairs, a book and toy shelf complete with several books and toys and puzzles. Well, six months turned into a year. We were all doing pretty great with this arrangement, but I noticed that I really did prefer to work with babies. As I question things, I always pay close attention to see if God is going to give me an answer.

As I was spending time watching Sarah learn and grow on so many levels, I kept feeling and hearing "MORE." More what? I had no idea, but it was like my being was craving MORE! One day, as Sarah and I went down into the basement to get something, I felt the potential of the space. When she went home, I decided I wanted to play with the energy I had felt earlier in the basement. Our basement was unfinished and just had boxes scattered around. So, as I just sat in the energy down there, I started to get excited. I had always wanted to build a home from the ground up, well, here was a piece of that. I could take this space and make it my own. But what did that mean? What did that entail?

That night I just kept thinking about the potential of our basement. I was asking questions of Spirit and waiting for the answers. Why would I need to have the expense of finishing our basement just so Sarah and I could have more room to learn and explore? What did the MORE mean? Was it time to create a home daycare for "more" children? How do I do that? And what children? The more questions I asked, the more answers I got. I saw how most of my adult life, especially after having Morgan, how people kept wanting me to take care of their children also. I had sooo many moms in Misawa, Japan, who wanted me to take care of their child along with Morgan. They saw how smart, kind, curious and engaged Morgan was, and they wanted that for their child also. I saw how God was opening a door to what I was supposed to be doing with my gift with children. I also saw how again and again, I was purposely closing that door by not working with children. Was God frustrated or disappointed in me? Of course not! But He was grateful that I was finally getting it.

When Morgan was little, I could feel the difference in both Morgan and myself when we were learning and exploring a new concept together vs. when we were doing it with a bunch of other children. I liked the feel and the flow so much more when it was just the two of us. I want to create that with this daycare if it moves forward. I want it to be that magical one-on-one connection that I experienced all the time with Morgan. So does that mean that I should only have one child at a time like with Sarah? Again I asked, then why do I need the expense of finishing the basement and turning it into a daycare business. I felt from my guidance there needed to be more of a separation between my personal life and the daycare.

I started opening up a dialog with Marsh and later with Morgan about the possibility of opening up a daycare in our basement. All Marsh could see was the expense. I needed to get some numbers to figure out if it would be financially prudent. Morgan knew how much I loved babies and encouraged me to speak to one of her friend's mom, who did home daycare. I told her, yes, please! Later in life, Morgan let me know that my having the daycare took the pressure off of her to have children to fill my need of... babies, babies, babies. But I really only wanted infants in the daycare. Was that allowed? Was that possible? And why only infants?

I see potential in babies that so few see. I see every moment as a teachable moment. With babies, everything they do is momentous. We are so present in those moments. As a child grows, they need more and more independence to find their own way, their own potential. I am wonderful at that too, but it is not where my heart of hearts lies. I LOVE doing the foundational work that is a part of their being the rest of their lives. So why didn't I do this when Morgan was little? I guess in a way I did, but always on my terms. I would have the three girls that lived in our 4-plex in Japan over to color Easter eggs, do science projects or just play. But I noticed that when I did, I was always asking Morgan to help with something, show them this, show them that, and it took so much away from Morgan being allowed to do her own thing. But maybe the advantage of having other kids around would have outweighed the disadvantages? We will never know because it's not the path I chose back then.

After speaking with the mom who did home daycare, I felt better and worse. I needed to find the truth and the lies in her words. I could feel a lot of ego involved in our conversation. She had been doing this for 20 years, and she took care of ten kids all by herself, but they took over her whole house. Yes, Spirit was correct. I needed to have a separate place for my babies and my home life. Marsh and Morgan needed to feel they could be upstairs living their own life and I would be downstairs with my babies, and at the end of the day, I could close the door on the daycare and be Mary Beth again. Yes, that felt like truth. This woman said there was no way that I was going to get the amount of money that I was looking at charging (lie). When we go for quality (my route) instead of quantity (her chosen route), people—parents—will be very willing to pay for that. That is what Spirit told me.

Next came getting quotes for the construction. Marsh needed numbers before he would agree to this. I found a guy that felt perfect. He and his son would do most of the work, but he would hire someone else to do the drywall work. Marsh agreed to it all, but I think it was not because of the numbers, but how he could see me lighting up from within. We were both scared, don't get me wrong. There were times I wanted to pull out. It is so much easier to be invisible. Why am I doing this? But I felt God's hands on my shoulder, and when I trusted, everything flowed, and when I resisted, everything stopped.

The process of starting the daycare reminds me of the process of writing this book. I really like my life. I'm ok with not writing my stories. This is very scary for me to put myself out there. To put my life out there for people to judge me again is terrifying! But God has asked me to be brave enough to do this. Even as I write this, I am crying because I don't like having to be brave. I like feeling safe. I also know that those moments when I was brave enough to do what was asked of me were life changing and I am so very grateful. For instance:

Trusting God knew what He was doing choosing Marsh as my life partner

Trusting God when I asked to live giving birth to Morgan

Trusting God when my back was hurt and paralysis started to invade my body

Trusting God when Dad wasn't ready to die

Trusting God when Morgan became sick

Trusting God about having weight loss surgery

Trusting God when I opened my daycare

Trusting God when I suffered from extreme anxiety

Trusting God when I was diagnosed with cancer

Trusting God when I was asked to write this book

There are hundreds of other times I trusted God, and they are my life-changing-for-the-better moments. I must also include this very important aspect of all this. God gives us free will, so I also TRUSTED MYSELF and my connection to all that is, in each and every one of those learning opportunities. I was not born to be invisible. I was not born to be mundane. I was born to be Mary Beth... an aspect of God. And I AM that, I AM!

I was caring for Sarah, while studying for my license, and handling so many questions about the construction of the daycare. The finished basement had a bedroom, full bath, main room with a wet bar and mini-fridge area to prepare food. I cannot begin to tell you how alive I felt. I always knew I had wanted to build a home. Well, this was close, I was creating my space. I decided where walls were going, and closets, and if I needed shelves, how high and how many. I got to design the wet bar area with kitchen cabinets that were big enough to store and organize things. The high chairs needed to fit in the closet quick and easy. But I was really picky about the carpet. I needed the best pad and thick carpet because I would be sitting on the floor all day.

I decided to go with a *Pooh Bear theme. I love Pooh Bear because it was about friends working together to overcome obstacles. That felt like a great concept for a daycare. Marsh, Morgan and I cut trees out of plywood. The trunks were covered in brown corduroy and the leaves with green felt. Then we hung a swing from one of the branches and had Pooh sitting on it. We even had a knothole in one of the trees with an owl inside that I could pull out to check the radon meter. My heating vents were on the ceiling so the babies wouldn't get burned. Yes, I really had thought of everything. The only thing I would have changed with hindsight is I would have put in a larger fridge. I had a glider rocking chair and two cribs in the bedroom and a rocker recliner in the main playroom.

Doubt would settle in for a while, and then I'd say, "No, it's Spirit who has been guiding me through this whole process." I could feel the babies that were going to be joining me in this adventure. No, I am going to trust my guidance, and my guidance said go for it with all your heart.

To become a licensed daycare, I had to take classes, including infant CPR and first aid. I also had a book I had to study and take a test after each chapter. Then came the scary part of being inspected. While I was doing all this and taking care of Sarah during the day, Marsh was learning the rules and regs from a business aspect. If I was nervous, Marsh was twice as nervous. I had told Sarah's mom that I was only going to keep babies until they were 18 months old. Everyone encouraged me to go to two years, but Spirit said 18 months and I have never regretted that decision.

On the day of my inspection, I had no idea what they were going to love and what part they were going to hate. I had been given a checklist, and every box was checked. I even had a fire inspector come and check everything out, and he was very impressed. My inspector was more thorough than I expected. I'm grateful, though, because that means my babies will be as safe as they possibly could be and that is my #1 priority. She loved my space and what I had chosen to do with it. I could tell she was looking forward to seeing me in a year to see if it was still going to look and feel this amazing—and it did!

Sarah's mom had a coworker that just had a baby and was looking for a daycare. We interviewed each other and felt it would be a good fit. She had another coworker that would need daycare in a few months. That would be perfect, ease into it slowly. Because I was only taking babies and only using the basement, I was licensed for three babies. That was perfect, I only wanted to have two babies at a time. But Sarah's mom was not getting my hints that Sarah would not be able to stay once my baby daycare opened up. Time to be a businesswoman and do the tough part. I explained that Sarah needed to find a new daycare by a certain date. She did not understand, so I put it in writing.

To say that receiving my letter with an ending date on it went badly is an understatement. She was so angry. She hardly spoke to me when she dropped off and picked up Sarah. Finally, she told me she found a daycare, but they couldn't take Sarah until a certain date. Crap. Sarah and my new baby were going to overlap for a few weeks. I didn't want to have them leave angry, but I really wanted this to be for babies. Sarah would be so bored spending her day with infants, and she was so highly intelligent and needed mental stimulation. Couldn't her mom understand that? I had no idea that Sarah's last day would be the last time I would get to see her. My heart ached for a very long time after she left. Her mom refused to answer my calls or anything. My whole family really missed her. Sarah had become part of our family.

When Sarah was eight, I saw her mom at the grocery store. Her mom was pregnant. I was so happy for her. I wanted to run up to Sarah and hug her, but I am always respectful with children. After greeting each other, her mom asked Sarah if she knew who I was. It had been six years. Sarah nodded and said yes. Her mom asked, "Who is she?" Sarah said, "She is the lady that loved me when I was little." That's right. If you remember nothing else, Sarah, the fact that you remembered that I loved you is absolutely perfect. I asked if I could hug her and she said yes. I cried after that hug as I walked away. Yes, my life is a blessing because a little girl knows that she was loved by me. My heart overflows with gratitude. Thank you, God, for that chance encounter. I needed to know that Sarah was ok, and now I do.

My first official day with my new baby daycare did not go as well as I had hoped. Sarah was very jealous. I asked her to help me with the baby, which she did. When it was time for lunch, I put the baby in a bassinet so I could prepare food for Sarah and me. As I was dishing out the food, Sarah snuck over by the baby and scratched her face. I was devastated. How was I going to make this work while Sarah was still here? Marsh and Morgan to the rescue! They both helped me as much as they could. It was a difficult few weeks but we made it. I kept my daycare open for over eight years. I was blessed with 12 beautiful babies that I was able to love and care for during that time. Each one taught me more and more about how to encourage them to learn and grow and keep them safe. My kids were so advanced, especially verbally because I talked and explained all day long. I had two sets of parents that really wanted me to teach baby sign language. I told them that there are many daycares out there that would be happy to help them with that, but I wasn't one of them. I know there are benefits to using sign language, but I didn't want them to have that crutch. I had a different vision. One of these parents later showed up on a Monday and hugged me and thanked me for sticking to my ideals about not doing sign language. He explained that they had gone to a 2-year-old's birthday party that weekend, and their son, who was 14 months old, had twice the vocabulary that the 2-year-old had. They were so happy to have that proof.

Because I trusted my guidance, I had a way of knowing what each child needed. There were a few that were more challenging to read (or understand) than others. One of my beautiful girls came to me at 13 months, and she had so many issues because the daycare she had been at, kept her in a highchair most of the day. I told her parents that I would be willing to keep her until she turned two so we would have enough time to reverse the damage (for lack of a better way to phrase it) the other daycare had inflicted. I needed to approach things gently with Macy (not her real name)to gain her trust. Each time we ate, I would invite her to use the high chair, but I never forced her. For about six weeks, she ate either while sitting on my lap or while standing near me, but eventually, she trusted me enough to go back in the high chair again. She was held and encouraged so much that after only a couple weeks, both her mother and I were so happy with her progress. Her vocabulary was increasing daily, and her willingness to join in with my other baby instead of staying on my lap was so wonderful to experience.

As I teach my babies the ABCs I also point at each letter, and I would sing a song with the phonics for each letter. As I was teaching Macy her animal sounds, and we were showing Mommy how quickly she was picking it up, she surprised me. She made the sound for the cow and the dog and cat, but when I asked what the bee said, Macy's response was buh-buh-buh—the sound the letter "B" makes instead of the "buzz" like the sound a bumblebee makes. Her mother and I were so surprised and impressed. Within a few months after starting at my daycare, Macy was more advanced than most kids her age. Thank you, God, for bringing her to my daycare and into my heart. That sweet child taught me so much about allowing and being gentle, and I am a better person because of that gift.

Another child I had was having difficulty keeping her formula down. On her first day of daycare, I was concerned that she would even live through the week because she was so thin and lethargic. I prayed and asked for guidance on that first day. I told her parents that I am not a medical professional, but it could be beneficial to try soy formula. The next day they showed up with the biggest smiles. The formula had worked and she kept her formula down for the first time. Soon she was gaining weight and had enough strength to do all the things an infant her age should do. The other baby that I had at the daycare during that time was so perfect for her. These two girls just hugged and kissed each other all of the time. I had never seen two babies that got along and loved each other as much as they did. I felt honored to be able to be part of such a loving environment each day.

During my eight years with my babies, I felt so seen, heard and appreciated by my families. I knew for the first time in my life that I was doing exactly the job I was supposed to be doing. My learning disabilities for once weren't an issue. I got to be 100% Mary Beth all day long. I got to give love and receive love on such a sacred level. I knew for the first time that the gift I had with children was a rarity. Not everyone had this ability, and I never before knew that with such clarity. I was in my element. Now I am not saying that every day was rainbows and sunshine because it wasn't. What I am saying is when we are doing a job we came here to do, you can feel it, and it feels so very wonderful! Thank you, God, for guiding me to this business where everyone won!

I believe that I would still be doing daycare today, except that Marsh was having to drive to Wyoming again while working midnights at the post office. He would tell me that he had no idea how he got home because he was so tired. Once he was home, he loved spending time with the babies and me until they were laid down for their afternoon nap. Only then would he finally give himself permission to sleep. He was so exhausted, and I didn't know what to do. I suggested he rent a room up in Wyoming and come home on his weekends. Because our house was more expensive than we could afford, he let me know that we didn't have the money for that.

Finally, after a really nasty snowstorm that Marsh had to drive in, I said that's it. We need to sell our house and move to Wyoming so I know that you are safe. I am a nervous wreck every night when you leave and I don't sleep well worrying about you coming home. It's just not worth it. You are more important than any house or business. We informed my daycare families, who were not happy about it, but they understood. And Morgan had just moved out, so uprooting her was not an issue.

After ten years, we sold my dream home, which was a financial nightmare, and closed my dream business that was very successful and moved to Wyoming. No one made me do this; it was my suggestions and our choice. I am so very grateful that Marsh no longer had that long drive, especially in the winter. And Marsh said I didn't have to work if I didn't want to in Wyoming. Without that enormous house payment, we should be ok financially. I didn't realize how guilty I felt that my dream home was causing Marsh so much financial stress. After we moved to Wyoming Marsh seemed to be more relaxed, and that ten-minute drive to work was a dream come true for him.

Chapter 24: Relationships Change

When I think of healthy relationships I often think of my supervisor during high school, Mrs. H. She was so kind and supportive to me over the years. When I wasn't sure about how to handle a situation, I would find myself asking, what would Mrs. H. do? Mrs. H. was a mother and a friend rolled into one. Mrs. H and I had some interesting conversations that went beyond surface stuff. I go bonkers talking surface stuff for very long. Mrs. H taught me about being present in a conversation and giving real life guidance that can assist someone.

During the time of Morgan being sick and shortly after that, Morgan and I were only talking about surface stuff. She was frustrated with how her life was unfolding. None of her doctors were helping much. Everyone kept telling her to eat more salt and drink more water. She was so very tired of it all. She was withdrawing more and more into herself. A part of me understood that Morgan was doing some self-preservation work. But I really missed our old way of being together.

Marsh and I had no idea what she needed or how we could help. Occasionally Spirit would give me a little bit of information, but mostly we were all doing the best we could with a difficult situation. Morgan was trying to keep everything to herself so I wouldn't feel anxious or worried. Morgan would always give me vague statements so that she wouldn't lie to me, and at the same time, she felt I would worry less. She was wrong. Not only had my daughter gone from brilliant, to at times not being able to complete a thought, but our relationship was constantly changing. Neither Morgan nor I knew how to be fully with each other anymore. No matter what I said, it was wrong. My joking was irritating, my loving was smothering, my leaving her alone meant I didn't care. I was losing my daughter and I didn't have a say in it. I know that's not true. I know it's a lie, but that's what it felt like.

So our new relationship began. This new relationship was... I let Morgan talk, and I try not to say anything. I don't give input, I don't say what I feel, just listen. I found that if I did that, then at least Morgan would talk to me. At least Morgan will allow me in a little bit. At least I will know what she is kind of thinking. Again, Mary Beth, don't be you. Don't show too much love, don't say what you think, just nod and smile. Holy crap, am I back to this again? I need Morgan to be ok. I need to do what I need to do so Morgan makes it through this very difficult time while she redefines herself. While she tries to figure out how to function in the world where her brain is not connecting properly.

For my birthday that year I went to visit my sister Christine. During that visit, Christine let me know that she and Morgan had spoken, and Morgan felt responsible for Marsh and my relationship. If she wasn't there, she felt we would fall apart. She felt she had to smooth the way for me because of my learning disabilities. In other words, she was taking on the responsibility of my life and Marsh's life. That is insane! How did she think we functioned on this planet before she had arrived? Yes, she has spoiled me by being my translator, but Marsh and I were actually very excited about it being just the two of us and what that will look and feel like. As Christine was speaking, I could feel Spirit putting me in a soft pink cocoon of light so I wouldn't go to a place of I-want-to-die, before the next part of the conversation. She let me know that Morgan felt that she had a very difficult childhood, having to deal with my depression and learning disabilities. Christine let me know that I needed to grow up and start standing on my own two feet so that my daughter can move on with her own life. When Marsh and I talked about this later, we were both so surprised. Morgan in our opinion had the very best childhood ever except for Utah, which wasn't something we did. Where is this coming from?

I was in such a very calm place as Christine told me all this. I was so proud of Christine being brave enough to say those things to me. I can't change if no one is willing to say what needs to be said. After that, Christine said some really horrible things about Morgan and that is when I came out of my calm place. I could kinda see and understand the other stuff, but talking about sweet Morgan in such a disgusting way was unacceptable. You can say what you want about me, but having one or two conversations a year does not make you an authority on Morgan! I'm not going to share with you what was said because that would not serve Morgan.

When I left Christine's home, I was not sure if I would ever really have a true conversation with her again. If she wanted to hurt me, she had done it in the surest way possible. Can I be in her presence and not want to scratch her eyes out? Needless to say, I was not feeling very God connected. When I got home, all Morgan kept saying was how perfect and wonderful Christine was. My heart was aching as Morgan told me all that Christine was, and all that I wasn't. Little did she know the horrible things Christine was saying behind her back. Please, God, let me die! I promised You that I would be a wonderful mother, and it looks like I had failed. How could I be so wrong? Of all the things I had done in this lifetime, the thing I was most proud of was how fantastic I was at being Morgan's mom. I guess my mother was right. I should never have had children. I should never have believed that I was good at something. Especially something as important as being Morgan's mom. Is there any part of my life that I have done right? Why do I even try? Lies, lies and more lies!

The good news, and yes, there is good news, is that when I go to this old place of belittling myself and replaying my old recordings from my childhood, I stay there for such a short time. Thank you, God. And thank you, God, for not allowing me to die when I asked for it again. I am so grateful that I was able to see that if Morgan had to believe that someone else would have been a better mom for her, at least she made good choices by choosing my sister Christine and my sister-in-law Janet. They are both women who have been a huge positive influence in my own life, and I get it.

I was still very angry and disappointed in Christine. Again, it was not what she said about me, but what she had said about Morgan. So a few years later, we were having a family reunion-type affair in Chicago when Christine's daughter asked me something. I have no recollection of what it was. I felt Spirit talk through me as I told my niece what her mom had said a few years ago. My niece was in shock. There was no way her mom would say such a thing. When she got back to her room, she asked her mom. Christine said yes, she had said that and she was so sorry.

I was frustrated that the truth was out there, and I had no way of getting it back. Why did I say anything? This was between Christine and me. Now her daughter was involved. Crap, crap, crap. How do I face them? I was crying telling Marsh what had happened. He asked me if anything I said was a lie. I said no. I could feel Spirit guiding my words. He said then you need to trust that there was a reason why this all came out now.

Of course, Marsh was correct. In fact, this ended up being a beautiful turning point in Christine and my relationship. I can't remember if she set up our meeting in the hotel lobby, or if we were all meeting to go do something we had planned. Anyways, Christine ran towards me crying, she was trying to get on her knees to beg my forgiveness. I was experiencing something so huge—and so important—in that moment. Christine cried and cried. She could barely get her words out. Please, please, could I ever forgive her? She was so wrong. She had no excuse. Could I please forgive her? I was sobbing, and she was sobbing as we held each other and I forgave her.

Christine and I talked as we had never talked before. For the first time, I told a family member the truth about me and it was so freeing. I told Christine about how I channel sometimes, and how God lets me be part of his healings and how God-connected my life was. I talked and talked and I was heard by my sacred sister Christine. She did not abandon me because of it; she was not ashamed of me. She simply loved me and understood me in a way she was never able to before.

We laughed and we cried. She said she always knew that I was holding something back, she just had no idea what it was. I introduced her to my spirit guide Charles, who had some funny comments for her. I felt so vulnerable and yet so very FREE and happy. My secret was out. I could come out of that closet I had been living in my whole life with my family. Charles said it was time for me to stop hiding who I am and instead be who I AM on purpose. That sure felt perfect!

Christine and I talk all the time now. She has learned to channel and she sees things sometimes in people's bodies and even has assisted in healing herself and others. All of this came from a most unexpected place. A place of hate and anger that just could not live in my being (body) anymore. I felt how wonderful and freeing it was to stop guarding my words and be who I am. To be ME... Mary Beth Smith, right here, right now in this moment. It was my moment. Why would I not live my moments to the fullest?

As time went on, I could broaden my perspective and see more of the whole truth of what had occurred. What I mean when I say broaden my perspective is I step way back to see more of the big picture. I then can see other's perspectives, not just my own. I try to do it without attachment to how it is supposed to look or feel. Like, who did what to whom and judging it. Instead, it is almost like watching a movie. I see how Morgan's words to Christine were words I needed to hear, but Morgan didn't feel brave enough to share them with me. I saw how Christine needed to say something so offensive that I couldn't let it go. So someday we would need to finally have the big talk, which would change our relationship to one of total honesty, where we talk about our God connections. Which would then open up Christine's connection to God in such a profound way. I even saw the significance of my niece's role in this whole thing. She needed to better understand my "God connection" so she could witness, understand and even participate in her mother's awakening. Yes, when we broaden our perspective, we have greater clarity and understanding. Especially when we are able to do it without making someone wrong and someone right.

Take this opportunity to look at a time in your life when you felt someone had wronged you. Now step way back. Step back ever further, and watch what happened like a movie playing in your mind. Allow Spirit to show you where the other person was coming from. Allow any past history to show up to explain why they are the way they are and why they feel the way they do. Again, I ask you, as soon as you go into a place of judgment, to soften it, until you can see the truth of it, instead of who did or said something wrong. Can you see and feel the difference? If not, just keep softening your thoughts, soften your feelings. Stop making it personal. I remember starting from a place of God watching two of his children having a dispute and He isn't taking sides. Does that help at all? Allow yourself to let go of the hate, anger or frustration as much as you can. Do this exercise again and again until you no longer feel those "negative" feelings and can let it go.

This is how we work on letting go of disease. Disease is being dis-at-ease with something. It festers in our thoughts until it starts to fester in our body. If we can let it go before we do all this unnecessary damage to our body, we are ahead of the game. The very simple version Spirit taught me in the beginning was something like this:

Heart disease = hardening our heart (arteries)

Urinary problems = being pissed off

Throat issues = not speaking the truth

Eyesight issues = not wanting to see the truth

Shoulder problems = you feel like you are carrying
the weight of the world

Skin issues = what or who had gotten under your skin?

These are just small examples that helped me to know where to start. We came here to experience our diseases, but they are a road map (in my opinion) to what is unresolved within us.

The next step is asking yourself honest questions, like why do I feel I need to harden my heart, or protect my heart? How has that served me? Do I still feel that I need to continue doing that? Am I ready to let that go? I continue that kind of questioning until I feel soft and comfortable in that aspect of my body (like the heart), and my thoughts and emotions are softer, too. The longer you can stay there, the more you shift. It is really amazing to feel the utter and complete difference when I keep going, asking more and more questions and being honest in my answers. Of course, it helps to write it down as you go through this process. This assists you in releasing on another level.

Eventually, I either feel spent (exhausted) or euphoric (happy). Then I know that I have gotten some of that out of my body. I do it again and again until all I feel is love and respect. I am simplifying all this to give you a place to start. Don't be afraid to feel things. Feeling and having emotions is our greatest way of releasing, and our greatest way of connecting to more. So cry, scream, whatever you need to do to let it out of your body without harming yourself or others. No more festering!

I also want to mention here that there is a divine plan that is playing out in our lives. Somethings that we are here to experience no matter what. When we can flow with those experiences instead of fighting and resisting, the whole experience shifts to something easier and more God connected. I hope that makes sense to you. Again, we need to experience something before we can understand it. From there we receive wisdom from it and we are changed on a very deep level.

Chapter 25: M & M & M & M

When Morgan started feeling better, she began looking for something she could do that wouldn't overtax her brain but was enjoyable. She found dance! I was so very happy for her. Her dad and I met dancing. I would tease that it was in her blood. In true Morgan fashion, she chose a dance that I knew nothing about, so it could be her own personal thing. Or maybe she just fell in love with it. Whatever it was, I don't care, it got her out of the house and out of her head. For a couple of hours, a couple of days a week, Morgan was happy. During her time of solitude, I think Morgan was better able to understand the depression I battled with off and on throughout my life. I would rather my child had a happy life and never understood depression, but this was Morgan's path, not mine. So Morgan needed to do what worked for her and her life. I will not have to live with any of the consequences of Morgan's choices, so why should I insist she makes certain choices, not that she chose depression. How are our children supposed to learn and grow if we rob them of their power to choose?

Morgan chose blues dancing. I had never seen anyone do blues dancing before and I had worked in a dance studio. The more Morgan learned the more self-confidence she gained. It came and went, but it was there and I was so grateful. Thank you, God. The first time I got to watch Morgan blues dancing, I was both surprised and impressed. It is very seductive, and yet I loved the way she and her partners had to communicate with each other and how she got the subtlety of the dance. As I watched her, I felt like this specific dance gave Morgan a permission that her life otherwise couldn't give her permission to let herself go and just feel. I have no idea if that is true, but it felt that way.

Morgan was seeking out some of the better male dancers so she could learn more from them. She lit up when she went dancing. She was working as a CNA at a nursing home when she started, and dancing gave her something to look forward to. When she came home, she would talk for hours describing every partner and every dance. I tried to stay up just so I could see happiness on my daughter's face. I will always be thankful to blues dancing for helping Morgan feel alive again. Morgan will be thankful to blues dancing because that is how she met her future husband.

Morgan met Michael at a house party. She was dating someone at the time, but I could tell that Morgan was growing bored with him and was not very stimulated by his intelligence. I had been telling Marsh since Morgan was in kindergarten that she is going to need to marry someone who is intellectually stimulating to her, more than any other quality. This guy she was dating, in my opinion, was not it. After she met Michael and danced with him, I knew that this guy was to be my future son-in-law. I had to tap dance around the subject because Morgan was a very loyal lady. So I said things gently, like, "I think this Michael guy sounds wonderful." Wait for her response. "He is!" Ok, we have our foot in the door. "What does he do?" "He's a student, and his major was in the science field." Oh, my gosh, he's a science nerd too. Play it cool, Mary Beth. "That must have been so awesome to talk science with someone again." She agreed. When I asked if she was going to see him again, she snapped out of her happy place instantly.

"You know I'm dating _____." I draw a blank. I don't even remember the guy's name. I asked her how that is going. Morgan makes a statement that makes it sound like she is starting to see this guy's true character, and it isn't perfect. I put one more thought in her head before I go to bed. "It would be so sad to miss out on a possible relationship with this Michael guy who you have so much in common with to stay with a guy that is ok and that's it." The next week or two I kept dropping hints when she said she might see Michael at some dance coming up. Next thing you know, we got to meet Michael after only two weeks of dating. Just like I got to meet Marsh's family after only two weeks of dating. We have so many sweet similarities. They met dancing, just like Marsh and I. Their initials are M&M, just like Marsh and I. Ok, I was stretching it a bit with that last one, but it worked well as an icebreaker when we met Michael for the first time.

It was Thanksgiving, and I told Morgan if she wanted to invite Michael, we would love to have him. It must be difficult being away from his family during the holidays. Michael is vegetarian, so we had cheese lasagna. Marsh and I danced in the kitchen as Morgan and Michael danced in the living room. We were separated only by a 4-foot-tall divider wall. Thanksgiving is my favorite national holiday because it's the only one that we are not in a space of gimme-gimme. Instead, we pause to give thanks for what we already have. What's not to love about that? So before we eat, I ask everyone to tell us what they are grateful for. Michael joined right in. He looked like he was very comfortable with us right from that first meeting. I told him the only reason we are letting him date Morgan is that his name has the correct initial. Even our dog Muffin had an "M" name. Michael said he needed to thank his mom for naming him Michael then. Yes, right from the start, we liked Michael. I must admit, I was a little jealous of how much Morgan and Michael had in common compared to Marsh and me.

What I have learned repeatedly from Spirit over the last five years is that Marsh and I are not here to be the same; we are here to complement each other. As in, he is good with computers, I am not. I am good with people, he doesn't feel he is. Because of this, I don't need to waste time and energy on things that he is very happy to handle because it is easy for him. We still encourage each other to grow and try things but sometimes it just feels like my energy is better spent on other things. It is more efficient to put my energy and focus where I can do the most good.

One of the things Morgan loved most about Michael was how they could talk and debate about so many subjects. You see, folks—Marsh, Morgan and Michael are all Libras. Libras, in my opinion, do not have balance; Libras are looking for balance. So they like to look at both sides of almost every subject.

Almost every best friend I have ever had has been a Libra, so I know that we are compatible. Michael challenged Morgan intellectually, but it was more than that. Watching Morgan be able to tease Michael and him being ok with it made me smile. Not everyone can handle Marsh and Morgan's sense of humor.

With Michael going to school about an hour away, and not having a car, Morgan was spending a lot of time on the road. I noticed one change after another with her. She began socializing a bit more. She started thinking about possibilities for her future again, and I was thrilled. Eventually, Morgan found a job at the local hospital near Michael's university. Morgan's experience with every job so far is that she is an incredible problem-solver. Unfortunately, the more problems she solves, the more they find for her to fix. And yet being a problem solver is part of who she is.

Just as there was a moment in Marsh and my relationship where his mother realized that maybe, just maybe, Marsh and Mary Beth were going to be ok, the same thing happened for me when Morgan and Michael went through some awful flooding. My brilliant child came up with the idea of renting a moving truck. Their apartment was half underground, so Michael was bailing water trying to keep it from entering their apartment. When they rented the truck, they were able to save a good portion of their belongings. But eventually, the waters broke through and the damage to the apartment was extensive. Drywall, carpet, cabinets, and appliances were all damaged. They needed to find a temporary home while the repairs were done. Through it all, both Morgan and Michael just did what needed to be done.

The moment I felt their relationship could really work was when I asked Michael how he felt about everything that had happened during and after the flood. His response was, "Well, now I can cross the 500-year flood off my bucket list." And when I spoke to him about how the Federal Government is willing to help out, he responded, "Why should the government pay for an act of God. Besides," he said, "we didn't lose much because of renting the moving truck." We stored their stuff until they were ready to move back in.

Morgan had let Michael know from the start that she is very close to her parents, and being an only child means she needs to actively be in our lives. I was so pleased that Morgan wanted to be part of our lives and yet have her own separate life with Michael. I had a blast watching them reason everything out in their logical way. Before Morgan, I had never really spent time with someone that lived from that place. Listening to them discuss the pros and cons of every purchase or decision was enlightening for me. Morgan loved the challenge, and Michael seemed to enjoy having Morgan as a sounding board. They do seem to make a great team.

Finally, the weekend came where they were going up into the mountains and Michael was going to propose. Michael had asked Marsh for permission to marry Morgan, so we knew what was coming. He did a scavenger hunt where Morgan had to solve clues until they ended up at a park where Michael had covered a gazebo with twinkly lights, and he asked Morgan to marry him. Her response... "Of course." The wedding was pushed back a year to accommodate other people, and it wasn't held where Morgan really wanted to get married, but it was a perfect Morgan and Michael wedding. We rented a house in the mountains that Morgan and Michael had chosen for the wedding location, and where my side of the family was able to stay. The ceremony took place on a huge balcony overlooking the mountains and trees... it was so absolutely perfect!

They have been married over four years now and have an incredible rescue dog named Cooper who is so entertaining. He is like Morgan and Michael as far as he likes to be challenged and he likes rules. Their favorite thing to do is to get away from the hustle and bustle of life and go hiking and camping. Michael has gotten his Ph.D. and is teaching, while Morgan has gone back to school. She needs to get two bachelor degrees before going to graduate school to wipe out all the F's she got during her years of being sick and not being able to attend classes. Many times these rules make no sense to me—what a waste of time and money. Eventually, Morgan hopes to be a Chemical Engineer. She wants to be a positive influence on our planet. What do you want to bet that her science background will be a part of her work?

I love who Morgan has become because of the choices she has made. She works full-time and takes about ten credits per semester. Last summer, she and Michael enjoyed helping with Special Olympics baseball. They help their community by assisting vets in learning to dance (for free). Morgan has probably made almost 200 knitted knockers for women who have had mastectomies. She knits and crochets hats for babies in the neonatal ICU. She donates blood or plasma when she has some time off and has grown her hair out 5 times so she could donate it to be made into wigs for cancer patients. Yes, I am very proud of the woman Morgan has become, and I look forward to seeing what she will do next! Thank you, God, for Morgan and her family Michael and Cooper!

Chapter 26: Healing My Birth as Family Members Pass On

Finally, my birthday was celebrated in a way that shifted me. On my 52nd birthday, Marsh and Morgan did a fantastic job of really getting me. When I was asked where I wanted to go to celebrate my birthday that year, I didn't hesitate... The Melting Pot. When we arrived, I asked for their server that was absolutely awesome at celebrating, and she was. I must admit that my favorite course was the cheese fondue. Doing one course after another was strange with my small stomach, but I was able to use restraint so I wouldn't get sick. Everything was yummy, and we all enjoyed having an interactive meal. We seemed to be basking in the happiness radiating from one another. I could tell that the work I had been doing over the years trying to learn how to celebrate my birth was paying off. The day before this birthday, I wasn't getting all quiet and starting to prepare myself for disappointment. I was happy and excited. Woah, what a difference. Is this how most people feel on their birthday? I choose to experience this every year.

Morgan made me some wonderful baby toys so that my babies in my home daycare had something soft to play with that is easy to grab and is washable. I loved all of us playing with them. Then Marsh gave me his gift. He made me a terrarium to remind me of Hawaii. He put sand in this large glass container. Next came blue bath beads that were the size of peas to look like water. He had seashells and bits of driftwood mixed into the sand. It was so very perfect. It took me to a place where my heart was so very happy and connected... Hawaii!

Marsh and Morgan kept looking at each other and giggling; I kept asking what was so funny. Finally, after our dessert, Marsh tells me that there is more inside my terrarium. I opened the top and looked inside, and there was a small glass bottle floating in the blue beads. Inside was a beautiful pearl necklace. The first necklace Marsh had given me in Hawaii was a blue pearl that we had gotten from an oyster and Marsh had it made into a necklace. This was a whole string of pearls, and it tied into the Hawaii theme so well. I was so happy I just cried. He got it, he really got it and so did Morgan. I love it when people do things or give me things where it shows how much they understand me and what brings me joy. In that moment, it felt like my birth was healed. On my birthday, my family understood my heart and I am eternally grateful. I know that it's not about the gifts, etc., but when you have had so many disappointing birthdays for me it takes something really spectacular to erase the pain and heal. This was that birthday for me! Thank you, God! Thank you, Marsh! Thank you, Morgan!

Since then, I have been happy to celebrate my birth. It no longer has a feeling of rejection and dread surrounding it. I like to spend a part of that day just being so very grateful for this life of mine and all of my blessings. Thank you, God, for helping me to learn how to celebrate this life you gave me. I am so very grateful!

When I was in my late teens and early twenties, one of my sisters every year for 4 or 5 years would say to me, "I was going to have a surprise birthday party for you but you know how it is after the holidays, everyone just wants to stay home." Or she would say that it wasn't convenient for people, etc. I think she thought this was going to make me feel loved and thought of. What it actually did was reinforce that I'm not a priority and that no one cares enough to celebrate my birth and that leads to my birth is a bad thing.

Marsh and my first Christmas and birthday in Hawaii, he took me around the BX and other stores and showed me all the things he was going to get me but he didn't. He was really proud of himself, he felt it showed how much he was paying attention, etc. But I asked him to never do that again because what it said to me was I was going to get this for you, but you're not worth it.

Now that we have celebrated my birth, it is time to walk you through some difficult times with the loss of some of my family members. The first one I lost was my dad in 2007. He had been sick on and off for so long that it was almost difficult to remember him ever being healthy. He ended up passing away during his dialysis treatment. I thought it was pretty appropriate since he really did not like doing the treatments. He said it didn't hurt, it was just uncomfortable and strange. Before he passed, my brothers and sisters did such an excellent job of making sure both Mom and Dad were taken care of in the highest way possible. It was incredible how they all took on certain roles to make Mom and Dad's lives better. I am so grateful to them. Marsh, Morgan, and I went home for the funeral. I was trying to process a lot and it was a difficult time. My dad was the person Spirit had connected me to the most as I was growing up. I understood Dad's damaged heart.

Connie and I got to butt heads during this trying time. I got to say "no" very clearly. Connie had a whole agenda of what I was supposed to do and when. I did some of it, but not all. I needed to process all I was experiencing, so I wouldn't have regrets later in my life. One day, before the funeral, I dropped off some pictures at Connie's house. Christine was in the passenger seat and Morgan was in the back. Connie was crying and very upset because I wasn't going to do everything she asked of me. She grabbed my clothes through the open window and said, "You don't understand, I just lost my daddy." I could not believe she was using those words with me. He had been MY "daddy" for over 30 years. Connie started calling him "Daddy" less than a year before he passed. I was so calm, which meant Spirit was talking through me. I said, "I'm very sorry you lost your dad, but in case you didn't notice, I lost my dad too." She screamed, "I miss you." I said, "I know you do." She said, "I love you." I told her that I loved her too. I could feel her frustration, but I couldn't put her needs before my own... not anymore. After we left, Christine said she didn't think it was good that Morgan witnessed that. I said, "Actually, it was the greatest gift I could give my daughter. For the first time,

Morgan got to witness her mom standing up for herself. I hope it empowers her to stand up for herself too."

Next was one of my brothers, who passed away in 2016. He is the brother I knew the least. He hated most people. He didn't want me to visit his home, but I did every time we were in town. He really loved my daughter, though. He told her that if she ever needed anything to call him. I was very grateful that he saw her amazingness. Even though we weren't close, I felt the loss of him.

My mother passed away in 2018. She was 94 years old and had been living in a nursing home. She got to spend her last day with all her special children. When I heard she was "actively dying," I contacted her church to see if a priest would go to give her the last rites. I asked him if he would place a rosary in her hands to bring her peace. Mom loved to say the rosary each night. I am so very grateful that he was able to be there for Mom. Connie, Grant and Charlotte did an incredible job of handling all the arrangements and honoring all Mom's wishes. Thank you, each and every one of you.

I did not go to Mom's funeral. I had warned my family decades in advance that I would not be going. Mom and I had found a peaceful balance in the last decade of her life. We loved each other in the best way we knew how. After all the kids had moved out, Mom seemed to like being a mother more. I enjoyed sending Mom new clothes. It seemed to be the one thing I did right in her eyes. We finally learned how to be with each other so no one felt sad anymore. I am grateful that because of my mom being the way she was with me, I wanted something different for my child. So thank you, Mom, for inspiring me to be an exceptional mother.

A little over a year after Mom's death, another tragedy struck our family. My brother Grant was diagnosed with Stage 4 cancer. The whole family didn't know how to respond to such news. I have been avoiding my pen and pad for days because I just do not want to go there. I don't want to remember that journey of pain. But go there I must, for it is part of my story. Grant was 58 when he experienced some discomfort in his arm while working out. He brought it up to a doctor who did an x-ray and then a CT. They did bloodwork and other tests, too. The doctor told him that he had a tumor in his esophagus, and the cancer was in his lymph nodes and his liver. He felt fine other than the pain of the knowledge that cancer resided in his body.

Grant was referred to an oncologist, the prognosis was not good. They informed Grant that he wasn't a candidate for this treatment or that treatment. They were going to start him on chemo. Every one of us was praying for him. His doctor appointments felt like our doctor appointments. We all waited for new numbers and new results. Janet and I asked Grant if he would like to do sessions with us. Janet's business is *State of the Heart*[9], and she does energy work. Her ability to do detective work to find the root of a problem is astounding. She does this with the help of God and all the Angels and Ascended Masters. She assists in finding the cause and core of a problem, and then Janet and Spirit go to work. It is an honor and a privilege to work with her and witness God's amazingness through her. Grant agreed to have a session. We found a time that worked for all three of us and did a conference call. Grant could not believe where our session went and what he was able to experience. He felt so at peace and he could feel things shift.

We would have loved to do a session every day, but Grant was very hesitant. Energy work is a very strange and wonderful thing. We never know where things are going to take us. Janet ran the sessions; I just supplied what I was witnessing happening in Grant's body. Sometimes Grant had no idea what Janet could be referring to, but since I had lived with him as a child, I could fill in the blanks. His progress was off the charts amazing. His cancer number kept dropping, and the doctor eventually said he was finally a candidate for these other treatments. We were all crying and thanking God again and again. I Love Miracles!

Then something happened. We have no idea what, but suddenly Grant was avoiding Janet and I and didn't want to do sessions. I could no longer see inside Grant's body. You see, we need a person's permission to do any work, and without Grant's permission, all we could do was pray. Not that praying isn't a good thing. Trust me, it is fantastic. But this was just so frustrating, Grant had been doing so well. Who got into his head? What happened? I told Grant to go ahead

---

[9] Janet, *State of The Heart*, 801-971-4556, stateoftheheart.jh@gmail.com.

and work with Janet alone if that was what worked better for him. It took months, but he did finally do a session or two with Janet. I felt helpless. I asked for God's help. I needed to allow Grant to make his own choices. We have a family group text, so we were still all keeping in touch.

After 15 months of battling his cancer, Grant made the decision to go into hospice. Unfortunately, Marsh had just had sinus surgery so we couldn't fly. We had to take the train, and there was severe flooding in Nebraska. The trip was so delayed that Grant had slipped into unconsciousness hours before we arrived. Morgan did not wait for us. She flew out there as soon as she could. Grant was her godfather and she loved him so much. I love watching Morgan love and care for people, it is truly a beautiful gift. The night before we arrived, Morgan stayed overnight at hospice with Grant's wife. She felt so honored to be allowed to assist in the best way she could at that point.

When Marsh and I arrived, we checked into our hotel and dropped off the luggage, then headed straight to hospice. Like I said, Grant had lapsed into unconsciousness about three hours before we had arrived. Morgan spent the night again with Grant's wife, and Marsh and I returned to the hotel. My most sacred husband held me as I sobbed. I felt robbed. Again I was last, and I didn't get to say what I wanted to Grant. I was so angry that everyone had gotten that except me. After grieving, I was able to refocus on being there for my unconscious brother and his wife.

The next morning we stopped at Connie's work, which was just a few blocks away from our hotel. We hugged and cried, and because it was Connie, of course we laughed, too. Back to hospice we go. What an incredible place that was. They had a lake out back and beautiful gardens. It was a perfect place for Grant to be.

I was grateful for having that time with both my brother and his wife. I got to hear stories about how they had met and their dating and their wedding. I told some stories too. We laughed and cried. One day as she was right outside Grant's room eating, she saw an eagle. She ran in and got her binoculars. She and Grant had been long-time birders, and it seemed a way for her to connect again with Grant. It made everyone smile to hear her talk about seeing an eagle. We all felt it was a sign. Morgan returned home the next day, so I stayed through the night in her place. After six days and nights there, I let Grant's wife know I was planning on seeing my other brothers and sisters for the next two nights. We all went to a Friday fish fry, which is a big thing in Wisconsin. Saturday, we all had dinner together as we told stories and laughed and cried together. Sunday night we left on the train. Monday morning Grant passed away. I understand that his funeral was so well attended and it was a real celebration of his life. Thank you, God, for our short 59 years with Grant. He made a lot of people happy, and the world is a better place because Grant was in it.

Chapter 27:
Challenges Surround Me

Writing about my challenges in life can be very difficult for me. I don't enjoy going back and reliving the things that triggered symptoms only five years ago. Because sometimes, it brings the symptoms back, and then I get to love them free again. When I am very strong and connected, I don't experience this at all. But if it does come back, it just gives me another opportunity to heal more of "my stuff" that still resides within me. Again, this tends to be my old lies, beliefs and patterns. As I elevate my energy or my frequency, by connecting to God more and living from a space of love, this old junk just can't exist inside me, it has to come out, even though this is not always very comfortable. It will keep showing up again and again until I am strong enough and wise enough to let it all go. Sometimes with baby steps, other times as giant leaps!

So what happened was, I was spending some time with some of my brothers and sisters, and at the time, Connie was suffering from anxiety. She needed everyone to talk about loving things, and couldn't have too much stimulation around her. Well, that's not the way our family works. I must admit I was not compassionate about assisting her. I only had a few days with my siblings and family and I didn't want to have to guard my thoughts and words. That was absolutely not the kindest thing that I could have done and it is only an excuse. Well, within two months of this experience, I started experiencing anxiety. It came on pretty harsh and fast.

At first, it felt like a nervousness. Within a couple of days, I began experiencing tingling around my mouth and hands. I wasn't sure if God was trying to tell me that my words were too harsh, or that I wasn't speaking my truth. I wasn't willing to stop and analyze things, I was too busy being happy... until I wasn't. Each day, I didn't know what my anxiety experience was going to be like. It felt like I was being immersed in a new culture and I didn't know the language or the customs. It became more and more difficult to stay in a place of peace. Within two months of the initial episode, I was totally immersed in experiencing anxiety every day and every moment. My therapist was helping as much as he could but I needed to see him daily. His schedule and my insurance wouldn't allow that. My physician that I had at the time was not willing to assist me in this aspect. She did, however, connect me to an incredible neurologist, who set up some tests for me. They discovered that I was having seizures. They put me on a medication that I had to build up a tolerance to slowly, and if I ever went off it, I needed to wean off it slowly. Well, I did not do well on this medication. I remember staying at Morgan and Michael's so I could see some specialists in Colorado. I had such paranoia that I was crawling on the floor because I knew I would fall over if I stood. Sometimes I thought the car seatbelt was trying to kill me. There were times I felt like a giant, and other times I was afraid people would step on me because I was so small. One day, I called Morgan at work and said, "I'm not ok." She said, "Mom, is that you?" "I'm not ok." She said, "Do you need me to come home?" "I'm not ok." She said, "I'm on my way, Mom. Michael should be there soon too." "I'm not ok."

When Michael arrived, I was sitting on the couch holding my shoes and purse and phone. I knew I needed them, but had no idea why. The best part was that I had an apron over my head and face. I couldn't figure out how to get it off, so I just sat there and waited for help to arrive. I know Morgan and Michael were trying not to laugh at me, even though I really looked ridiculous. Morgan and Michael took me to the hospital, but I couldn't go in. We sat outside in the car for a long time. Finally, Morgan took me to the park. Swinging is very soothing for me, and it helped. When I talked to my doctor, she decided I was having an allergic reaction, and weaned me off the pills. She also retested me for seizures by having electrodes placed on my head for three days, and found I wasn't having seizures after all. Maybe it was already healed, or maybe I never had them. Either way, thank you, God!

As time went on, I was afraid of so many things, and it would come and go. I was no longer on those meds, but the anxiety had progressed to paranoia. I was afraid to go to bed. I was afraid to get up. I was afraid of certain foods, sometimes all foods. I was afraid to go to the bathroom. I was afraid of the tub. But most of all I was afraid to leave my house. I remember one day in the spring, about five or six months into this anxiety stuff. I was feeling pretty good, so I decided to go for a walk. Usually, I just went around my block, that's all I could handle. This day, I was feeling very brave, so I ventured a little further. I was about three blocks from my house when I went into a panic. I didn't know where I was. Doesn't this sound like Morgan's experience during college? The more I tried to logic it out the worse I got. I couldn't call Marsh, he was sleeping and didn't have his phone with him, so I called my guardian angel Janet. I was so grateful she answered. She sent me some energy which calmed me, and then she kept talking to me until I made it home. I was so happy to be able to get into my house and close and lock the door. Thank you, Janet, for saving the day!

During this period, my brain was buzzing so much I couldn't hear Spirit very often. My neurologist was trying different medications and nothing seemed to help, and some medications made it worse. Poor Marsh was beside himself with worry. I didn't want him to go to work, but I knew he had to. I tried to logic things out, but I couldn't make sense of my thoughts. Then things got even stranger. I noticed I would just freeze. I couldn't move, I couldn't really think, I would just freeze. I could see everything but I couldn't talk, move or think. Then slowly, I became more aware of my surroundings again and could figure out what was what, but it would happen in slow motion.

More tests and more meds. I finally found a medication that calmed me enough that I could again logic out the situation somewhat. Then finally, we had a diagnosis for this "freezing" aspect of my anxiety. I was experiencing dorsal vagal shutdown. When I read the write up from the *American Counseling Association, it fit my symptoms. When the dorsal vagal nerve shuts down the body, it can move us into immobility or dissociation. The way my neurologist explained it is that there are animals that experience this when they are being hunted. They just shut down and pass out, confusing their predators. Some believe it is a more peaceful way to die than experiencing being clawed and attacked. Sometimes the predators just walk away and never touch them. Eventually, the animal comes to, shakes itself off, and walks away unharmed. I can't live like this, I can't drive, what am I supposed to do?

Help came in the form of my beautiful sister-in-law Janet. I can never thank Janet enough for the love, patience and wisdom that she bestowed on me. She asked me to text her when I needed her. Some days all I could text was "help." I just couldn't find any other words. Because Janet does energy work as her job, sometimes she would be busy with clients, but I always knew she would get back to me eventually, even if it was just five or ten minutes in between clients. Janet and I worked a lot on my family's history of dealing with anxiety. When I was young, anytime someone did anything, even spilling milk, my mom would take a nerve pill (Valium). After experiencing this anxiety myself, I understand how very difficult it must have been for my mother to have so many children and no time or space for herself to deal with all the chaos in her body, mind and life. I'm so sorry I didn't have more compassion for Mom at the time. I cannot fix what I don't know or understand and mom never spoke to me about it. That is why I was constantly talking to Marsh and Morgan about what I was experiencing. That way they could assist me and understand me as best they could, instead of watching from the sidelines.

Janet's business, *State of the Heart*, and all her training was a true lifesaver for me. Some days we would connect several times a day. Thank goodness, the work Janet did with me gave me some tools so I could do things on my own to help myself also. I'm going to briefly teach you some of the most beneficial techniques now.

To me, the one I remember assisting me the most was softening and allowing. What I do when I soften and allow, is I just give my entire body, mind, spirit and emotions permission to relax. I notice every part of me getting softer and softer. I carry no tension in my body. I check it, and if I notice tension, I go to that part of my body and I am present with it, and I ask it (no demanding) to soften. Then I ask it to soften again and again until it feels so relaxed. I allow myself to feel what I am feeling (that is the allowing part). I notice thoughts and feelings but in the place of allowing, there aren't the judgments and attachments I usually encounter. Because I am coming from a place of softness, I'm not thinking about who did what to me at all. I can soften my thoughts if I do go there. As I am in this incredible place of softness, I see all the judgments fall away and I let go of being a victim. I feel myself relaxing so much that anxiety is just a faint memory that, again, I have no attachment to it. I feel peace spread through my nervous system. I can even notice light coming into my body. I allow all of it. If a scary thought comes in, I allow it. I look at it from a place of detachment. I notice the frequency it carries. I ask it what it wants to tell me. What message does it have for me?

I will give you an example. I am softening and relaxing, and I notice a nervousness in my brain. I invite my brain to soften and relax. I allow my thought to come in, and I hear and feel, "I'm going to die." This was a common one during my times of anxiety. I ask my brain in a very calm voice, "Do you really <u>know</u> that you are going to die?" I wait for an answer. "Well, no. But it sure feels like it at times." I soften my words. "That must feel scary." My brain says, "Yes." "Is there anything going on that might make you feel that way?" "I feel like everything is on high alert." I ask, "Everything?" "Well, not exactly everything." "Ok, well, what doesn't feel on high alert?" My brain starts listing parts of my body—my legs, my throat, my back, my elbows. As things are listed that are doing ok, I notice my brain calming down. Finally, I ask specifically which parts of my body feel like they are on high alert. "My hands, my nervous system, my brain and my heart a little." I thank my brain for giving me such accurate information. I say let's go to the nervous system since that could be a main source of anxiety. I ask my I AM Presence to take me to my nervous system. I wait until I feel or see something. I notice it is vibrating very fast. I ask my I AM Presence (which is an aspect of God that resides within me) to assist my nervous system in softening and allowing. Almost instantaneously I notice it calming down. I stay present until everything

237

feels calmer. I ask my brain if it is feeling softer and less fight or flight. "I feel it is!" I thank my brain, my nervous system and most importantly my I AM Presence for assisting me in becoming more whole, more connected. Thank you, God!

I know that this is a lot for a beginner, but I wanted to show you a long version. The short version is to just soften your body, soften your words in your thoughts, soften your emotions. Soften anything and everything you can notice and just allow it to be what it is. No making yourself or your body bad or wrong. It simply is. When we fight or resist looking at something, or feeling something, it persists. That old adage "What we resist persists" is so very true. So when you notice something come up for you, allow yourself to feel angry, or whatever emotion comes up for you. Do whatever you need to get it out of your body. Cry, yell, whatever works for you. Just don't harm yourself or someone else. Allow yourself to feel the pain. And then try to soften where you felt the pain. I am not telling you not to see a doctor. I see my doctor quite often, we work as a team. You need to decide. This is simply something that I did to help me through my anxiety and physical pain, and I continue to use it today. Another aspect of this that Janet taught me was that healing decades of old issues can take time. I continually remembered that each time I released a layer she taught me to see it as a layer of an onion. There are a lot of layers to be gone through so be patient with yourself. I noticed also that when a new layer of pain showed up for me to heal, it was less and less intense with each layer. Thank you, God!

I actually found that softening and allowing was able to assist in almost everything I was experiencing. Panic, nervousness and even physical pain were part of this and it was and is so beneficial for me. Even with Marsh, when he gets a headache, I ask him to just sit or lie down and soften and soften some more, and it seems to help him also.

Another tool Janet gave me was trusting, knowing and believing that it is not a matter of IF I will be healed, but WHEN. When she said those words to me, I would always smile. I told myself something similar when my back was hurt. I just knew that someday it would be fine. So each day I would ask... is today the day I'm going to be healed? Just like when the doctor told me Morgan would always be smaller than other children and not as smart. I knew it was a lie, as soon as he said it. I laughed about it with baby Morgan. "Can you believe that doctor? He sure doesn't get it, does he, Morgan? We know that you are going to grow healthy, strong and intelligent!" And she did! I know what I know. Thank you, God.

I want to share with you something that has really helped me when I try to quiet my mind to meditate, or go within, my mind keeps talking and talking, which is very distracting. Sometimes I have found listening to my "self-chatter" helps me to understand better where I am at in my head, and what I might want to work on next. But for those times that I really do want to quiet my mind, I simply say, "Thank you for sharing," and my thoughts stop for a while. And when or if they start up again, I repeat, "Thank you for sharing." That saying acknowledges—I hear you. We all want to be heard and acknowledged. Why would our thoughts be any different? I hope those of you who struggle with this aspect of meditation give it a try and see what happens.

I watched a lot of comedy like *I Love Lucy*[10] during my anxious moments because laughter can shift us so quickly. Placing myself in positive situations helped me to move on sooner also. However, I noticed that if something less than perfect came up I would talk myself through it by calling out the lies. "I'm going to die right here, right now." Am I really? *No.* Another choice for me was that I could leave. Just walk away from the situation. However, if I was going to get better, I needed to be ok no matter what was going on around me. So I would continually tell myself, "That went so much better than I thought it would." "Wow, I am doing better than I used to do." If I had a bit of anxiety and got through it, I would say, "Wow, that was so much easier than a month ago, or a week ago," whatever worked as truth. My mind and body needed to be able to trust my words completely. So give yourself pep talks at every opportunity, but only say what is The truth. "Wow, that person was really trying to put you down, Mary Beth, and you were not buying into it. I am so proud of you. Ten years ago, those words would have felt devastating to you. You've come a long way, Mary Beth. I'm so proud of you."

---

[10] *I Love Lucy*, American television show, 1951-1957.

Walking through my old stuff was a daily activity. Janet taught me something called *Ho'oponopono*, a Hawaiian practice of forgiveness. It has 4 steps to it. It can be used in forgiving someone you feel wronged you, or when you need to forgive yourself.

#1 I love you _____ (State their name)

#2 I'm sorry, _____ (List all the things you are sorry you said or did. If it's about someone doing something wrong to you. It's something like "I'm sorry you saw me as a victim. I'm sorry you felt you had a right to abuse me." Go on and on until you have said everything you have ever thought or felt with this person. Get it all out.

#3 Please forgive me. Please forgive me. I ask you to please forgive me. (Then wait until you feel you have been forgiven) For me, I usually experience a big sigh. This can be different for everyone. What you are looking for is a feeling of release.

#4 Thank you, thank you for forgiving me, all is forgiven.

If you need someone to apologize to you for something that was said or done to you, it can be beneficial in step #2 to imagine them asking you for forgiveness. For example, imagine your parents saying to you, "I'm sorry I didn't listen to you. I'm sorry I spanked you. I'm so very sorry I never took the time to understand your point of view." Keep going until everything you experienced was apologized for. Then in step #3, they would ask you to forgive them. Now I do all of this in my head or on paper. You can do it with the other person present, but I have never done it that way. I feel the reason we do exercises like this is to get all of that old junk out of our body. We don't need to carry it around anymore. It doesn't serve anyone, especially not you! Sometimes I am so surprised by how deep the pain is for me. I need you to understand how important it is to keep going until everything that needs to be said is said. If you would like more information on this practice, please look it up on the internet. I am not an expert, I am only sharing some things that were helpful for me.

From start to finish, this whole process or journey took about a year and a half to two years, but by 12 months, I was doing so much better. Janet and my therapist were my lifelines. I really felt like they were talking me off the edge of the cliff. Janet's tone of voice alone is so very soothing to my soul, and when she combines it with her wisdom and abilities, I felt there was nothing we couldn't accomplish together. I owe Janet more than I can ever express for her willingness to keep walking this journey with me. I love you, my sister, my friend, more than words can express.

My therapist Robert really, really allows me to be 100% me, and that is so freeing. I was concerned that he wasn't going to be able to allow me to talk to Spirit and about Spirit during our sessions. Or maybe this guy wasn't going to believe a word I said. Neither of those has been my experience. Robert allows and allows and allows. I feel so seen, heard and understood during our sessions. I am able to show more of who I am to the real world because of the work we have done during our therapeutic sessions. I wish Marsh and Morgan could find a Robert to help them let go of their baggage, too.

Some of the tools Robert used continually during my anxiety/paranoia bouts were tapping (also called Thought Field Therapy), and EMDR (Eye Movement Desensitization and Reprocessing). I absolutely love EMDR! I hold a little pad in each hand, and the pads take turns vibrating. I am able to take my thoughts and feelings so much further when we do EMDR. I was concerned about having a male therapist. I now know that Robert was a gift given to me by God, and I am so grateful he is exactly who he is! Thank you, God, for this man who takes me so much further in my learning and understanding of myself.

The thing that almost always helped with my anxiety was to have Marsh enfold my body in his. He would have me sit between his legs. My back rested on his chest, and he would wrap his arms and legs around me, encasing me in his cocoon of love. I would feel my anxiety melt away. I could feel my thoughts becoming more clear. I was so grateful that the thing that assisted me the most was Marsh's love. Unfortunately, we did not discover this until I was over a year into my anxiety experience. What matters most is that we did discover it. I understood on a deeper level why God picked Marsh as my life partner. Marsh's frequency is soothing and loving to my frequency and they meld together! What that means is his energy is calming to me. Thank you, God, thank you, Marsh.

Another thing that really helped me came from a very unexpected place. I found that baking calmed my anxiety. My spirit guide encouraged me to bake, and I had no idea why. What I learned was that baking gave me something to concentrate on. If I focused on measuring, mixing and baking, it was a distraction from the anxiety. If I could distract long enough, I began having days with no anxiety. Now what to do with the three batches of cookies I made in one day? At first, Marsh's coworkers enjoyed them, but eventually, a lot of them were making a lot of comments about gaining weight and high cholesterol. He wanted me to be healthy and happy, but they just weren't appreciating the cookies if they got them every day.

That's when I found out hospice was very happy to receive my goodies. I brought 10-12 dozen cookies to them 2-3 times a week. It was a win, win for everyone. Our grocery bill had tripled, but Marsh was so grateful I was doing better. My happiness and health is so very, very important to this man that I love so much. As I got better, I noticed I was baking less. Then someone at hospice said that I couldn't bring anything into the building that had any connection to nuts at all. I started worrying ... what if I missed a spot washing the cookie sheets. I felt sad, but it seemed it was time to stop supplying hospice with homemade cookies. They were ok with store-bought, but that's not me. You see, Marsh found me a cookie cookbook at the used book store. I wanted to try to make all 230 recipes. As I was reading the different recipes, I found that one of the recipes was from my home economics teacher from high school. That was such an incredible, heart-touching moment. I loved my Home Ec teacher, she had a lot of patience with me.

So as you can see, assistance in the healing of my anxiety came in so many forms. It really does take a village! I tend to avoid people that tell me this is the only way. God puts many angels and options on our path, we just need to pay attention. After Janet began helping me, I only took about 20 more pills to medicate myself out of my anxiety. I still connect with Janet when I need assistance with anything, and she is always a gift from God. Robert and I still meet once a week, and I am learning so much about myself and where I still have issues. I only send cookies to Marsh's work 1-4 times a month. I am so very grateful to God for the learning and growth I was able to experience from my anxiety. The most surprising part of this was that I learned to understand the shift in my frequency or my energy and what to do when it happens. What a gift. Thank you, God!

A couple of years later, as I was opening my heart more and more along with elevating my frequency so that I could connect to Spirit more effortlessly, I learned something. While yes, I was experiencing anxiety, much of it was my frequency raising, which activates our nervous system. You see, as we notice our nervous system vibrating faster, ask Spirit if this is our body getting an "upgrade" or is it truly anxiety. Eventually you will recognize the difference.

Chapter 28: The Day of Recovery

According to the book *The Secret Language of Birthdays*[11] I was born on "the day of recovery." I'm going to give you the first three paragraphs written about those born on the day of recovery:

Recovery is a central and recurrent theme in the lives of January 5 people. Not ones to be kept down for very long, those born on this day have a surprising capacity for comebacks—gradual or dramatic recoveries from disadvantageous situations, either of a personal or social nature. On the personal side, this may mean overcoming illness, catastrophe or just plain bad luck; on the social side regaining lost status or leading a group to restore its standing.

Needless to say, January 5 people are resilient. They bounce back from injuries and accidents of all types. Even more impressive is their ability to recover from emotional disappointments or rejection. This is due ultimately to their bedrock of self-confidence and their capacity to leave the <u>past behind</u> and move on.

---

[11] Gary Goldschneider and Joost Elffers, *The Secret Language of Birthdays*, 2013.

This does not mean that they are superficial individuals for whom loss has little meaning. On the contrary, they are highly involved committed people, and therefore the wonder is even greater that they can recover from setbacks which are doubtless deeply felt. Part of their strength lies in an acceptance of the fact that one cannot win all of the time.

My brother Grant, who passed away this last summer, came through to me via channeling and asked me to put this quote in my book. It's the only thing he has brought up to me since I started writing this book. At first, I didn't understand why. Then when I reread the section, I got it. I was born on the day of recovery. I am grateful that I am so proficient at recovering, but I would really love to live more of a life that I don't NEED to recover from. The quote above talks about leaving the past behind. That has been the most difficult aspect for me. I spent the first 30 or 40 years looking at how everyone wronged me. That is the victim mentality. It doesn't serve you (or me)... let it go!

In September of 2018, I was doing really, really well. I was happy. Marsh and I were very close and loving to each other. My anxiety was minimal. Morgan and I were finding our groove more. Many of my siblings are on a group text together, and we were all enjoying being part of each other's lives. A major, major negative during this time was that my brother Grant was going through Stage 4 cancer. We were all there together for him, and that felt so incredibly sacred to all of us. He didn't have to call each one of us and let us know the latest test results which could be so daunting. We could all ask questions not only of Grant but each other and sometimes we would get answers. Sometimes we ended up with more questions, but my inner core was strong. I was happy, except for feeling helpless with Grant. He didn't want my help, only my prayers, which I gratefully offered up. My life was feeling like I could breathe again. Maybe someday I could even fly again. I had such incredible HOPE. I had become terrified of flying and driving or even riding on the interstate during my anxiety episodes, and that was the only part that still wasn't healed. I occasionally have a flicker of nervousness, but I just soften and allow and move on.

Then in September of 2018, I was diagnosed with uterine cancer. This can't be happening! This absolutely cannot be happening. As I came out of the doctor's office after having a biopsy, she let me know that she thought it could be cancer. She would get the results Friday, but she was going to be at a conference. Would I be ok with her giving me the results on the phone, or did I want to come in on Monday? I wanted her to call me on Friday. As I got into the SUV that we had purchased that month, I saw ravens on a fence in front of the car. As I cried, more ravens were landing on the fence. There were over 25 birds looking at me crying. It's strange, but it felt like they were there to be supportive and let me know that I was going to be ok. Ravens are a symbol of magic. I could use some magic!

When I got home, I woke up Marsh and gave him my news. Marsh enfolded me in his love and said, "You're going to get through this." I told him that I had no doubt I was going to live, but it did feel like I had cancer. I cried a lot. Everything made me break into tears. I hated the waiting. On Friday afternoon I got the call. It was cancer! My doctor explained that uterine cancer caught this early was taken care of by having a hysterectomy. No radiation—no chemo! Did I want her to put me on her surgery schedule? I said yes. She said she would call me Monday to let me know when my surgery would be.

I cannot describe the moment that you are given a diagnosis of cancer. There is a feeling—at least for me—that your life will never be the same. In that moment your life is changed forever. I went to a place I had never gone before. I don't know if I can do this. I doubted everything. I couldn't remember ever being connected to healing. I doubted God's love for me. I doubted Marsh and me making it through this. I doubted Morgan being able to handle this with all she had going on in her life. I felt like all the old recordings were coming back, in loud stereo. I deserve nothing less. Did I really think I mattered? I went to such a dark place I even felt my mom must be happy knowing I was going through this. I had to allow myself to feel it and think it all. I needed to get all the pain, doubt and frustration out of my body. None of it was wrong and bad, it just was my experience.

Calling Morgan was very difficult. How do I try to be optimistic when first, I need to allow myself to be angry and sad? Morgan was extraordinary. She asked a lot of questions as she took it all in. She was not happy with how my doctor was handling this, and she wanted to go to my pre-op appointment with me. She needed more information. I told her there was no pre-op appointment. That was unacceptable to her.

Morgan started doing what Morgan does so well. She researched and talked to all the doctors that she had access to at her work. She found me an incredible doctor in Denver who was a Gynecologic Oncologist. I still wasn't convinced. I hate being on the interstates; Denver was pretty far; winter was coming up. I can't drive to Denver in the winter, even as a passenger. I kept coming up with one excuse after another, and Morgan, knowing how I process things, was stepping back and allowing me to process. Then she would give me another tidbit, like one of her coworkers had this particular doctor, and she loved her. She was a rare case and this doctor saved her. But I don't need all that. I just need a hysterectomy. She found another coworker who had this same doctor and loved her, did I want to talk to her? Finally, I saw the pattern. I used to ask God for three signs if I was supposed to do something. Morgan had provided me with way more than three. Ok, I would do a consultation with this doctor.

I called my doctor in Wyoming and told her I was getting a second opinion. She wasn't happy, but oh well! It's hard to believe, but we left a week later to go to Wisconsin. We had been planning this trip for months. This trip would give me time to work on healing my body! This trip was part of the reason we bought the SUV when we did. I needed to see Grant now, more than ever before. Grant and I have never had a heart to heart talk, just him and I. How do I tell him that I have cancer too? Will we cry together? Will Grant's sense of humor help me navigate this? I needed to be with family. I needed to feel all of their love and support. It was my turn to have my family be there for me.

Ken, Janet and Morgan joined us as we traveled. Ken was an incredible driver! Janet and Morgan were amazing too, and this, along with Janet sending me energy, helped my nervousness. I was constantly reminding myself... look how far you have come, Mary Beth. Three years ago, you could never have even thought about doing this! I felt that having it take two days to get to Wisconsin gave me more time to get used to the idea of having cancer and what to do. This was done in a vehicle filled with people that love me.

Things did not go the way I planned it in my head. I was trying to make sure everyone was taken care of. I was trying to make sure I was coming from a place of honor and respect. I was respecting Grant's desires and needs so much that he was avoiding us. I know that our family can be a lot for a healthy person, much less someone with Stage 4 cancer. I got to speak with him at two gatherings with lots of people around, so no one-on-one time. No using humor to navigate our new commonality of cancer. I was never given the opportunity, nor did I insist on having the conversation about cancer with Grant. I could feel the last thing Grant wanted was to talk about cancer. That is all anyone wants to talk to you about once they hear you have had a "cancer diagnosis."

I was really feeling more confident during this trip that I was really going to be ok, even though nothing looked, felt or seemed like what it did in my head. Then at Connie's apartment while I was sitting on the floor, I watched Morgan step over my legs so she could go over to Aunt Christine and do some energy work on her. I blinked several times, trying to take this in. Did my daughter just bypass her mother who has a cancerous tumor in her, to go help my sister with energy work? I had to excuse myself so I could go into the bathroom and hold towels over my mouth as I wailed. I was back to feeling invisible and crying in a bathroom instead of a closet. This slight from Morgan was not intentional, but that didn't make it hurt any less.

I left Wisconsin feeling more alone than I had felt in a long time because I never found the right moment to tell people about my cancer. I wanted and needed alone time to have a really big pity party for myself. Grant's cancer was so big, my cancer wasn't, does that mean my cancer experience didn't matter? Hell no! Cancer was a word I could barely utter back then. If I don't say it, maybe it doesn't exist. All the tools I have spoken of on the previous pages were so far removed from my moments during this new cancer experience of mine. Later I used every one of them, but first I needed to process and get all of this fear out of my body.

When we got home, I had my consultation with the oncologist in Denver. Morgan was so right, this doctor was incredible. We were there for hours asking and answering questions. My surgery was scheduled for the beginning of November. It should take two to four hours, and was going to be done laparoscopically. They were going to tilt the operating table 40 degrees so my head would be down and my feet would be up. This was to help my intestines gravitationally move towards my head so she could operate behind them. If my blood pressure went up too much, they would straighten the table and open me up to perform the surgery.

I worked every day preparing my body for what was coming. The really bizarre thing was that I was having a difficult time with not being able to have more babies. I had not had a period for over six years. I didn't want to have a baby at my age, but not much about this was logical. I did not want to lose these organs that defined me as a woman. These organs needed to be loved, not ripped from my body. I had to deal with more rage from my past and being sexually abused. Is this because I didn't heal all of that thoroughly enough? I wanted to hate me again. The interesting thing was I didn't hate my body or what was happening to it. Janet, my beautiful angel, was doing sessions almost every day with me. My sister Christine was connecting with me all the time, letting me know how much she loved me. Morgan was handling everything she could, because of her love for me and so I wouldn't back out. And my sacred Marsh was getting very quiet. He would let me vent as much as I needed and just held me and loved me. The only thing he would really say was he needed me to be ok.

The night before the surgery, I could feel Spirit inside me, and I felt so calm and confident that everything was exactly as it was supposed to be. Morgan, Michael, Marsh and I stayed at a nice hotel in Denver, and we played games and talked. I could tell Morgan was gauging me continually. Is Mom really ok, or is she putting on a brave front? The next morning everything was great except I had apple juice because my surgery was later in the day, and I got diarrhea. I was so afraid of having diarrhea during my surgery. I was joking with everyone about it. I was so grateful that Michael was truly being part of our family during this scary time for me. Again, Morgan just handled everything that she could from the sidelines. Once

I was in the surgery, it was her job to keep Marsh sane. My surgery went for 7 ½ hours. I did perfectly as far as my blood pressure and vitals, but the cancer had spread to the cervix. The uterus had torn during the operation, and they needed to move slower and more thoroughly. But they got it all! Hallelujah, Thank You, God, and all of you beings of light that assisted me. No cell was left behind!

Morgan said Marsh wanted them to close me up and start again tomorrow. I guess he was pretty frantic and pacing. They had no idea what was going on in my surgery. Morgan said they went on a tour of the hospital critiquing all the artwork. I'm sure Morgan had Marsh laughing. Thank you for doing such an incredible job, Morgan. You are priceless and so important to our lives. For some reason, in recovery, I didn't want to go right up to my room. I think I wanted to be monitored as closely as possible for as long as possible. Because of that, I didn't get to my room until 12:30 in the morning.

Marsh and Michael went back to the hotel. My precious angel Morgan stayed in my room to help in any way she could. I remember someone coming in around 8 A.M. to let me know I could leave. I was freaking out. There is no way I was ready to go home! They agreed to let me stay until 10:30. Marsh and Michael arrived, and we needed to accomplish so many things before I left. We sent Marsh to the pharmacy to get my prescriptions filled. I sent Morgan and Michael to get me some soup. I was hungry but didn't want to overdo it. I laid back in my bed to recover more, but then a young woman showed up with a wheelchair. She said that I had been discharged, and she was here to transport me to my car. My doctor came in to tell me how well the surgery had gone, but I couldn't really hear or understand her because I was still so groggy from the anesthesia. I do remember her saying I would need radiation therapy. I thanked my doctor and hugged her. This young woman with the wheelchair was getting a little impatient with me. I was trying to collect my stuff because I didn't want a stranger to do it, and thank goodness Morgan had done most of the packing already. As I was being wheeled down the hallway, I realized my family didn't know where I was or what was happening. Where was she taking me?

My transporter asked me which exit I wanted. I only knew one exit, and that was near my doctor's office. I asked for my phone. She handed it to me, and

I foggy-groggy texted Marsh, telling him I would be at the cancer center exit waiting for him. He contacted Morgan and Michael. He found me sitting in a wheelchair outside in 40-degree weather with my coat half on. My purse was on the handle behind me, and I had stuff on my lap and stuff behind me. Anyone walking by could have taken everything. I kept thinking foggy-like, what the heck? Is this normal? Nothing felt normal. Of course, I was in pain, I had just had surgery, but this whole process made no sense. Who dumps a patient on the curbside and leaves them there? There were lots of people around, but I didn't know any of them.

Finally, Marsh pulled up in the SUV, and Morgan and Michael appeared from somewhere. I needed to go to the hotel because I was not ready for a 2.5-hour drive to Wyoming. As we settled in at the hotel, I was feeling paranoid. Everything was moving so fast and nothing was making sense. I should be in a hospital bed. I just had a 7.5-hour surgery 12 hours ago. I wanted to stay close to the hospital, but Morgan reminded me there was supposed to be a snowstorm that night. Do I still want to stay in a hotel in Denver? Crap! She was right, ok, let's head home. Michael left for their home, but Morgan was going to stay with us for about a week. Both Marsh and Morgan had taken off from work, Morgan for a week and Marsh for two weeks.

Finally, I was home. Morgan and Marsh helped to get me settled, but I was having a lot of pain on my left side. I was not being a good patient. I felt like everything was outside of me. I was lost and loopy. Morgan called the on-call doctor, and he was concerned about an obstructed bowel. So guess what... back in the car, back to Loveland, Colorado, to the ER... an hour away! Are you kidding me! I had just gotten settled! But the pain was pretty bad.

They did a CT scan, and everything looked normal for having just had surgery 12 hours ago. I was dehydrated, though. Once they got a couple of liters of fluids in me, my mind was clearer. I needed to drink more water. NO, I need an IV in a hospital room! This insurance game is so ridiculous. So back home we go... again.

Those first two weeks were so difficult. The most difficult part was showering. Marsh got me a shower chair, which really helped, but eventually, he just came in with me because lifting my left arm could put me in extreme pain.

As much as Morgan was helping me, I was not a good patient, as I said. I didn't want to mask symptoms with pain pills. I had to be so careful about what I ate because vomiting was so painful and could rip something out. I felt like all decisions were out of my control. Of course, that is a lie. Marsh and Morgan asked my opinion on everything. The truth is I felt that my surgery pain and having Stage 2 cancer was affecting me and causing me to take things out on the people that I love most. And now, I was going to need radiation treatments!?! I'm so very sorry for all I put you through, Marsh and Morgan. You deserved my gratitude, but what you got was my bad attitude. Please forgive me?

How can I have cancer? How could the cancer have progressed into my cervix? I had so many questions and so much anger, but few answers. I know eventually it will all make sense to me, but for now, I only get tidbits of answers. I have too much of an attachment to the answers. I want to blame all my ancestors. The truth is my ancestors didn't have cancer, except my mother had lung cancer from smoking so much. Some of my siblings and I are the first to take cancer on. This makes me mad at myself. I knew that saying the word cancer really affected me. Why didn't I take the time to look at that?

Time to go back to Denver to talk to my oncologist. She wanted me to see their radiation oncologist. I did, but her energy made me feel wonky, though she was very kind and patient with me. Morgan was there taking notes during our appointment so I could be reminded of the information later. As this radiation oncologist spoke, I started feeling something happen inside my body. It was familiar, yet put panic in me. What was it? I needed to define it. Morgan was able to help me; I was starting to experience dorsal vagal shutdown. Marsh immediately stood beside me so I wouldn't fall over. The doctor was very concerned.

The next day when I was able to step back and broaden my perspective, I could better understand aspects of what was happening. My body was screaming at me. Are you kidding me? You just took away our organs, and now you want to radiate me? My body was asking, what do you have against me? The radiation oncologist wanted to do 25 external radiation treatments and two to four internal radiation treatments. The external radiation was bad enough, but over the summer, Christine had come for a visit, and she told me about what her mother had gone through having radiation during her female cancer experience. I was terrified. Yes, Christine's mother went through this about 65 years ago. I know so much has changed since then, but the story was fresh in my mind. This poor woman with four young children and an infant was diagnosed with "female cancer." She was desperate to get better, to be there for her children, so the doctors did some radical things. One of the things they did was place radium up inside her cervix and sew it shut. She was in so much pain. She may have even been buried with it still in her; we have no one to ask. I can still feel this beautiful mother's pain.

And now, this radiation oncologist wanted to put an apparatus up inside of me and radiate more. Gee, I wonder why I'm experiencing dorsal vagal shutdown! But Morgan took excellent notes. She was better able to explain things to me when I was in a calm, safe environment. Morgan also asked if I could have the treatments up in Ft. Collins. My doctor said yes, as long as she was kept in the loop. Thank you, God. It would have cost us thousands of dollars for me to stay in hotels in Denver and eat out most meals. In Fort Collins, I could stay with Morgan, Michael and their dog Cooper, and it wouldn't cost anything.

When I met my Ft. Collins radiation oncologist, I loved him right away. His quiet compassion just radiated from him. He spent a lot of time answering my questions. He was willing to let me wait until the beginning of February before I had to decide about the internal radiation treatments and whether I was going to have them in Fort Collins or Denver. I could tell Morgan wanted to shake me, but she was allowing me to process. There had been so much, so fast. I had a mapping appointment, which was a CT that mapped me internally. They needed to know where my organs and everything was so they could target the radiation so that I wouldn't receive more than I needed. I got three tattoos the size of a dot to line up three small laser beams to make sure I was in the correct position for each treatment. I stayed with Morgan and Michael during this process, and I met with a cancer counselor or therapist. I found everyone to be very kind and compassionate. They were here to help me through a most difficult time in my life, and I was so grateful. I was to start treatments the day after Christmas.

My cancer counselor told me that they had several homes that the hospital rented to cancer patients for $20 per day during treatment. These houses were only a block away from Morgan and Michael's home. I could have my own space and my own food, and yet Morgan and Michael were very close if I needed help. I decided that was what I wanted to do. I did not realize how much it was going to hurt Morgan. This was nothing against Morgan. I know they were excited about teaching me more about being vegetarian while I was with them and that it could assist me, but I had enough to deal with, without having to navigate new food (excuses, excuses, excuses).

In 2017, Marsh, Morgan, Michael and I made over 5,000 cookies over the 4-day Thanksgiving weekend. In 2018 we made zero. I told Marsh, please no Christmas tree and lights and presents. So on Christmas Eve, Marsh brought me down to Ft. Collins so I could check into my new home for the next 5-7 weeks. Our extra car was already there, so I would have some way of getting around. We opened a few presents for Christmas, and Morgan gave me such a precious gift. She had knitted me seven new hats in all different colors and styles. I could donate them to the cancer center as I wasn't supposed to lose my hair with these treatments, or I could keep them. That gesture really touched my heart. When we had gone to meet my gynecological oncologist doctor for the first time, Morgan had taken a large bag of baby hats to the neonatal ICU. Morgan has such a beautiful, giving heart!

The cancer center called about 40 minutes before my first radiation treatment to let me know the machine was down. They would call when it was back up. I had to drink water before my treatments to protect my bladder as much as possible, so a delay was very uncomfortable. Two hours later the machine was back up, but I said why don't we start tomorrow? They were so very grateful because they still needed to get everyone from the last two hours treated. The next day I showed up with my family. I had drunk a liter of water. I lay down on the table, and they gave me a warm blanket to cover myself because I needed to slip down my pants so they could line up the lasers with my three tattoo dots. I had been asking everyone how long the radiation exposure would be. That day I found out it was 2 minutes 12 seconds. Once the techs leave the room, I have to remain still as I watched these four huge arms rotate around me. They had to do a quick scan, I found out, before each treatment to make sure my bladder was full enough and everything looked ok. If it did, the arms moved into a different position, and the radiation treatment started. We were a go. I started counting and watching everything. I smelled something funny, but not terrible. I could feel my organs reacting, and I cried. As I pulled up my pants before getting off the table, I started singing, "Another one bites the dust, and another one's gone and another one's gone and another one bites the dust."[12] I make up songs when I am nervous, but this one was not made up. This was my way of saying this is only temporary!

During my 25 external treatments, there were four times that I did not have enough water in me, so I upped it to 1.5 liters, and eventually, it took 2 liters. On Tuesdays, the radiation oncologists met with every one of their patients. It was crazy. I liked having someone with me on those days. Michael took me twice and Morgan did two others, and near the end, Christine flew in from Florida to help me out. By the end of the second week, diarrhea became a problem. I never knew when it was going to hit and if I would be able to make it to a bathroom. I started to carry a very big bag with extra underwear and pants and large baggies for soiled clothes, and lots of wipes. I tried to limit going out in public, but going out to eat is one of my favorite things. It was something that made me feel normal.

Then I had a very difficult day. I had so much diarrhea that I called and left a message at the cancer center. By the time someone was able to get back to me, I was feeling off because of dehydration. Thank God it was a day when Marsh was there. We ended up in the ER where I was given two bags of fluids, and I had already drunk 3 liters of water, and I was still dehydrated. I needed to up the amount of Imodium I took each day. At 14 sessions in, I was thinking about stopping. I talked to Marsh and Morgan about it, and Marsh said it was my call. Morgan said, "Mom, if you quit now and the cancer comes back, you will be so mad at yourself. Is it worth it?" I decided to continue. I continued to have very strong stomach pains, but I could find no patterns as to why other than that my organs were being radiated daily!

[12] Queen, *Another One Bites the Dust*, 1980

I was having difficulty with the energy of the house I was staying in. Janet and I worked on it a lot. Because I work with energy, I could feel the sadness and desperation in the house. It had been decades and decades of people living in these houses short term, the whole time putting dread and fear into the house. Think about it; years of no one caring about the building's wellbeing. Even a rental has that. The house felt very lonely and unloved. This was difficult for me, and it's one of the reasons I like newer homes; there is less drama held in the walls and space.

During a mindfulness class I was taking at the cancer center, one of the assignments we had was to pick a task we do daily and try to be as mindful and present with it as possible. I chose my radiation treatment. As I felt the techs manipulating my body, I could feel my girth. There was no judgment, just experiencing it. Then, as the techs left, I heard Spirit say, "This is your moment, Mary Beth, what are you going to do with it?" And I said so quickly and effortlessly, "I'm going to dance." And I did. I saw Connie, Christine, Charlotte and I in the '80s all dancing together to *We are Family*[13] at a disco. The joy and solidarity came back and I was smiling. I saw Morgan in my arms as a little girl, and we were dancing and twirling as she squealed with joy. Then it switched to Marsh dancing with me in the kitchen. I felt our bodies moving as one in a rhythm and I felt so loved—so very, very loved! The machine stopped. I know it was not what my teacher intended for mindfulness, but I was very mindful of that experience and I am grateful. Thank you, God!

Both Janet and Christine had offered to stay with me from the start. Finally, I gave in and asked Christine to please come help me. Christine was retired, so I thought it would be easier for her. I was wrong... Christine could only stay 10 days which wasn't enough. While Janet can do her business from anywhere, I just didn't want to inconvenience her more than I already had. We were having sessions almost every day, and they were really helping me. Marsh spent two days a week with me the first couple weeks and three days a week for the next two weeks. Christine coming would help with all of that. Morgan would stop by on

---

[13] Sister Sledge, *We Are Family*, 1978.

her way home from work, and visit on the weekends. So having Christine around 24/7 would be wonderful.

Again, it was frustrating for Morgan. She wanted me to stay with them. Having Christine come was a pretty big slap in the face to her because she wanted to be there for me, helping me every step of the way. It was not my intention to hurt her. When Morgan spoke up, I felt awful. How had all of this gotten so messed up? I needed to do what I needed to do, but not at the expense of my relationship with my daughter. Will the trauma and drama never end with this experience?

Christine arrived with five days of external radiation remaining. I had no idea how much I needed her until she arrived. She kept me calm and rational. Marsh and I took her to Red Lobster, which is a favorite of ours. Christine got to see firsthand how the stomach pains would come on with no warning. Then she got to witness me running to the bathroom several times only to sit down and then need to jump up again without even taking a bite. She texted about it on the family group text the next morning. It was fascinating to see my experience through someone else's eyes, and I was grateful for it.

Christine enjoyed being part of these relationships I had developed with the other cancer patients receiving treatments. She had no idea that this kind of bravery along with needing to go with the flow was part of all our lives there, and she was so honored to be a part of it. It was such a relief to be able to share my burdens with someone. I didn't realize until then how much I was holding back from Morgan and Marsh so they wouldn't worry. Christine made everything easier and more doable.

My daily routine was that I had to eat a very small meal as soon as I woke up, then start drinking water. Now remember, because of my stomach surgery I can't eat and then drink. But God helped me each day with this. The thought of putting water inside me was repulsive, but it had to be done. My body seemed to know that after the water came my radiation treatment. I took tiny sips and gagged. After the first liter, I could gulp more. But If I drank too early, I'd have to pee. Then I'd have to drink more and hope it would get to my bladder in time for my treatment. Then I would be hit with sharp, bend-over-in-pain stomach pains. Through it all, Christine was my cheerleader.

There was a young man going through treatments that I would sometimes see in the waiting room. He reminded me so much of my brother Grant. Christine saw it too and commented on it. I told her how I felt guilty complaining about my experience when what Grant was going through was so much worse. She and Janet continued to help me understand that my experience and Grant's experience were totally different. And neither one was better or worse, just different.

On my last day of external treatments, I got off that table singing I have, *I have rocked this!*[14] As I came up the ramp leading from the treatment room to the waiting room, there were about ten staff members applauding me. I cried so much. Marsh gave me a huge bouquet of flowers. When Christine met my radiation oncologist, she asked him if she could hug him. That touched my heart so much. She thanked him for taking such good care of her little sister. A nurse read a poem about being powerful and overcoming. I wished it had been more God-centered, but I realize some people might be offended. Then I hit a little gong and walked out feeling free... but I would be back.

Throughout my treatments, Morgan continued to make more and more hats for me. I kept four of them and donated the rest. The day after donating a hat, I would always check, and Morgan's hat would be gone. Each one had so much detail and was made with love and healing light. No wonder why they went so fast. Thank you, Morgan, for sharing your talent with people who really needed it. Morgan also made Grant a big, thick hat to wear during his treatments in Wisconsin. She is such a gift to this planet and my life.

I had four days free before my first internal radiation treatment would begin. Christine went back to Wyoming with us, but she would be leaving in a couple of days. I wanted to beg and plead with her to stay. We had packed everything from "the cancer house." Marsh would be taking me down to Fort Collins for my four internal radiation treatments and we would be coming back home after each treatment. I was relieved to be in my own space at home again, even though I now felt like a stranger in my own home. I couldn't find my groove.

---

[14] Queen, *We Will Rock You*, 1977

I couldn't figure out how to be Marsh's wife again. I didn't feel like I belonged in our beautiful rental home anymore.

I had to stop and see my wonderful friends at my favorite Asian restaurant right away. Ever since living in Japan, I have loved Chinese food. I had never liked sushi until the owner of this restaurant gave me a free sample of something called White Mountain. I was hooked. I would stop in 2-4 times a week, and the wait staff has come to feel like family to me. If I was going to get back to my normal life, I needed to go to my favorite restaurant! Christine had been there with me in July when she had come for a visit, so she was happy to return with me. I was greeted with such huge smiles and even some hugs. I could see the relief on their faces. I was back and I was alive. I could feel them wanting to ask questions and yet wanting to respect my privacy. How do you explain diarrhea to someone that English is not their first language? I still carried my diaper bag and continued to use it. Geday's smile made me feel a little bit more "home." Geday has been such a sacred friend to me. He lets me talk about spiritual things (whenever there are no other customers) without judging me. As Geday would speak about spirituality and different religious beliefs, he would say, "The end goal is the same, it's just different paths to get there."

Christine and Geday both enjoyed teasing and laughing together. Christine would look at me to see how much she should say. I gave her free reign... truth is truth. Marsh just stared at me all the time. He was so grateful to have me home again. Christine and I talked about it several times. She said, "You really do need to realize how much Marsh loves you, Mary Beth! You are everything to him. He would be so lost without you." So I tried to reassure Marsh that I was back, and I was going to live and live fully! I just didn't know what that meant yet.

The moment of Christine's departure came. I drove her to the shuttle, and I wanted to throw myself down and beg her to stay two more weeks until this whole aspect of my life was complete. Part of me felt it could be healing for her to stay after what her mom had gone through, and another part felt like it was too much to ask. My heart missed her the moment the shuttle door closed. How would I navigate this without her? I understood the significance of Christine being there with me. I needed to connect to the knowing that on a very sacred level, someone from my birth family wanted me to live and participated in bringing that forth. It sounds ridiculous because they all want me to live, but I can be so ridiculous sometimes. You see, no one has ever flown in to help me when I was injured, sick or dying before. This was a first for me. Thank you, Christine, for answering my call and being willing to move beyond who I was as a child and see the woman that I have become. I am so very grateful!

I was so grateful that Marsh and Morgan were both there for my first internal treatment. I was crying as Dede, one of my favorite techs from my external treatments, came to get me and take me in. We laughed and joked as we had always done, and it greatly assisted me. June would be the one putting the wand up inside of me (yes, I want to call it a wand so it can do its magic inside of me). June had such a gentle, loving presence and I needed that. My radiation oncologist was there. He had never been there before for anyone during the internal treatment, but I had asked him if he would be willing, and he showed up. My heart was so touched as person after person just loved me through every step of this most difficult part of my healing process. I saw Rose, my dad's first wife, as I laid there having this "wand" inserted into my vagina. She was there for me, to let me know that all is well and I was showing her that I was doing this to heal this wound from their family line, even though she was not my mother. Tears were streaming down my face as once again my vagina was being violated. But this time I was radiating my abuse and every aspect of <u>him</u> from my body. It was like the fires of hell were not nearly as strong as the love God was placing inside of me to rid myself of the pain and abuse of my innocence. Never again would there be anything less than love inside of me.

June connected "the source" (that's what they call it) to the wand. Another tech would stay in the room with me. He was covered in a lead apron to protect him from the radiation. I saw everyone behind a glass window. I was told this would last 2 minutes and 20 seconds. Would I like a countdown every 30 seconds or so that passed? I said yes, please. I had to hold as still as possible as I allowed and encouraged the radiation to flow into any part of me that needed it while releasing any part that was excess and not necessary. The tears silently flowed into small puddles at my shoulders. The wand gave a startling pulse and then stopped. Startling pulse and then stopped. 60 seconds remained. Startling pulse and then stop, just like the radiation had a pulse, a heartbeat. Finally, I was told we were done. I could breathe. I didn't realize how afraid I was to breathe. I didn't want to breathe in this experience, but I did it. I could feel Rose and all of my family on the other side celebrating with me. My mother was not happy I had cancer. Instead, my mother was happy that I was brave enough to lie there and radiate any cancer that may have remained. Thank you, Mom. Once June removed the wand, I hugged her and thanked her for all she is and all she does. I hugged my doctor too. I thanked the brave man who stayed in the room with me standing at the controls. I changed back into my clothes and just needed to collapse into Marsh and Morgan's love for me.

Now that I knew what to expect, the second round was so much easier, and there were a lot fewer tears. Afterward, I spoke with my radiation oncologist about something that I felt needed to be addressed. When I was having my external radiation, by the third of 25 sessions, I was experiencing discomfort in my hands. Spirit showed me how having my hands at my sides put them in the field of radiation. I had asked the techs if I could put my arms above my head, but they said I couldn't because it would change my anatomy, and where I would receive the radiation would be off. So my hands had to endure 22 more influxes of radiation for no reason other than no one realized this. So I told my doctor it would be beneficial to have the mapping done with the patient's arms above their head if physically possible to minimize the amount of radiation the arms and hands received. I could see how surprised he was to hear this, but he seemed to be really excited about it too. I felt like I understood another reason why I had been given this cancer experience and I am grateful if I can help others by changing the way treatments are done. I am not saying this as a form of bragging. I am saying it because I want everyone to understand how what we do affects others.

On the morning of my third internal treatment, I felt apprehension and dread. I felt absolute dread, like if I go in that building, I will die. Marsh was by my side, but he didn't know how to help me. I was crying again. I talked to God, "Ok, you guided me to do this here at this facility with these people and the equipment they have here. You guided me to do four less-intense internal treatments rather than two more-intense treatments. Why then do I feel like I am about to face my doom? Please assist me in the highest way possible to do what is the highest good for all concerned." When we arrived at the cancer center, my legs were trembling and I was barely able to stand. Everyone greeted me with a huge smile, but then saw my agitated state and retreated. June was at a conference and wouldn't be there. The person at the controls was a woman I didn't know. Everything was tilted—I was tilted. I heard and did everything like a robot. I was not working with the radiation as it went into my body. At one point, I left my body and was floating above my body just like I had done while being sexually abused. I spent a couple of days trying to regroup. Again Janet was there assisting me from such a genuine place of love and respect for me and my wellbeing. Because of her and God's assistance, I could go into my final treatment with my eyes and heart wide open. I later learned I had told my body we would have two internal treatments. I never corrected this when I changed to four with a smaller dose. This is how much my body and I communicate.

The day had come—my last day at the cancer center. I had touched so many lives here, just as so many had touched my life. I had shown those that were ready, a new way of being. I had loved people exactly where they were. I loved being surrounded by people who wanted another way to live, people who were seeking answers to questions that were too big to say out loud. And in return, I had been changed forever. I learned how to receive love and compassion on a new level. So many people saw me. But I was being seen in a new role and in a new way. I am here to touch lives, affect lives, and teach new possibilities. There was no apprehension this time. Let's do this! I am ready to move on to the next chapter in my life, whatever that may be.

I was in and out of my treatment so quickly. I was ready to be done and I was. Marsh and I went to lunch and I was able to talk and talk about my experience, the people, the joy and the pain. Marsh listened fully engaged knowing that this was important to my moving on—moving forward. Thank you, Marsh, for always being my love, my heart, my rock, my shoulder to cry on. You do it so magnificently and I am so very grateful. Thank you, God, for showing me so much good that could come out of something so bad. Thank you, Morgan, for continuing to love me even if I wasn't doing what you wanted or thought I needed during this experience. I love you, baby girl! What I realized later was how again and again I would prepare my body for something and then not follow through. For example, my body did magnificently during the surgery because I had prepared it (told it what was going to happen and how it was going to help me). I had not done any work on what would happen after the surgery. So chaos was my experience. The same thing had happened when I changed my internal treatments from two treatments to four. My body wasn't prepared. And I again did not prepare for what would happen after my cancer experience, so again I was lost and in chaos. Just like I had visualized the outside of my yellow Victorian home, but not the inside or how to pay for it. All of these were important life lessons. And I am so very grateful!

Chapter 29: In My Moment Now

We need to participate in our lives and our own healing. As I bring all this knowledge, wisdom and experience to a space where it all comes together, I see how much I needed to experience something so I could understand it and grow from it. For instance, I needed to have the mother I had so I could choose to be something more—something different as a mom. I needed a father that thought boys were everything and girls were to be tolerated, to see that when his heart had failed him, it was the nurturing of his daughters that brought him comfort, and he was grateful. I needed to want to die for years and years and years so that when I finally chose to live, it was not going to be "living" a mediocre life but a "fully embracing every aspect" kind of life. I needed to only have one child so I would yearn for more to the point where I opened a daycare so my love of children would have an outlet. My whole life is an example.

I can see the consciousness of all of my experiences creating who I am, what I think, and what I believe. I am the sum total of all my parts. So to miss one part—one aspect—of my life is to not be who I am in this moment. And I truly love who I am in this moment! I can see good in my moments, even the horrific ones. Sometimes they teach me what I don't choose to create anymore. That was my past. It is not my present. It is not my future. Knowing what we don't want can come from those challenging moments in our lives. We can stay there always dealing with one negative experience after another as a victim, or we can quiet our being and soften, then soften some more. From this softened space, we can get clarity and insights so we can become who we came here to be.

When we understand with every fiber of our being that we matter and our planet would not be complete without what we came here to be and do. As we raise in frequency, we get a clearer picture of what our purpose is. Our purpose for being here is usually something that when we talk about it, we can feel an energy flowing through us that feels so very right. Our words come out so clearly and concisely that we pause and say, "Wow, where did that come from? I love it!" People take notice and want to hear more. They want to understand what you know on a deeper level because they can feel the truth in your words. Not everyone is going to get what you are saying, or even care about what you are saying. But the ones that do will be touched so deeply, so profoundly that it makes everything that led up to that moment worth it. Like a huge crescendo in a symphony.

They say that when we die, our whole life passes before us. I feel aspects of that sometimes when I am so centered and doing exactly what I am supposed to be doing and saying exactly what I am supposed to be saying, to exactly the right people who are supposed to be hearing it. And in that moment, I knew that I needed to experience all the things I had experienced so I could come together with these people from the depths of understanding about abuse, neglect, obesity, sickness, loss, and victimhood. And then show them from the ashes of the phoenix to rise into Joy, silliness, intellect, knowing, understanding, compassion, presence, aliveness. It has been my experience that when we have come from a place of adversity, we can stay in a place of victimhood or we can choose to appreciate the simple goodness of life so profoundly.

I love to feel things. I notice as I allow myself to feel more fully, I can connect to Spirit more and more. I take my experiences to a whole new level. I love the word JOY. When I feel joy, it makes me feel so happy inside. And then if I take it a step further and EXPERIENCE joy, it makes every cell in my body come alive. I am not just feeling joy, I am BEING joy. Can you feel the frequency change from feeling joy which is absolutely wonderful to BEING joy? Every bit of you is alive with giggles. Your thoughts are joyful, your heart is wide open and you can't imagine a better moment than this one right here and now. Everyone around you can feel it coming from your being and it is contagious. I was so happy the moment Spirit showed me that Enjoy = In Joy!

This is what I do with my moments with God. Some people are very happy to repeat prayers that someone else wrote, maybe even thousands of years ago. And that works for them, and I truly celebrate that. I want more. I want to take out the middleman (the person who wrote the prayer) and create my own relationship with the creator. I want to talk to Source (God) with my own words, from my own heart. This is called heart-<u>felt</u>. It is a heartfelt prayer because you felt it in your heart and you spoke from your heart. I recently heard someone say the rosary. I had no idea that the rosary could be said at that record-breaking speed. How many of those words came from the heart? How many of those words were heart-felt? Again, I am not judging or condemning—simply asking a question. When you recite <u>any</u> prayer, how many of the words are coming from <u>your</u> heart? Did you feel each word IN YOUR HEART? Now have a conversation with your creator FROM YOUR HEART. Which one do you think was heard and felt more by your creator God?

Again, I'm not trying to tell anyone that they are bad and wrong, I'm just suggesting that they take a moment and try to see some things in a different way. See with new eyes, hear with new ears. Some people may want to do both traditional prayers and heartfelt prayers. There is no right or wrong answer here, just different options and possibilities.

So, with hopefully a greater understanding of repeating something vs. really feeling and experiencing something, and reciting someone else's words to God vs. speaking to God from your heart, now comes my next giant leap for you. Are you content with living your life feeling God once in a while vs. experiencing God in your every moment? This is what I am allowing in my life more and more. It is why I keep saying "Thank you, God" all throughout this book. I saw God's hand in that experience and I want God to see that I noticed and appreciated it. I noticed how I could not have assisted my father in being healed without God doing the work, showing me where to go next and telling me what to do. Thank you, God!

I could not have heard Spirit as I was writing my suicide letter if I had not opened up my heart and mind to God or even just wanting another way of being. I say it that way because when you are at your lowest points in life, in all honesty, you would not be feeling what you are feeling if your heart and mind were open to God. I had done the work of connecting with God earlier in my life and then stopped. But I was still wanting, needing and praying for another way of being. My prayers were answered, and I thank you, God! Not only were my prayers answered, but I was given hope for a better future so I continued to walk in faith and trust in God's words to me until I met Marsh two and a half years later and beyond. Thank you, God!

As I lay there dying on an operating room table and I saw my angel, I was still saying thank you, God! Why? Because my heart and mind are so open to God's plan and God possibilities. This means that I am every moment allowing God and my I Am Presence, my Higher Self, to guide my path. To put the best people on my path to learn from. We humans have taught God that we will take the time to talk to him—to pray to him—if we are in the midst of turmoil. If our lives are going great, do we even remember God had a hand in that? Do we say thank you during a normal boring workday? Sometimes our cage needs to be rattled to get our attention back on God. This is a lie, but it is the way <u>we</u> have created it to be. Because if we do not involve God in our lives unless we are going through a crisis, guess what we get? More crisis!

I believe that when we talk to God all day about everything like he is our very best friend, less cage-rattling happens. We don't need to be reminded of how very blessed we are to be alive if we are living a blessed life in every moment. Remember how I learned that for me, when I experience bouts of depression, God is simply trying to get my attention because He wants to have a conversation with me. That conversation is always that I have gotten off my path again and I need to reprioritize. I always come out of my bouts of depression changed for the better. Also, a God-centered life cannot exist in fear, doubt and lack. So on our journey to God-consciousness, we must release anything and everything that is connected to fear, doubt, and lack. Anything that is less than love must go. So you really have to walk through your old stuff and see what parts are true as in God's truth vs. your own truth. Our truth is what we believe, but we could be lying to ourselves. We do that by holding on to those old lies, beliefs and patterns that are not true... like I am unlovable. It is an old <u>pattern</u> that plays in my head. Because of it playing in my head so often as a child I <u>believed</u> it. It was a <u>lie</u>, just ask Marsh—I am very loveable! So even though <u>my</u> truth during my childhood said I am unlovable, God's truth is I am loveable! Can you see and feel the difference?

I had a very short friendship a couple of years ago that taught me so much. One day as my girlfriend and I were walking around a small lake talking about spirituality (my favorite subject), she wasn't getting what I was explaining. I was shown by Spirit that her religious background was limiting the way she could look at things. Spirit gave me a brilliant idea. I said, "Imagine everything you say is a prayer to God. My life sucks. God hears you say that and says, oh, Dinah would like her life to suck more. I love you so much, I am willing to give you what you ask for. Soon you're saying I am so angry. Again God hears your prayer and gives you what you ask for... Dinah would like more anger in her life. Next, you say... nothing in my life turns out in a good way. Guess what God is willing to give you as an answer to your prayer. You guessed it, even more things are not turning out positively."

Ok, we are going to increase the momentum here. Do you believe God can hear us talking in our heads? I don't know about you, but I am always talking and praying to God in my head. The answer for me is, yes, I believe God hears the talk in our heads. What if every thought we think is a prayer to God? As we are driving, we think I HATE driving behind slow people. God in his benevolence says... Oh, Dinah wants to hate more people and driving slow seems to assist her in this, so let's slow down all the traffic around her. I love her so much and now she will feel My presence with her even more. I know by now you are probably getting really mad at me because I am acting like God doesn't get us. Nothing could be further from my intention. However, as we connect to God more and more, we notice our verbiage changes, our thoughts change. We very seldom hate things. And if we do feel hate, we step back and look at how we can shift it to something softer. We come from a place of what we want instead of what we don't want, and this is very important. From there, a connection is made that what we say and think, we can create.

269

Here's another tricky part of creating with our words... we can take it to a place of manipulation, and that is not a win-win. We go to a place of saying and thinking things that we don't really believe. For instance, "everyone thinks I'm perfect" or something similar to that comes from a place of ego. You really do not believe that "everyone thinks you are perfect." It's not a <u>pattern</u> you bought into and you know it's a <u>lie</u>. So the frequency is coming from a different place and therefore does not stick or work. Like I hate driving behind slow people. You believe that you hate driving behind slow people. You have noticed it again and again that when you drive behind slow people, you start getting angry and frustrated, creating a <u>pattern</u> and a <u>belief</u>. Can you feel the difference in the sincerity of the two statements? "Everyone thinks I'm perfect" was not sincere, so it carries a very different frequency than "I hate driving behind slow people."

So how do we change this? Well, as I said before, we start changing our verbiage. We usually start out very slowly. We catch ourselves saying my life sucks and we stop ourselves. How can I soften those words and yet speak the truth? So it can be changed to something like... my life is not what I was hoping it would be in this moment, but I know that can change for the better at any time and I am ready for that change.

Making the decision to live, think, speak and be at a higher frequency does not usually happen quickly, so don't despair when you revert back to your old ways. You will most likely feel the difference when you go back to your old way of thinking and being and it does not feel good. So one thought at a time, one word at a time, and you will get there. And when you do, you will notice your whole life transform right before you and it is magical! Thank you, God!

As you do this shifting, you will begin to notice how people around you are treating you in a different manner. The words they use when speaking to you and about you are softer and kinder. Even the way you are being seen is beyond anything you could have imagined. Now this usually does not happen with family members as quickly as it does with strangers. That is because we have a past with family members. They have a belief of who you are, because of their past experiences with you. Just let go of the thought that you NEED them to see the changes in you. You NEED them to say how proud they are or even acknowledge your growth. No, you don't need anything from them. This is about you and your growth. You are doing it because it is so incredible to feel and experience or whatever your reason may be. If someone notices or acknowledges it, that's simply a bonus. Keep your focus on living from a place of truth.

Spirit keeps telling me I need to address distractions. Distractions are at a level of epidemic proportion on our planet at this time. We are spending hours and hours of our day avoiding our lives. If this rings true with you, please take the time to ask yourself honestly why you are avoiding your life? What is it you are not wanting to look at or deal with? When you finish with your distraction, your life is still there, your problems are still there. Another thing that we are experiencing is the need—a desperate need—for other people's approval. We want to post everything we are experiencing so everyone can let us know how acceptable we are. Why? What are you lacking that you are not enough already? Now take the time to shift whatever it is. How does someone giving you a thumbs-up make your experience even better? This feels like the energy of "I'm not enough until you tell me I am." Now look at how getting a thumbs-down affects you. Why are you giving another person that power to affect you?

We all need to stop looking outside ourselves for everything. The answers you are looking for are not out there... I promise you. What you truly want and what you truly need can only be found inside. Go inside and ask your questions and then wait for the answers. But you must be open and you must be willing to hear the truth. Not what you hope the answer will be, not what you hope the truth is, but the absolute truth.

Going outside yourself to get approval from others only creates more need. The more approval you get, the more you need it, until nothing you think, do or say is ever enough unless someone outside of you tells you that you are. How many times a day are you telling people what they want to hear instead of the truth? How often are you telling someone that you like something when really you think it is mediocre? How is this lying assisting them? They may feel better for a moment, but they will stop trying to be more, because you keep telling them that mediocre is perfect and wonderful. And then they lie back to you that everything about you is wonderful. And it is. But ... are you learning, are you

271

growing, are you being more? Are you enjoying more of what you want and like or what others tell you that you want and like?

I try to stop my routines every once in a while to see if they are still serving me. Am I stuck in a rut or am I trying new things and expanding who I am? We are as limited as we <u>believe</u> we are. Take a moment and really take that in. We are as limited as we believe we are. When I hear those words, I see how I constantly told myself every day that I can't read. I can't understand the words and the flow. My brain just stopped functioning when I would look at a page of words. So I had to read one word at a time, and fully understand that one word before I could move on to the next. By the time I saw a period at the end of a sentence, I had no idea what was said. And teachers would always say to me, "What does that mean, Mary Beth?" I would freeze. Go into a panic. I could maybe remember the last two or three words. Do any of those two or three words give me a clue? I hated school because of this one aspect. It took all the good that happened in a day and obliterated it.

I <u>believed</u> I was stupid. I <u>believed</u> I was untrainable. I <u>believed</u> reading was the worst part of living. And here I am writing a book. Talk about coming full circle. Thank you, Morgan, for not buying into all those lies, that I turned into my beliefs, which then became my pattern about reading. I see how reading children's books for years and years with Morgan prepared me for reading more, learning more, being more. So put down those distractions for a while and see what you are without them. See how differently you are experiencing your life because you don't need to wonder what others will think. Recently, a friend came to visit. I paused several times noticing how when we stopped to take pictures to remember this moment, we broke our connection to the moment. The funny thing is, I liked the pictures from her trip that were not posed, but instead we didn't even know they were being taken. I especially like the picture of Marsh and me dancing in the kitchen. Thank you for that moment.

Again, I am not telling you that you are bad and wrong. I'm just giving you an opportunity to change. If you are avoiding your life, maybe change is a good idea. The choice is yours. The choice is always yours.

Chapter 30:
Let's Break Those Patterns!

I would like to assist you in understanding your lies, beliefs and patterns on a greater level now that you have heard about them again and again. The easiest way that I feel you can truly understand this is ... when someone tells us a lie, for example, "You were a mistake." There is something about those words that you felt were true. The words resonated with you or you would have shrugged them off. They assisted you in having an excuse so you didn't have to be more. In fact, they gave you an excuse so you could purposely be less. If "you are a mistake," then you can't be expected to be exceptional. For me that would have been— now I understand why no one loves me... "I was a mistake." So you took that concept (that lie) on as your belief of who you are. "I am a mistake." And then you look for evidence to validate this new belief of who you are. For instance, yes, look how Dad pays so much attention to the boys, they have importance and I get so little attention because "I am a mistake." We do this again and again, trying to find proof of why we are less and others are more. This is the perfect excuse so I don't have to step up and be more. You can stay in victim mode the rest of your life because "You are a mistake." Some people do just the opposite. They look for proof that others are less so that they can <u>believe</u> that they are more.

As time went on, whenever you felt you were less than others you would repeat the lie that "You were a mistake" until it became a pattern in your thoughts and in your belief of who you see yourself as. All of this makes so much more sense as we break it down. Now let's look at how we let that lie go and make it a truth instead.

How can I be a mistake? God doesn't make mistakes and God made me. Even if by some stretch of the imagination I was a mistake, which I am NOT, we can learn from our "mistakes" and move on. But the truth is that there are no mistakes, only misinterpretations of the truth. So that person that first mentioned that "You are a mistake" was buying into a lie also. This is how collective lies start. Collective lies are when a whole group of people buy into a lie together either to make themselves <u>believe</u> that they are better or to make themselves worse than others. For example... "We are the Chosen Ones." Yes, we are all chosen by God to be on this planet at this time. But to believe God chooses us over all His other children would be a lie. When we take God into our heart, into our entire being, we see more of the truth. God simply loves. God is love. How can God believe someone is better and someone is worse when God simply loves all his children? You can say God loves some more than others but that would be a lie. To love more or less is conditional love and has no connection to God's truth. That is a human belief, a collective belief.

Spirit laughs at us a lot. I hear them all the time laughing at how silly we can be when we believe such crazy ideas and then they watch as our crazy ideas take hold and manifest in our lives. Think about how many beliefs you have about food. You have convinced yourself that certain aspects of food are good and certain aspects are bad. And then your body reacts accordingly once it becomes a part of your truth, and your belief. What if you changed your truths and your beliefs, would your experience be different? Marsh's Grandad lived to be 93. He was in excellent health his whole life even though he lived on bacon, sausage, eggs and biscuits every single day. And he chewed tobacco. Why was it ok for him? And no, I am not encouraging you to do this same behavior.

I would like to show you how lies that we have bought into personally and collectively have affected the way we look at and experience just one aspect of our lives... aging. We can do this with any topic or belief at all, but I thought aging would be perfect as an example. When I was young, we didn't see old people as senile and weak like we do as a society in this country today. Back then I only knew one person until I was 30-plus years old that was senile. My dad's mom had Alzheimer's when I was a teenager. It was very sad to watch this strong, vibrant woman diminish right before our eyes. This was not a common thing in society back then. I found out later that my mom's mother suffered from it too. So I have an opportunity to buy into "it's in my genes" or not. There are many whose ancestors experienced something medically, but they never took it on as theirs. But because our society in the west has chosen to laugh at our elderly instead of showing respect, dementia and Alzheimer's is a normal way of life now for our elderly. We watched it in movies and TV shows how if you are over 50 you are going to have "senior moments" and forgetfulness is now considered normal. Then companies decided to make some money on these new beliefs we took on as a collective. If you do the puzzles or mind games we sell, you can keep your mind young. If you keep moving you will stay young so you need to buy more stuff to assist with that. While yes, there is truth to these concepts, we have made them bigger and given them more power because of what society keeps flooding us with. I was shocked to see advertisements for adult diapers for people in their 40s and 50s and we keep buying in and buying stuff. So dementia is affecting people younger and younger. Yes, I know science has proven this and that. I'm talking about miracles, not science. We are our beliefs. Again, are we looking for proof to prove we are right?

Let's look at what we believe about aging in this country. You are going to have wrinkles and wrinkles are bad. You are going to have arthritis in all your joints. You are going to have hip and knee replacements. You are going to fall down and break bones. You are going to be weak and frail in body, mind and spirit. You are going to forget everything and everyone. You will lose your eyesight and hearing. You will lose your hair. Every part of your body will hurt. You won't be able to write anymore because it hurts too much. The list goes on and on. I call bullshit! I choose, as some of these aspects show up in my life (if they show up in my life), to take the time to call out the lies and reverse these symptoms of what

I bought into. Better yet, when I hear or see something that goes against what I want my experience to be, I'm going to call it out. Again, I choose to live in a space beyond what society and science dictates (and I love science). I choose to live from a place of God-connected miracles! This is my new normal. How can we create incredible change, if we don't believe we can change in incredible ways? And if some of these things happen, so be it. I will look at them and work toward shifting them.

I'm not saying that any or all of those things aren't true, what I'm saying is... the more WE believe they are true, the more likely they will be <u>our</u> truth. And when we buy into a truth as a collective, it gets to be all our truths. The more emotion we have about something the stronger it will be for the individual. Again, I want to remind you that love is always stronger than fear. Allow yourself to feel your fears deeply. Allow every bit to play out in your head and in your heart. When it is complete, bring in the love and compassion. Tell yourself all the things that you wished others would have said to you. Be the love of your life in this moment of NOW!

To be clear, I am exercising, I am working on expanding my mind—my thoughts. I am not doing it from a place of fear. Oh no, oh no, I didn't exercise today, now I'm going to have arthritis as my experience. Nope, not my mindset. I say, wow, I feel so much better when I exercise. My body moves more freely and that feels wonderful to my being, so I am going to keep it up. Do you feel the difference? Science and spirit can become one. Another thing I notice is when I pick up my feet more, and walk with purpose, I carry myself differently. And I like the difference!

Now look at other beliefs you have about anything—like driving, buying a car, going to school, going to work, having a vacation. You name it and you will find that you have many beliefs about it. Now see if those reasons or beliefs are what you want to believe or not. Time to figure out what is serving you and what isn't. Who do you want to be and who do you want others to believe you are? Now go out and be that—go out and do that!

Chapter 31:
What Are We Observing?

As I work at keeping my frequency up by living from a place of love, respect, compassion and kindness both towards myself and others, I notice my old recording looping in the back of my mind gets more and more quiet. The way I see myself and my place in the world shifts. I notice I love myself so much more than ever before. I look forward to my exchanges with others instead of dreading them. I see the magnificence in each and every one of my family members. Can you believe that!

Do you want your moments to be more? Then you need to be more, by thinking differently, treating yourself and others differently. For the first time, come from a place of complete honesty. Not what you want your experience to be, but the truth. From there you will be able to recognize what needs to shift and in what way. The only one that can change you is you. We can't change others, we can only change ourselves. If you could change one aspect of you, what would it be? How can you start to move towards that change right here, right now? For me, it is by changing my thoughts. I let go of the "I can't" thinking and look at what I can do. For instance, with wanting to make better choices to lose weight. I stopped drinking soda and started drinking water. Then I slowly or quickly depending on how I'm doing with it, I increase the water. I go from "That's not too bad" to "Now I prefer water." Next I eliminate sugar. I showed myself when I ate sugar yesterday, I felt worse and it showed up on the scales.

Notice how I don't shame myself and feel guilty when I slip back into eating sugar, I simply observe the consequences when I do. That empowers me to make different choices. I can continue with sugar or not, I can gain more weight or not. Every choice we make is a choice. We chose that. No one chose it for us and if they did, we have the option of saying "No more." I love the frequency of "No means no."

Now I would love for you to take the time to play with the concept of living from a place of observation. Notice things around you that you have never noticed before. Look at the clouds. I love clouds, they take me to a happy place. Observe people around you. I love to observe people that I don't know without an attachment. I observe their choice of words. No judgment, just noticing how interesting the multitude of choices they are making. I continually stop myself if I go to a place of judgment and say, "How interesting they chose to say that, think that, or buy into that." I can feel myself softening as a human being. I can feel myself coming from a place of trust, then compassion, and then finally love. It is a process. I am a process. I need to be patient with both.

After many years and even decades of waking up more and more to who I am and who I am becoming, I see so many changes in me. For instance, the way I do healings. I don't usually see different-colored lights coming in like I used to. I don't need that proof anymore that God is doing his amazing work. I simply feel, know and trust. That doesn't mean I wouldn't welcome the colored lights because I would. I love them. I don't see as much when I look at someone's body, because I am learning more about how that person may need to learn from that experience. God's will trumps my will every time. If I see something, I speak up and assist however I can. I notice that I am not channeling as much either. I don't need outside conformation like I used to. I trust myself more and my own inner guidance. This inner guidance almost feels like channeling, but it is different... more connected, softer, more quiet. When and if I need to channel, it's always an option. When I look at the world and all its chaos, it reminds me of my childhood of living in two worlds. One that makes no sense to me and the one I still live in inside my head and heart with Spirit. I'm able to merge the two worlds now because there are so many more of us that are living from a place of love and not fear. I see the chaos as people who are lost try to navigate their lives. Been there, done that. Why would I judge someone else for needing to go there? Also, some people need the chaos to wake up and make new choices.

Of course, as our frequency raises, our old stuff can't reside in our thoughts and in our body. So those old lies are going to come up for us and they're going to be very loud and in our face. This is a good thing, because when that happens we can see and understand exactly what we still need to look at and let go of. As we let go, we become lighter in our thoughts. Lighter in our way of being with each other. We no longer want to live from a place of heaviness. Looking at what is happening out there on the planet we see how all this heaviness or density is coming to the surface for everyone. This is because our frequency on the entire planet is raising and so all the old patterns and beliefs have to go. We have a front-row seat to watch the old ways of government, of money, of corruption not being allowed anymore. Once we get to the other side of dissolving all this old negativity what will be left is oneness, connectedness and love. So buckle up during this ride of dissolving the old and bringing in the new. Just like you are doing within yourself. As above so below.

I am so very grateful that our planet is shifting. Sometimes that can look and feel like chaos during the shift. You see, to change, we have to shift. And to shift, we have to change. So let's try to be patient with ourselves and others as we navigate these changes. Let's be patient with each other as we figure out our places in this new way of being. Try not to get caught up in the drama, by staying connected to the truth of what is going on. We asked for change and we are certainly getting it!

When the dust settles, we will be living on a new earth. One that goes so far beyond what we have experienced so far. And it all starts by letting go of those old lies, letting go of those old patterns, those old beliefs. Do you see now how that old heaviness or density is not serving you? It's time to let it go and live from your open heart. Let's shift this planet one thought at a time. One kindness at a time. One knowing at a time. We've got this, especially when we do it together.

I am not a lie, and neither are you!

I see your magnificence and I thank you for joining me on this ever-changing, ever-evolving journey called life. Now go out and be the change you wish to see in the world. And know that I am so proud of your willingness.

As Pooh Bear[15] says, "You are braver than you believe, stronger than you seem, and smarter than you think." That Pooh Bear really knows his stuff!

[15] A.A. Milne, *Winnie-the-Pooh*, 1926.

Chapter 32: Know that I AM

I, Mary Beth Smith, am an aspect of God! It is not something I need to aspire to, or work towards... I AM that, I AM. I was born an aspect of God and I will leave this planet an aspect of God. There is nothing I can do or be that will change that. Knowing that—I mean really taking that in and knowing that—takes a pressure off me that I put on myself. I don't have to do something or be something so God will love me. He already does. So I can let go of those huge lists of why I'm not good enough. What does that mean? I am good enough, I always have been good enough, and I always will be good enough!

I realize that I want to be the highest vision, of the highest version, of who I am. Not because maybe then God will love me and I will go to heaven. No. I choose it because it's who I want to be. Who I choose to be. Because an aspect of God is Love. And Love will always be more powerful than Hate. Love will always be more powerful than Fear. Love is my divine right. Anything less than Love is a lie and as I told you in the beginning, I choose to live from a place of honesty and truth, not lies.

I don't have to do the journey alone. I have so many on the other side helping me... helping us! We can hold the energy or frequency of Love together. We can transform this planet to heaven on earth if we, moment by moment, let go of the old lies. Let go of comparing who is better or worse. Who is successful and who isn't. Who deserves and who doesn't. And simply realize, we are each and every one of us, different. We are supposed to be different from each other. We all have worth. We all have something to share and contribute with one another. We are all an aspect of God. We are all Love. Some days are easier than others to remember this.

I choose to live on this new earth that is composed of Love, peace, kindness, wisdom, compassion, abundance, health, joy and oneness. Yes, that is a planet I would love to live on. Where respect is a way of life. Willingness to be of service instead of gimme. Yes, yes, yes, I want in! Gratitude is in every breath, every thought, every deed.

This separateness from God is a lie. For we are all connected. We are all one and there is no separation. I AM that, I AM. And so it is.

Chapter 33: Epilogue

In August of 2019 I was told by Spirit that it was time to write my book. The window of opportunity was closing. And this book needed to be completed before the summer of 2020. Well, no pressure there! How was I supposed to write a book? At that time, Janet and Ken were traveling with us. We were heading to a 5-day spiritual retreat in Arizona. Janet told me how much she loves my writing. She said that she has saved many of the cards that I have sent her over the years because of how incredible they had touched her heart. Then listening to people speaking to us for 5 days about God and possibilities and making a difference, I decided to give it my best shot. I knew I wanted to write about simple, basic things to get people started on their own spiritual path by teaching them some important things that have helped me.

Of course, I asked for guidance from Spirit through every step of this journey. Writing this book was so transformational for me. I was able to see where I still felt stuck, where I still believed certain lies and how it was time to step up and become more. Sometimes I spent days crying and avoiding, especially when it came time to write about both my brother Grant's cancer experience along with my own. The experience was too fresh in my mind and heart and I miss my brother so much. There have been times that I even felt guilty because I lived and Grant didn't. Grant had so many friends and people that really cared about him.

So as I wrote and processed, rewrote and processed some more, I actually finished way ahead of time. I finished in December of 2019. I knew it was going to take a lot of editing so I was grateful for the extra time. As luck would have it, my best friend was going to be coming and staying with us for several days after Christmas. I was so excited about her reading my book. I had it all ready for her to dive into. I was looking forward to our conversations after each chapter. That wasn't what happened (notice the expectations). I did a lot of channeling for her. I let her talk about being with her family for Christmas. We laughed and had a wonderful time. But every morning I would wake up to her on her phone for several hours either in her room or in our living room.

After several days of this and bringing up my book multiple times, I just lost it with her. How could she sit there and tell me how excited she was about my book when she won't even open it up and read the first page? I ranted at her. I could see the shock on her face. The fact that she wasn't even saying anything angered me even more. It had been so very long since I had felt rage like this. Finally she let me know that she wanted to give me the opportunity to get everything out that I needed to say. Then she let me know that she didn't want to start it until she could read it uninterrupted. She wanted to get the flow of the book and really immerse herself in it. It made sense, but I really wanted/needed a dialogue. She left with my book and a promise that we would connect and she would let me know what she thought and would give me editing ideas.

In the meantime, I was told that there was an organization in our town that helps people in the Arts, so I checked them out. I found out they no longer help new writers, the only thing that they could suggest was that I could enter an upcoming writing contest. That would get my name out there if I won, and it would get my book noticed. I spent time trying to figure out what part of the book to enter in the contest, and rewrite it so it could stand on its own. It was during this pandemonium time that I finally heard back from my best friend. She wanted to know if I would be willing to put the book into 3 books in one: My life, my spiritual journey, and my spiritual advice. I told her that I would consider it. Here she was practically rewriting the whole book, I guess.

She let me know that we could work on the corrections together on the computer. I said I can't until this writing contest is over in a couple of weeks. Then I found out she was going to a 10-day meditation retreat, followed by a trip to another country. Well, I have no idea what she was going to do with the book or how her meditation went, or even how her trip went, or if she had even gone on the trip, because she just disappeared from my life. I was worried she was hurt, or sick, or dead. This was when Covid-19 first started. So my best friend, after reading my book, left my life forever without talking to me, which she promised she would never do. I did get her to respond to me over the summer when we moved and I needed to find out where she wanted me to deliver the stuff we were storing for her. She did the bare minimum on information and civility, but at least I now know that she is alive and ok.

So now it was time for Morgan to step up and help dear old Mom edit my book. She was working full-time and taking 10+ credits per semester. We got 1 ½ chapters edited before she became too stressed out and had no time to help me. I told Spirit that if they wanted me to publish it, they needed to put someone on my path that wanted to assist me and believed in my story. In the meantime, my story was not chosen for the writing contest.

All went quiet. The planet was going crazy with the Covid-19 lockdown. I was witnessing how this was bringing the entire planet together. I told Spirit that I don't know why You had a before-summer deadline, but I have no idea on how I am to move forward. Then at the beginning of May, my gynecological oncologist ordered a CT of the abdomen because I was feeling strange lumps there. The next day someone from a urology oncology office called me about setting up an appointment with a kidney oncologist. I freaked out. I told her I had no idea what she was talking about. Why would I need to see a kidney oncologist? She apologized and said I should talk to my doctor. I called my doctor, and of course she wasn't available.

I talked to Marsh and Morgan. I took some deep breaths to calm down, and connected to Spirit. When my phone rang later, it was my doctor and Morgan on a conference call. My doctor said that the CT showed something in my right kidney that they believed was renal cell carcinoma, which is a cancerous tumor in the kidney. She can recommend a really good kidney oncologist if I wanted that. I told her that I value her opinion, so yes I would like to meet with this doctor. Morgan wrote down the information for me. I asked what tests they would need to do to find out if it was cancer. The doctor said that they would find out when the results of the biopsy came back after the surgery. I was going all over the place. What if it isn't cancer? I would put my kidney through all that for nothing? The doctor said that I needed to ask these questions with the urology doctor. I couldn't believe how just hearing my doctor's voice was calming me, and yet the words she was using were freaking me out. She told me that it was caught very early. I was told all that was required was surgery, no chemo and no radiation. I also was told that this cancer was not connected to my endometrial cancer. In other words, my first cancer had not spread. That was the turning point for me. Ok, let's do this. Let's get this tumor out and move forward with my life. That was on a Thursday. On Monday, Marsh, Morgan and I had a teleconference visit with my new doctor. We had to do a teleconference because of Covid-19. I was told that the surgery would be done robotically, and that the tumor was so small that I would be able to keep about 90% of my kidney. Oh, Thank You, God! Because of the Covid lockdown, the doctor guessed it would be about 8 weeks before they could fit me on the surgery schedule because I was a low priority with the tumor being so small. I let them know I preferred sooner rather than later. They called me on Saturday to tell me my surgery would be in 11 days. Thank you, God!!

As I was getting used to all these changes happening to me emotionally, physically and mentally, I started looking for things outside of myself to help me. I was looking at astrology and asking people's opinions trying to find something that was going to tell me what I wanted and needed to hear, which was that I was going to be ok. I had to laugh at myself. I know from experience that the answers are within me, not out there. So time to get to work.

I felt some very wonky energy surrounding the word cancer, my having cancer, and the surgery I was about to have. I wanted to connect with Spirit and see where it would take me. First, I asked for some guidance. I asked God (Spirit) to guide every step of this cancer journey, in the most divine way. I decided to call on Saint Germain. He is a very powerful healer and he loves assisting us. I started taking some deep breaths. The next thing I knew, I was in a surgery suite. I knew it was me on the table, even if I didn't look. The whole room was filled with beautiful sparkly light. The light almost felt alive. I was taken to the machine that my surgeon was sitting at. Her head was down in the machine. I watched Saint Germain step into her. Actually, he was larger than her. His whole body encapsulated hers. His body extended out about 6 to 8 inches beyond her body. I saw how he was guiding her. Their thoughts and movements were one. I was so very grateful, and I told him so.

Next, I watched as he became one with the nurse that would be putting instruments on the robot. Suddenly I noticed that Saint Germain was connected to everyone in the room. So much connectivity, so much oneness. I felt such gratitude.

Then I was taken inside my body, like I was a camera that could go anywhere inside of my body. I realized I was close by my right kidney. I thanked my kidney for all it had done for me and will continue to do for me. I apologized to my kidney for being so PISSED OFF for the first 40 years of my life. I watched as an instrument came over and removed the tumor. I said no cancerous cells can be left behind and Saint Germain pinched his fingers and picked up one cell and placed it in the basket with the rest of my tumor. He showed me the cancer was encapsulated in a membrane so it wasn't a danger to me. The basket was closed up and pulled through my port (or incision). It was then taken to be biopsied. Everything was closed up and I was sutured. When I felt assured that all was exactly as it should be, I came out of my body and was back in my room in Cheyenne.

I was crying as I thanked Saint Germain and God and any other being of light that was going to assist me before, during and after this cancer experience. I apologized to my kidney that it had to go through all of this. I let it know that we would do this together and that I love it so very much. When things got bad as a child, I learned to leave my body. I don't do that anymore. We are one and there is no separation.

During my therapy session 6 days before my surgery, I was telling Robert how I feel like my body and my kidneys are so mad at me for creating this. He told me, your body and kidneys are not mad at you, or disappointed in you. It is grateful to you because you are removing this tumor which is causing problems, or will cause problems. Also, he said after this surgery my kidneys can heal and feel whole again. My cells can merge and feel safe. This is so wonderful.

I was now ready to have this surgery. I had no reservations, no hesitations. After Saint Germain walked me through everything, I felt at peace and knew all would be guided. So at 5:30 A.M. on the day of my surgery, Morgan and I checked in for my operation. Because of Covid-19, neither Marsh nor Morgan could be in the hospital, except to check me in. So Marsh gave me hugs and kisses as he waited in the SUV. Once they called me back to pre-op Morgan left. I would see them tomorrow when they picked me up to go back to Morgan's to recuperate.

Everything felt so divinely guided. In pre-op I had been told that my doctor had decided to do the surgery from the front, not from the back. I was comfortable with that decision—in fact, I preferred it. I noticed how I was just flowing with everything. How nothing was throwing me off balance. I noticed the differences between my two cancer experiences. The first one I tried to micro manage everything and left little room for flow. This time I just surrendered and allowed, and boy, did that make a difference. Every time I would try to vibrationally assist with something I would hear... It's already taken care of. So there were very few bumps on my path, in fact I can't think of a single bump, just flow. I felt so alert as I was taken into the OR suite. I was so grateful Morgan had shown me ahead of time what the equipment would look like. There were several enormous pieces of equipment in this average size room. I felt like the OR table was one of the smallest things in the room. My anesthesiologist asked me what I was going to dream about during my surgery. I told her I was going to fly and play with Spirit. I loved my anesthesiologist.

I don't remember waking up in recovery. When I woke up in my room I remember being surprised at how little pain I was experiencing. Everyone who entered my room was kind and respectful. I went for several walks to get the anesthesia out of my system and to see how I tolerated walking. I remember watching how easily and effortlessly my body was working. There was no strange pulling like last time. Instead all I had was discomfort. I video chatted with Marsh and Morgan. They were impressed with how alert I was. The doctor said everything went according to plan with no issues at all. The next day at Morgan's house, Marsh kept staring at me. No one could believe how well I was doing. Like I said, the two experiences were so very different. We watched movies and just enjoyed each other. We walked in the park the next day, and my phone said I had walked 2 miles. I felt discomfort, but otherwise I felt fantastic. We stayed with Morgan and her hubby for several days and it felt like Morgan and I were able to heal some of the discord that we experienced with the last cancer experience. Morgan and I had both had agendas last time. This time we both flowed and just enjoyed each other.

So the reason I feel I didn't move forward in having my book published was I needed to learn, understand, experience and then share this experience of shifting and where it can take us. I connected with Spirit a lot during my first cancer experience, but there was a desperation involved. I want this over and I want it over now. Again, that frequency of, if I do this, can I be healed. I could feel how much my body did not want to experience the radiation. There was discomfort in my body at every turn, yet there had been supreme moments of flow. When I allowed, flowed and trusted with the second cancer experience it was a completely different vibration. My physical body recovered so quickly. Emotionally, I felt loved and cared for by Spirit. Mentally, I was empowered. Oh my gosh, what a difference!

Three months after my second surgery I had another CT and met with my kidney oncologist. She said everything looks so perfect and that she doesn't need to see me for a year. So it's a year later, I have had my CT and have seen both of my oncologists. My latest CT shows I have some small gallstones, which I knew about from my other CT scans, otherwise everything looks great. My urology oncologist said everything looks wonderful, and she will see me in a year. My GYN oncologist also said everything is doing well and they will see me in 6 months. So it is time to move forward with my life. I'm ready to share my wisdom by publishing my book. The first version of this book was so very different from this version. My first version was filled with anger and pain. As I was able to heal, my words became softer with every edit I completed. I am no longer that wounded victim.

The reason nothing made sense to me when I was younger is because my childhood had been formed from lies I was told, patterns I created to help it all make sense and then wrap it up in a nice bow with the beliefs that I used to justify it all. It served its purpose and I am grateful for each and every experience that got me to this moment. This is MY moment and it is filled with truth, flow, kindness and love.

I still have my moments of doubt, but I am able to recognize it and shift it so much more quickly now. I know fear once in a while. I spend time with it to learn what it wants to tell me. I ask it... what are you here to teach me or show me? Where did this come from? What do I choose to do to resolve/shift it? I love my gift of a question. Remember, if we don't ask the question, we can't get the answer.

Another essential thing I learned from the frequency of all this was that I came here to have these cancer experiences in this lifetime. They were necessary for my growth. I no longer blame my thoughts or what I ate or the anger, hate and frustration from my childhood. Knowing that on a deeper level has freed me up. I no longer have to micromanage every thought. I allow myself the freedom to think what I think because it tells me so much about where I am and what I believe.

Now I understand why this book needed to be written before the summer of 2020 because by then I would have been able to process and resolve so much within me that by the time of my diagnosis in May of 2020, I was ready for a "whole" different experience. Thank you, God!

I came here to experience certain things, like I was going to have the experience of almost dying when I had my baby so that I could have an opportunity to finally choose to live. I came here to experience my hurt back and being bedridden to help me wake up and connect to God and my spirituality more. I was born to the family I was born to, so I could experience the belief that I didn't matter. My needs didn't matter, my desires didn't matter, my existence didn't matter, what I thought didn't matter, what I experienced didn't matter. Nothing about me mattered. So one day as I connected to my inner strength, I could have the profound realization that not only did I MATTER, but my existence was important to our shift on this planet.

Another example is when Marsh and I were first married. I had asked him what he had imagined his wife was going to be like and look like. His answer was always "I don't know. I never really thought about it. I just knew that someday I would get married and have kids." I now see how having Marsh almost die when he was 11 and Morgan letting him know that he had to go back into his body so that she could be born, that he understood on some level that he would be getting married and having this child. He didn't need to imagine it because he knew it and he trusted it.

It would be beneficial for us to realize that most of the "big things" we experience are predestined before we are born. That's why even when I was little the word "cancer" bothered me and I didn't even know what it was. The "free will" that we are given has a lot to do with how we respond to what comes across our path. Are we going to come from a place of fear, blame and doubt, or from a place of trust, love and flow. I can tell you from experience that the choice you make— makes all the difference.

Because of all the work Spirit and I have done over the years, the lie that I had become was transformed to the truth that I AM.

I AM THAT, I AM.